Humiliation

Humiliation
Claims and Context

edited by
Gopal Guru

OXFORD
UNIVERSITY PRESS

OXFORD

UNIVERSITY PRESS

22 workspace, 2nd Floor, 1/22 Asaf Ali Road, New Delhi 110002

Oxford University Press is a department of the University of Oxford.
It furthers the University's objective of excellence in research, scholarship,
and education by publishing worldwide in

Oxford   New York
Auckland   Cape Town   Dar es Salaam   Hong Kong   Karachi
Kuala Lumpur   Madrid   Melbourne   Mexico City   Nairobi
New Delhi   Shanghai   Taipei   Toronto

With offices in
Argentina   Austria   Brazil   Chile   Czech Republic   France   Greece
Guatemala   Hungary   Italy   Japan   Poland   Portugal   Singapore
South Korea   Switzerland   Thailand   Turkey   Ukraine   Vietnam

Oxford is a registered trademark of Oxford University Press
in the UK and in certain other countries.

Published in India
by Oxford University Press, New Delhi

ISBN-13: 978-0-19-806030-7
ISBN-10: 0-19-806030-0

Typeset in ITC Giovanni Book 10/12.7
by Eleven Arts, Keshav Puram, Delhi 110 035
Printed in India by Repro India Limited
Published by Oxford University Press
22 workspace, 2nd Floor, 1/22 Asaf Ali Road, New Delhi 110002

Contents

Acknowledgements

This volume comprises papers that were first presented at a conference on humiliation held in Ranikhet in 2002. Both the conference and the volume form an integral part of my commitment as a C.R. Parekh Fellow at the Centre for the Study of Developing Societies (CSDS), Delhi. My foremost gratitude is due to the Nirman Foundation that instituted the C.R. Fellowship at the CSDS. I thank the members of the Nirman Foundation Fellowship Committee, particularly Dhirubhai Seth and Ashis Nandy, for choosing me for such a prestigious fellowship. I owe special thanks to Bhikhu Parekh who showed sustained interest in my research persuasion of the theme of humiliation. Rajeev Bhargava deserves special mention for more than one reason. He not only made one of the lead presentations in the seminar but also took personal interest in helping me find an appropriate location for the seminar.

Though I am indebted to every participant in the seminar, I need to thank all the contributors to the volume for their patience and commitment to my endeavour. Their endurance has made the volume an original. Special thanks are owed to Peter Ronald deSouza who has remained a consistent and constant interlocutor in the dialogue on humiliation. Gurpreet Mahajan, Valerian Rodrigues, and Sanjay Palshikar took out their time and offered valuable suggestions particularly on the introduction of the volume. This helped me discipline my thinking. Tani Sandhu deserves special mention for her capacity to morally force people to ethically edit their personality, which otherwise forms the basis of the experience of humiliation. I found her sense of practical reason quite inspiring.

Last but not the least, I must thank Hema, Ashu, and Himanshu, who, without any grouse, supported the absentee member of the family.

Preface

As a C.R. Parekh Fellow at Delhi, I tumbled on divergent responses that came from a number of concerned friends, colleagues, and commentators, both in and outside Delhi. When I shared the theme on humiliation with them, some of these scholar friends found the theme quite exciting, particularly in terms of the promise it offered for doing theory differently. Some of them went ahead and suggested the need for humiliation studies in India. Few of them wasted no time in reading into the theme of humiliation, a powerful moral source that brings out an element of guilt from among those who are aware about the structures of humiliation in Indian society. The third kind of response was more encouraging in the sense that it found resonance of this theme with the language being used in everyday forms of social interaction. Ultimately, this divergent feedback—that I was fortunate enough to be offered—suggested the need for pursuing the theme from more than one theoretical perspective. The purpose of organizing the conference on humiliation and finally producing a volume out of the proceedings was not to help socially sensitive sections to transcend either personal or collective guilt, but to interrogate the system that underlies and renews the structures of humiliation. I feel happy that this volume does not feed into efforts that seek a connection between guilt and theoretical transcendence. It offers a kind of guarantee to those scholars like Sundar Sarukkai who also argue against this link.

Some friends who saw the theme replete with a strong element of phenomenology also voiced their scepticism. Some critics of phenomenology would further argue that it is not a phenomenological analysis of humiliation that can provide an opportunity to gain an understanding of social reality. Since phenomenological move involves individual response to existential humiliation, it would insulate the larger structures of humiliation. If the structures of friendship also underlie and renew the possibility of humiliation, those in question would certainly deploy phenomenological moves to cope up with social infirmities. Surely, at some level, the experience of humiliation and need to cope up with this experience, particularly by the social groups that are put to servility, does involve a phenomenological move. In the social and cultural context of India, which is overwhelmed by what is called 'caste of mind' and the archaeology of untouchability, reference to phenomenology becomes imminent. Some of the essays in this volume do address the question of humiliation by using the framework of phenomenology. Thus, the volume points out at the necessity to deploy multiple frameworks in order to make a more or less accurate sense of social reality. Consequently, some of the essays would treat humiliation as a lived experience, as matter fit only for the scientific investigation of the social relations.

Thus, the Marxist scholarship and its theoretical engagement with issues like exploitation and alienation did form the major theoretical concern for the scholar working from this vantage point. Yet, such preoccupation forecloses the possibility whether humiliation and exploitation or alienation could belong to the same logical class, where these could be understood as neighbouring concepts, existing side by side, harmoniously. On the other hand, the studies in social psychology do focus on prejudice and suffering, hate, envy, and shame but without relating much of it to concepts of exploitation and domination. This would have also made it necessary to explore whether humiliation as a category has its own autonomy to exist between exploitation and suffering. However, in the realm of literary studies, particularly from Dalit literature, humiliation has been the recurrent concern, principally autobiographies, short stories, and poems, and not so much the novel which Dalit literature has so far failed to handle successfully. However, the theme of humiliation in the literary genre has operated through very powerful allegories, thus giving vent to the experience of humiliation through metaphors like poison bread or *zoothan* or branded. Though Dalit literature writings proved an important medium of articulation, such a format could not unfold to us the many nuanced aspects of the experience of humiliation. They could not be the adequate substitute for the theory of humiliation. Some of my colleagues and friends have also asked why I need to invoke the moral category of self-respect and its opposite humiliation when the Indian constitution has provided for the protection of self-respect. Such observers might argue that terms like equality and justice and freedom have already taken care of setting people free from possible humiliation. The question that needs attention is: do these terms accommodate the essence of self-respect? The practices of civil society seriously challenge this constitutional essentialism. The twice-born character of civil society seems to have overwhelmed the essence of constitutional intervention.

Much more interesting was the observation made by some of the colleagues who seemed sceptical about the language of articulation of humiliation. They somehow acknowledged that the language of communicating humiliation is specific and does not form part of the canonical genre. Their scepticism was understandable particularly in the context of public discourse in India which seems to be dominated by a pet language; for example, of democracy, civil society, and secularism. The use of such language did suggest that certain concepts are the final and complete vocabulary of discourse. However, such a vocabulary could be treated as final only in the absence of the language of humiliation, and not before it is overwhelmed by certain other vocabularies. In the literature as produced in the realm of social/political theory, social science, and humanities, there has been discussion on issues like discrimination, deprivation, exploitation, and marginalization. However, such literature tends to focus more on the phenomenon that has happened or has been practised. There is hardly any literature that could suggest caste of mind, that is the repository of humiliation and archaeology of untouchability, as the minefield of humiliation. For example, the discipline of sociology does offer very detailed accounts of the practices of untouchability but hardly gives us any idea of the psychological preparation of those particular practices. Finally, the universal and the particular context of humiliation makes for an understanding of the social reality involving an experience of humiliation. I was also advised to whether it was analytical or allegorical?

The present volume thus is a modest attempt to make theoretical sense of the phenomenon of humiliation. The contributors to the volume are aware and informed by the discourse on humiliation in the West, and yet a majority of them have enriched our understanding of humiliation by bringing in fresh insights to the humiliation that is specific to India. The essays point out, along interdisciplinary theoretical grounds, the different aspects of humiliation. Thus, these contributions incorporate within themselves the moral, cultural, legal, constitutional, sociological, psychological, and political. They have succeeded in throwing up categories that are constitutive of humiliation. Finally, most of the articles offer both the universal context as well as the local context of the theory of humiliation. While they reveal the universal patterns in terms of the experience of humiliation, some of them also delineate for us the context-specific forms of humiliation. This volume thus seeks to reorient the established theoretical framework in a different but ingenious way.

Gopal Guru

New Delhi
28 October 2008

Introduction
Theorizing Humiliation
Gopal Guru

Humiliation is almost endemic to social life that is active basically through asymmetries of intersecting sets of attitudes—arrogance and obeisance, self-respect and servility, and reverence and repulsion. It continues to survive in different forms depending upon the specific nature of the social context. For example, in the West it is the attitude of race that is at the base of humiliation. In the East, it is the notion of untouchability that foregrounds the form and content of humiliation. This endemic character of the concept of humiliation can be explained in terms of the social paradox produced by the socially dominant elite from different societies. This paradox involves the dynamics of social life with contradictory responses offered by the modern elite. Thus, on the one hand, the dynamics of social life shakes this social elite from the humiliating social protocols that regulate feudal society, on the other, these so called modern social elites tend to reproduce structures, both institutional (state) and moral (friendship), that underlie and renew the phenomenon of humiliation. Those social elite who were the object of humiliation at the hands of the estate and caste lords, or the colonial masters, somehow become the source of humiliation/degradation of which they were victims in the first instance. The reorganization of modern society based on the division between the private and public spheres was accompanied by the possibility of misrecognition, degradation, and humiliation. Transgression of the boundaries between the private and the public was considered as the context for humiliation (Habermas 1991: 39). Secondly, the capacity to control the corporeal body (both male and female) in the public domain defines individual dignity and decency of the bourgeoisie society (ibid.). The emergence of the modern self with an intellectual capacity to control, combined with the confidence to conquer vast areas of knowledge, can also produce a tendency to despise those who lack the same capacity for knowledge.[1] Thus, the emergence of modern society is both enabling and constraining at the same time.

However, recognition remains a vital need of human beings who form the part of moral life based on face-to-face social relations (Taylor 1997: 225). There is a line of thought both in the West and also in the East which has paid continuous attention to the ethical/moral reorganization of society within which this normative need could be realized. The modern strand of thought seeks to define ethical reorganization of society in terms of the search for 'recognition' and 'respect'. The philosophers/thinkers in the West seem to have made sustained attempts to philosophize and theorize the experience of humiliation and suggest its elimination in favour of respect, recognition, and dignity. This, in effect, has led them to focus on the question and to understand and interrogate a set of concepts that form into a logical class comprising humiliation, shame, degradation, insult, indignity, and misrecognition, as also the opposite set of values, that is, respect, dignity, and recognition. Following this line of thought, Rousseau, Kant, Hegel, and Adam Smith appear quite prominently in imagining a more ordered, decent, and just society. For example, in Hobbes and Machiavelli's thought the struggle for self-preservation through extracting recognition from others, or racing for it, acquires seminal importance (Honneth 1995: 5).

Rousseau's republicanism on the contrary seeks affirmation of the ordinary self (Walzer 1983: ch.11). However, the concerns for dignity, recognition, and respect figure more prominently in Kant, and later in Hegel's writings. According to Kant, a capacity to not humble one before others but to subordinate oneself to moral law constitutes self-respect (Seidler 1986: 45). In Kantian writings, respect and dignity become a possibility within the sphere of the intelligible world that is related to the inner and essential autonomy of the will which is separated from the everyday empirical self (ibid.). In Kantian reading, it is the sensible world that is the sphere in which one could lose dignity. This notion of the sensible world in Kant relates to the empirical self (ibid.). Hegel's notion of recognition moves from the asymmetrical relationship between master and slave to the inter-subjective relationship between person qua person (Westphal 1984: 79). This inter-subjective dimension in Hegel could be understood in terms of its absence in the master–slave relationship, which, according to Hegel, is irreconcilable (Williams

1997: 2). In the liberal moral thought tradition Adam Smith is another leading thinker who has addressed the question of humiliation quite centrally. In his monumental work Smith has expressed concern that a person should be able to appear in public without a sense of shame (Smith 1966: 371). Hence, according to Smith, appearing in public with pretension can become the source of humiliation, as pretension is vulnerable to deflation (ibid.). According to Smith, a man who ascribes to himself any other merit besides that which really belongs to him fears no humiliation (Smith 1966). On the other side of the spectrum of imagination stands Karl Marx, who in his early writings has paid some attention to the question of humiliation (Marx 1975: 247).

Thinkers who belong to the liberal philosophical tradition of the West have further enriched our understanding of self-respect, as also its opposite, humiliation.[2] However, the intellectual/theoretical initiative taken by these thinkers need not be interpreted as something natural or innately radical. As mentioned before, the early arrival of modernity to western societies seems to have caused decisive disruptions in the existing social hierarchies thus undermining derogatory social protocols with a universal language of dignity and self-respect. Thus, in the western intellectual tradition, the theorization of humiliation takes shape and orientation basically within the local configuration of power suggesting tension within the bourgeoisie pubic sphere based on new and, perhaps, secular social hierarchies.

In colonial societies, traditional elite develop an insight into humiliation. However, they acquire this insight not because they have an innate moral capacity. In fact, a colonial configuration of power, produced by western modernity, necessarily disrupts their feudal complacency and awakens them to their own subordination within this framework of power. They are unable to retain their power to distribute recognition and social worth to others. In fact, the social disruption caused by the colonial configuration of power forces them to seek recognition from others. This colonial configuration of power compelled thinkers to offer a radical and immediate response to the humiliation emanating from the asymmetrical social relations in colonial India. Thus, Bankimchandra Chatterjee's experience of humiliation, emanating from an arbitrary act of cultural and social exclusion by the British family, encouraged him to fight for Bengali self-respect (Roychoudhury 2002: 116). Tapan Roychoudhury terms this discrimination and exclusion of the Indian as 'racial humiliation' (ibid.). It could be argued that the colonial configuration of power produces experiences of racial humiliation, which could be universal in character. Colonial rule in different parts of the world have subjected local people to both crude and subtle forms of humiliation.[3]

Interestingly, racial humiliation, which is at the base of the colonial configuration of power, undergoes inversion into caste humiliation at the level of the local configuration of power. Within this configuration, the function of caste-based humiliation, it could be argued, is to compensate for the loss of prestige and honour that the dominant social elite tends to lose in the colonial configuration of power. The celebration of India's spiritual superiority over the material West could be understood in the context of nationalist imagination. Invoking spiritual/cultural superiority by the nationalist thinkers and leaders by implication seeks to ignore the internal forms of humiliation that emanate from the social practices based on caste, untouchability, and gender discrimination. Nationalist response which remains silent over caste-/gender-based humiliation and shows hyper-sensitivity over racial humiliation necessarily acquires janus face. This face, thus, looks internally conservative and externally radical. In this regard it is interesting to note that Bankim was radically against racial humiliation but inconsistent over caste humiliation (Alam 1999: 106). Indian thinkers do not seem to have a hold over the nationalist imagination which ignores the question of self-respect for women and the lower castes. In fact, they tend to produce the same mechanism of humiliation of which they were the victims at the first instance.[4]

Conversely, the colonial configuration of power also plays an enabling role in that it creates the condition within which those who are at the receiving end of degradation begin to assert against the locally rooted structures of humiliation: caste and untouchability; they begin to question the karmic theory of servility.[5] The karma theory (Sharma 2000: 98–102), particularly in the Indian context, does not provide any scope for the lower caste untouchable to stake a claim against humiliation. This is because a slave in the grip of fear of death finds it impossible to stake a claim. Similarly, the theory of karma constructs a person in such a way that he/she finds it unnecessary to take the moral initiative so necessary for making the claim. However, it is necessary to point out a major difference between servility in the master–slave relationship as visualized by Hegel and the theory of karma as given by Manu. In the Hegelian master–slave relationship, the fear of death in the slave leads to the diminishing of moral capacity that is so important for assertion that defines humiliation. Humiliation is a struggle concept in the sense that it is both a struggle with the self and with the other. Compared to servility in the master–slave relationship the attitude of resigned fate in the theory of karma is much more baffling as it effectively arrests the growth of moral insight into the experience of humiliation. It leads the victims to adopt an attitude of resigned fate. The theory of karma, from the point of view of those who are reduced to servility, seeks to manipulate the servile into acknowledging their contemptuous and repulsive image as the part of a natural social arrangement. This acquiescence necessarily leads to the diminishing of moral initiative that is important for making a claim against humiliation.

Thus at one level, the idea of the public sphere based on the language of rights does help the slave and the untouchable to successfully overcome the element of fear and fate. At another level, the reorganization of society on modern lines also creates the condition for the production of humiliation. The ideological spell which necessarily arrests the growth of assertion against humiliation begins to fade away particularly in modern social conditions. These are twofold conditions that provide a formative context for the definition of humiliation. First, an element of comparison generates within a person the capacity for self-reflectivity necessary for gaining insight into oneself and others. Second, the emergence and the articulation of the language of rights make the assertion against humiliation possible. The language of rights helps the previously servile classes to achieve self-definition through detecting/resisting humiliation. Modernity plays an important role in generating among the servile a critical consciousness about actual and possible forms of humiliation, emanating from the local configuration of power. The historicized view of humiliation, which includes the experience of caste-based humiliation faced by Jotirao Phule[6] and Bhimrao Ambedkar (1993: 666–77) and their people, therefore becomes necessary for an understanding of both its definition and its complexities.

Although humiliation as a theme finds its expression in both the nationalist and socio-political thought in modern India, it calls out for a more detailed theoretical treatment from scholars. In contemporary social and political theory we come across intellectual efforts that would involve a serious theoretical follow-up of the theme of humiliation that finds its early expression in the socio-political thought in India. In the absence of these efforts it is quite encouraging to come across scholars, who, in their works, give definite hints towards the theorization of humiliation (Alam 1999: 67; Bhargava and Baxi 1987: 122; Desai 1995: 254; Kaviraj 1995: 303; Parekh 1974: 220–34). These are simply hints and are not adequate enough to capture the meaning, context, forms, and language of humiliation, which is complex and varied and hence requires a more sophisticated treatment for its better comprehension.

THE MEANING OF HUMILIATION

Defining humiliation is one of the central theoretical concerns common to most of the articles in this volume. These articles have adopted a distinct method to approach this definitional concern. First, in their attempts to define what humiliation is, they seek to unfold the meaning of humiliation by juxtaposing it with other concepts such as shame, disgust, discrimination, degradation, and segregation. This method is similar to the Apoha tradition in Buddhism.[7] In these traditions, the definition of a particular phenomenon is achieved through the negation, interrogation, and rejection of other concepts. Second, these articles also seek to define humiliation not simply at the level of empty abstraction, thus jumping from one concept to another, but by unfolding its complex meaning and providing concrete evidence within which this concept acquires a definite shape and an orientation. The articles therefore suggest the possibility of multiple meanings of the concept depending on specific socio-cultural contexts. This cultural specificity provides a vantage point that could be deployed in order to develop a comparative perspective on humiliation. At another level, it is also interesting to note that the attempts at theorizing humiliation made some of the contributors to the volume also suggest that this concept may not remain confined to a single disciplinary location. On the contrary, as the articles suggest, it could be cast into an interdisciplinary framework implicating several disciplines from psychology through political philosophy to jurisprudence.

Like the Apoha tradition, Bhikhu Parekh defines humiliation in terms of what it is not. He seeks to negate other concepts in favour of humiliation. He argues that causing physical cruelty or insulting someone does not involve humiliation. According to him, the term degradation would not constitute humiliation. Or, that degrading someone may not lead to humiliation. He seeks to defend this argument by citing pornography and prostitution, which, according to Parekh, may degrade women but would not humiliate them. For Parekh humiliation involves disrespecting and demeaning others, damaging their self-respect, and causing them moral hurt and pain. Although Parekh does draw on Kant's notion of self-respect, he finds two difficulties with the latter's notion of self-respect. First, Kant's doctrine of self-respect has a deeply homogenizing thrust and cannot provide the basis for the respect of individuality and difference. Second, Kant's notion of respect is more intellectual and a matter of individual achievement and hence it fails to appreciate the vital role of social structures, one's treatment by others, the conditions in which one lives, etc. in the development of self-respect. Parekh's understanding of humiliation thus suggests that humiliation as an inwardly driven feeling (falling in one's own eyes) gets defined in terms of the reception (acknowledgement) of the humiliating meaning that the tormentor assigns to the victim. This sort of communication of humiliation involves an element of passivity. There could be active ways through which humiliation could be defined. In the former, one confirms humiliation by not internalizing it but by rejecting the meaning that damages the self-respect of a person or group. In the second sense, humiliation acquires an active angle to the extent that it is externally driven against the tormentor. The rejection of an act of disrespect or maltreatment may take place through various levels of protests. Sanjay Palshikar elaborates on this dimension in his article.

Palshikar, like Parekh, approaches humiliation by juxtaposing it with other concepts. He also excludes other concepts in favour of humiliation. Palshikar argues that the concept of sad-masochistism does not involve humiliation because it makes pain or humiliation enjoyable or welcome. A victim begins to enjoy his/her humiliation. For Palshikar, humiliation in a radical sense is an unwelcome assault on human dignity. Similarly, Palshikar excludes the concept of shame in favour of humiliation. For him shame is a passive concept, which makes a person more inward-looking. Shame does have moral power, but only to transform a person from within. Shame thus does not prompt a person to either interrogate or communicate his/her displeasure to what Judith Shklar would call continuous devaluation by a tormentor (Shklar 1984: 232). Shame, according to Palshikar, is caused by a person's authority which comes from inside. This internal authority can lead to self-humiliation. Humiliation for Palshikar, therefore, is a claim of some sort. According to him the claim 'I am humiliated' is only half a claim or no claim at all. It becomes a full claim by offering a radically creative response to the present order and a need to create an entirely new vision of social relations. In short, Palshikar argues that if humiliation is a claim made complete only by incorporating in it the proposed responses to the alleged humiliation, then those who make that claim must face a situation of choice and attain the clarity required for making the choice. It could also be argued that humiliation cannot be defined in terms of a passive acknowledgment of the fragmentation of a morally integrated personality. Humiliation, as hinted by Palshikar, has the discursive power that is available to both the tormentor, who has capacity to assign differential moral worth to individuals, and the victim, who acquires the power to question and complain against humiliation. Humiliation in this sense is coefficient. This coefficient angle of humiliation also forms the core insight of Ashis Nandy's article.

Ashis Nandy argues, 'humiliation is a form of human relations that can never be a one-way exchange'. It is clear from his article that both the tormentor and the victim retain power within this particular social relationship. For Nandy, it could be argued, the role of the victim is more decisive in defining humiliation. He argues that unless the humiliated collaborate, by feeling humiliated, one cannot possibly humiliate people no matter how hard one does try. Thus, no humiliation is complete unless the humiliated oblige their tormentors by validating their desire to humiliate. He further argues that the humiliated do have some control over their tormentor. For example, Dalits have traditionally controlled the *savarnas* through their power to pollute. The Dalits, as untouchables, can thus act as poisoned weapons to produce a crisis for the twice-born in the Indian context. At a different level, Nandy brings out another important definitional dimension of humiliation. According to him, humiliation is a feeling that could be carefully cultivated for political purposes. Ethno-nationalists perceive humiliation as a potent weapon to inferiorize others on the basis of categories that may not have been historically present. For example, Hindu as a category is a recent construct and the humiliation of a Hindu is also recent. In this reading, humiliation does not have history but only a present. For Nandy humiliation is also a means to reassert the old hierarchies increasingly under stress. Strangely enough, as Nandy rightly argues, humiliating occupations like scavenging become available for Dalits to gain some social worth. Quoting his own study of Partition, Nandy observed that the Karachi elite and Pakistan's political leadership had to cajole the Hindu Dalits of Karachi to stay on in the city when ethnic cleansing was taking place all over northern India. He shares other perceptive insights in as much as he sees humiliation as a substitute to genocide, particular during the social holocaust of either Partition or Nazism. For Nandy, humiliation thus is a joint venture of both the tormentor and the victim, and is constitutive of this logical relationship.

Upendra Baxi, in his contribution, lays down a wide conceptual canvas covering a complex conceptual dimension of humiliation. The analysis of humiliation in Baxi's reading implicates the usual suspects like deference, degradation, decorum, aggression, violence, and violation, as also the opposite of humiliation—pride, honour, dignity, and self-respect. Baxi then argues that humiliation is not a stand-alone notion. According to him, the meaning we choose to invest in vis-à-vis associated notions will condition and even determine our understanding of humiliation. In analysing humiliation, Baxi draws our attention to crucial distinctions that relate to two dominant intellectual traditions. First, he argues that one should remain sensitive to the distinction between humiliation and exploitation, alienation and repression, truth and power, and governmentality and truth and juridical form. Second, he draws our attention to two etymological standpoints—the conventional and the critical. Conventional etymology, which existed from the eighteenth century in the Euro-American social experience, connected the humiliation experience with the experience of mortification. Baxi cautions that a Eurocentric take on humiliation needs to be fully understood, if only because socio-linguistic practices often express epistemic domination. Critical etymology on the other hand involves the critique of terms which could be quite deceptive. Baxi argues that the canvas of Hinduism involves the notion of *punya, sadachar, satkarma, namrata, sistachar,* and *vinamrata* or *vinay.* According to Baxi, all these ineluctably relate to *Dharmic purushartha* in the great cosmic chain of karma. If one reads this from the lens of conventional etymology, then it might appear to be an act of epistemic violence. He thus suggests that the very task critical etymology would pose is to search for the words of the humiliated that correspond to the above-mentioned six terms. He rightly suggests that the critique of these terms was undertaken by Buddhist, Bhakti, and Sufi traditions in the past, and the subaltern, led by Ranajit Guha, in the present.

V. Geetha gives a different angle to the understanding of humiliation. She seeks to define humiliation as an experience because it is felt; it is held and savoured in the very gut of our existence, in the core of our being. In this formulation, the understanding of humiliation is contingent upon the understanding of an experience of untouchability. She argues that we need to understand untouchability both as layered experience and as an evil that is stunning in its banality. Following her formulation, the Dalit body becomes the playfield of humiliation. The Dalit body is the prison for the Dalit human and his corporeal being precedes him and is itself considered as evidence of its lowness. Following the description of Cornel West, Geetha says, the body itself becomes an 'ontological wound'. Geetha, taking her cue from Kate Millet, argues that the ontological wound (in the Indian case it is caused by the practice of untouchability) assists the tormentor in exploring the dark depths of his soul. Geetha indirectly invokes Gandhi, who, in Bhikhu Parekh's words, would suggest moral surgery of this soul by cleansing it of untouchability. Thomas Pantham in his article provides a detailed overview of the dialogue that took place between Ambedkar and Gandhi over the question of untouchability. Pantham's article looks for the grounds of compatibility and complementarities between the two thinkers. It provides a background context for the larger understanding of untouchability, which could be linked up to the theme of humiliation.

Servility is another form of untouchability that denies authenticity to a being, for a servile person is the expression of another being. Thus, an untouchable as a slave is the living embodiment of his/her master's manhood and honour. As mentioned earlier, this kind of asymmetrical social relationship does not provide any moral condition within which a claim about humiliation could successfully be made. Servility necessarily postpones the possibility of an insight into humiliation; it exists because the untouchable or the servile person lacks the capacity to aspire for self-respect. To put it differently, a person who lacks self-respect, and does not aspire to attain it, cannot be humiliated. The questions that need to be raised here are: What is the social basis of humiliation? Under what conditions does it occur? It could be argued that humiliation is a modern phenomenon, which occurs within the conditions that make it possible for the servile to acquire both assertion and autonomy so necessary for self-respect. The struggle for humiliation and its contestation becomes more acute under the modern condition. The tormentor's ideological weapons like caste and karmic theory begin to lose the hold on the imagination of the servile who also become active to resist his/her humiliation and demand more and more recognition. This becomes possible only with modern conditions. In fact, these conditions, which offer space for self-definition and its assertion, enable us to make theoretical meaning of humiliation. Contributions to this volume clearly unfold to us this meaning.

The Context of Humiliation

Humiliation as a claim does not choose its context. On the contrary, the context plays a far more determinative role in terms of deciding the form and content of humiliation. It can be generally observed that society of the socially dead cannot provide the active context for the articulation of humiliation. Or, that a society with heaven on earth would make humiliation redundant. In fact, it is the context that decides the nature, level, and intensity of humiliation. This context could be varied and thus would play out itself differently in historical, institutional, and structural form. In its historical turn, it would suggest the shift in the forms of humiliation. However, humiliation looks endemic when understood from the structural point of view. It is going to be there as long as structures that underlie and renew the need for inequality and subordination/servility exist. However, as Parekh observes in his article, not all unequal societies involve institutionalized humiliation because much depends on the nature, extent, and basis of inequality. Humiliation is also institutional in the sense that it is rendered more acceptable if not natural through the complex process of mediation and moderation that works as its processes. The articles in this volume seek to capture this multilayered context of humiliation. Bhikhu Parekh, in his contribution, argues that colonial societies involve a certain kind of humiliation which could be called as racial humiliation between 'white' and the 'brown'. He offers British colonialism in Africa and India as the context that generates racial humiliation. Apart from Tapan Roychoudhury (referred to earlier), Dipesh Chakrabarty locates racial humiliation in the colonial context (Chakrabarty 2002: 76). Parekh, Nandy, and Palshikar locate caste-based humiliation in the local configuration of power. The local configuration of power inverses the relationship thus transforming the victim (in the colonial configuration) into the tormentor (in the local configuration) who uses caste-based humiliation against the untouchables. Nandy adds another interesting dimension to the humiliation that takes place in the local configuration of power. This claim to humiliation acquires a complicated dimension because it also defines the quality of the tormentor. For example, look at the following complaint that Nandy records of a Muslim who is reported to have said, *'ham ko achhuito se pitwaya'* (they [the Hindutva forces] had us thrashed by the untouchables). This indirectly suggests that if someone powerful thrashes a person, the person is concerned about the 'dignity' of the tormentor and not concerned about his/her self-respect. This lament ironically confirms the social hegemony that seeks to differentially accommodate people in the hierarchy thus creating an ascending sense of reverence for the socially dominant, but at the same time possessing an ascending sense of repulsion for those who constitute the lower order. This is the typical social charter of the Hindu social order. What about the other so-called liberal societies?

Parekh perceptively argues that institutionalized humiliation is largely marginal to a 'modern liberal bourgeoisie society' even though such a society is marked by deep economic, political, and other inequalities. He further argues that in such societies the poor and the powerless are exploited, coerced, manipulated, and even, from time to time, humiliated. However, they are not subjected to a systematic regime of humiliation, to use a phrase coined by Parekh. He offers reasons as to why humiliation is marginal to such societies. According to Parekh, in liberal societies inequalities are relatively fluid and allow for vertical mobility in principle, and, to some extent, even in practice. Finally, clinching his argument, Parekh observes that since one's place in society is contingent and not fixed forever, no major group has an interest in establishing a humiliating structure of practices lest it should itself one day be subjected to itself. This, according to Parekh, makes it easier to agree on the moral minimum (these are basic conditions for a reasonably decent life) to which all are entitled.

In continuation to Parekh's argument it could be argued further that in such modern liberal societies an element of rationality tends to minimize if not completely eliminate the possibility of humiliation. The twofold conditions based on equal opportunity principles and rule-bound competition should remove the reasons that would make the claim for humiliation valid. For example, the context of competition that is organized around certain commonly agreed upon rules, leaves little scope for the feeling of humiliation for those who have lost in such a competition. For example, a 100-metre race assumes that everybody is equally competent and hence those who do not make it have no reason to lose their self-esteem. Such people tend to reason out their failure on the grounds that they are 'more or less equally competent' with the successful one. In other words, both cultivated talent and skill form the background conditions that help in avoiding humiliation. If one takes this bourgeoisie rationality seriously, then, to use as example, the defeat at the hands of a relatively less skilled or less talented player of a team can lead to a deep sense of humiliation that a more competent team is likely to develop. Hence, the relatively less competent team ceases to have reasons to feel humiliated although it may inflict self-humiliation on itself. Such people through their instrumental rationality can avoid humiliation by staying away from the competition. Ironically, 'commonly agreed upon rules' force people to moderate their aspiration to a subsidized level where they tend to 'reason out' their exclusion as a natural fallout of their inability to participate, and hence nobody is to blame but themselves. This individualization of blame removes the possibility of making claims for humiliation that is internal to such rules.

Parekh, in his attempt to define the social context of institutionalized humiliation, points at such societies which are based on slavery, racial segregation, hierarchical status, untouchability, and caste system. For him, humiliation is built into the very structures of these societies. For Geetha, Hinduism provides a social context within which humiliation finds its most obnoxious expression, particularly in the form of untouchability. From the above account of liberal and not so liberal societies, it looks pretty clear that it is the traditional institutions based on caste, gender, race, and ethnicity that harbour humiliation. However, from here it does not follow that modern institutions based on universal secular principles would be devoid of humiliation. The division between the private and the public sphere helps in eliminating the possibility of humiliation from the public domain—both civil society and state institution. The 'public gaze' (mostly middle class) tends to define what is decent and what is not. This gaze therefore strictly monitors actions in the bourgeoisie's public domain. People are forced to drop their humiliation out of this public domain. On the one hand it is the force of social vigilance that keeps the humiliation out. The language of communication, based on communicative competence, removes the possibility of any condescending language. Humiliating language gets completely obliterated from the societies based on the logic of argument. However, the articles by Valerian Rodrigues, Peter Ronald deSouza, and Upendra Baxi seem to question this sequential notion of decency that is germane to the progressive transition of societies from the natural to the cultural, and from the barbaric to the civilized.

Valerian Rodrigues argues that the public domain, which could be called the bourgeoisie social order, at the theoretical level promises people a sense of respect and dignity. This is so mainly because this 'modern' sphere assigns equal status to people. The question that Rodrigues raises is, has this domain emerged in India? According to him India was expected to seek cultural departure from humiliating practices that colonial rule adopted against the Indians. In what way, he further questions, is the modern public sphere of independent India different from the colonial public sphere that was divided on racial lines—civil line and bazaar line, the latter being treated with deep derision. He argues that the public domain in India continued to be a space for squalor. Like every scholar in the volume, Rodrigues too reaffirms the concern that the biggest challenge for the constitution of the public domain in India was to include within it the Indian untouchables. What follows from Rodrigues' article is that the untouchables are not treated as part of the public domain which continues to be based on the ideology of purity and pollution. And, it is the public domain that has relegated the untouchables to do the unclean job. To paraphrase both Rodrigues and Geetha, it could be said that the untouchable is dirt and that dirt is the untouchable, both completely indistinguishable from each other. Yet, ironically, this shit is not disposable, as it is required to dispose the emitted shit. Nandy makes this complex but painful reduction of the untouchable to shit very clear, particularly with reference to the

Karachi Muslim elite during Partition. Rodrigues, with a lot of moral force, argues that the constitution of the public domain in India is impossible without the elimination of untouchability. Both Rodrigues and Geetha seek to link the persistence of untouchability to the public domain that according to them is deeply Brahmanical in nature. It is distinct by its capacity to fragment the untouchable's body by deploying the ideology of purity-pollution.

However, dirt does form the generic problem of the public sphere in other societies as well. Yet the idea of dirt in India is unique and deeply structural in nature. In western societies, for example, it is the corporeal body that carries physical dirt and hence can become an object of humiliation. As Marglit has observed, the sweating bodies are looked down upon (Margalit 1996: 104). Bodies are sized up and down through the humiliating gaze. Put differently, the notion of hygiene puts organic bodies to humiliating classification thus making some sanitized, and others dirty. Similarly, in British society, the elite classes carefully avoided mixing with pollutants (Ogborn 1998: 112). In England, the organization of the public sphere involved gender-based discrimination, as only men were admitted to coffee houses, while in French society the bourgeoisie was excluded from state and church and who, in the event of this exclusion, went to the salon (Habermas 1991: 33). In the Indian social cultural context one might hold the Brahmanical social order responsible for producing and reproducing the idea of dirt and squalor. The ideology of purity-pollution that is so central to the definition and survival of Brahmanism primarily aids the politics of cultural metamorphosis that involves the conversion of the corporeal body into what Barrington Moor calls the walking carrion[8] which thus becomes deeply repulsive. Walking carrion is the concentrated expression of repulsion. Within the Brahmanical mode of conceptual construction the untouchable represents the combination of multiple stigmatized images which make him/her untouchable, unseeable, unapproachable. It is in this sense that the untouchable's body is perceived and treated as a 'sociological danger'. As discussed in my own contribution to the volume and also through hints in Nandy's article, the stigmatized body is also available for counter-hegemonic purposes. The untouchable can also resignify his body and use it as a poisoned weapon to create a sense of anxiety in his/her tormentor.[9] It is in this sense that the body of an untouchable becomes a field of an insurmountable conflict. The untouchable's body, ridden with conflict, plays out across both time and space. One also comes across humiliating remarks from an upper caste person who says, Thank god Dalit women are dirty, otherwise they could be the easy target of vicious gaze and sexual assault of the male'. As has been argued by Rawls (1972: 431) and later by Margalit (1996), democratic institutions based on egalitarian principles do not humiliate people. In fact, they are supposed to create the conditions within which every person enjoys equal recognition. For example, these spheres of recognition are created through constitutional provisions and the state then subsequently tries to create institutional spaces for the realization of self-worth and dignity. However, deSouza and Baxi challenge this liberal theoretical commitment that promises to keep humiliation out of public institutions. Based on his study of Panchayati raj in one of the villages in Goa, deSouza presents a contrary thesis to the constitutional commitment. He argues that public institutions like the Panchayati raj become instrumental in sustaining humiliation as inflicted by the socially dominant forces. He further argues that such institutions provide a context for practising discrimination which is humiliating for some social groups. In his case it is the Mahars of some villages who feel humiliated in such structures. The cremation ground serves the basis. Chandhoke locates her argument in the larger theoretical context provided by Kant, Hegel, and other contemporary continental philosophers. She argues that the issue of recognition could be located in the interface between individual and community. She, in her essay, further argues that the prospects of basic self-confidence is inherent in the experience of love, self-respect in the experience of legal recognition and family. Self-esteem, according to her, is found in the experience of solidarity. For her, self-image of individual is correspondingly based on the experience of recognition. She links the question of recognition with cultural well-being. Inferring from her overall argument, it could be summarized that any cultural marginalization, happening even in the institutional setting of state would lead to a loss of recognition. This question of cultural marginalization, according to her, should warrant the attention of the critique to the relationship between the distribution of material resources and recognition. Baxi and Parekh also argue that public institutions in India entail elements of humiliation. Baxi further argues that certain constitutional provisions like reservation may regulate and reinforce humiliation of those who are the beneficiaries of such provisions. The question that needs greater attention is this: Why do people walk into the disciplinary regime of the state? Suhas

Palshikar also holds the state responsible for not removing the conditions that lead to humiliation. In his article, Palshikar tries to situate humiliation as an unfortunate fallout of the industrial breakdown in Mumbai. His narrative of the humiliation of the working classes operates in the conditions of servility and helplessness created by the industrial strikes in the textile mills in Mumbai. Palshikar seeks to focus on those textile workers who have lost their job due to the textile workers' strike in 1982. His narrative of the working classes in Mumbai brings out the humiliation that workers face, both at the level of the 'intimate' and also at the level of the more anonymous, which he calls the sphere of civil society. In the intimate, the jobless worker is looked down upon by other family members; in the anonymous, the civil society humiliates the worker. For example, the wife of the worker becomes the maidservant and hence becomes the object of ridicule and suspicion (Haldar 2006: 144–5). It is suggested that normally maidservants in India do face this problem.

Finally, humiliation is not so much a physical or corporeal injury; in fact, it is more a mental/psychological injury that leaves a permanent scar on the heart. I argue in my own contribution that the cultural reduction of a human being from the cultural to the natural (anti-civilizational) takes place through the infliction of mental/moral injuries that assigns differential inferior/hierarchical meanings to the corporeal body. This reduction of a decent body into a decomposed body (walking carrion suggesting a concentrated expression of repulsion) introduces a fine distinction between human rights and humiliation. One of the ways to define human rights is to place an absolute premium on the integrity of the physical body, which may be the source of humiliation. It is in this sense that the one-sided and limited understanding of human rights may put the latter in direct contradiction with humiliation. On the other hand, the Kantian notion of human rights would treat the corporeal body as a repository of dignity and respect and not a storehouse of humiliation. It is for the first reason that Kant would oppose the annihilation of the human body, which, according to him, has the moral stamina to reproduce as also human values like dignity and the capacity to respect the self and others. The argument against capital punishment has to be understood within this kind of human rights discourse. Thus any physical injury to the corporeal body is absolutely unacceptable in this kind of understanding. Thus guarantee to physical existence in such understanding gets privileged over other moral goods. Humiliation on the other, as Orlando Patterson has observed (Patterson 1982: 37), can lead to social death. According to Patterson, servile attitude and slave mentality, which kill a person symbolically, may look preferable to self-respect that cannot be gained without struggle. Struggle for self-respect may cause real death. This fear of death suggests the slave mentality, which makes mere physical survival more precious than survival with dignity. Taking cue from Judith Shklar (1984), it could be argued that people facing a threat to their lives tend to make choices that could be morally problematic. They would ironically find humiliation to be a lesser evil than physical threat. Thus, an insult for some becomes preferable to total physical annihilation. This raises a question of who can be humiliated?

A person or social group who is not only sensitive about self-respect but can also protest cannot be humiliated. To put it differently, as Richard Rorty and others have argued, a thick-skinned person cannot be humiliated (Gender 1999: 94). The target of humiliation as the contributors to this volume have noted, could be an individual, or a group, community, and even an entire country. Bhikhu Parkeh gives different examples so as to show how re-description of a person or the entire community can lead to social degradation. Parekh further argues that pathological re-description, which is based on race or caste, region and gender, does constitute humiliation. Parekh, Geetha, and Nandy have dealt with these forms of humiliation in their contributions. Parekh argues that the tormentor deploys humiliation to hit more than one target. He cites the example of Serbian soldiers raping a Bosnian Muslim woman. Nandy makes a similar point in the case of the women raped during the Partition in 1947. Geetha argues that sexual assaults on Dalit women by the upper caste are conducted with the intention to assert virility, and also to shame untouchable men. Sanjay Palshikar maps out different and more contemporary forms of humiliation which suggest that it is not human beings but geographical regions which place humiliation at a symbolic level. He substantiates his classification of humiliation by referring to what Habermas says about the US attack on Iraq. Habermas, as quoted in the article by Palshikar, said, 'US attack on Iraq was the humiliation of the Islamic world'. In any case, the attack on the two towers is seen by many observers and commentators as the national humiliation of an American. As the articles to the volume suggest, the culturally specific practice of humiliation produces its different forms across both time and space. These forms however do not provide the conditions for their expression for in order to communicate their expression they require language.

Humiliation does have a particular vocabulary, which decides the depth and intensity of the former. In fact, the language of humiliation introduces a certain economy of scale that has a bearing on the impact that the tormentor intends to produce. The words that carry and communicate humiliation can achieve a huge impact with less investment. For example, words referring to women's modesty are deployed with the intention to produce a paralysing effect on the victim. Words have an enormous impact and this fact is corroborated in the local saying in Hindi, '*Goli maro parantu gali mat do*' (shoot me with a bullet but do not shoot arrows of abuse at me). The use of language for producing humiliation also makes the moral passage of the word/vocabulary quite painful. For example, look at the journey of the term scheduled caste, which is a modern, universal term. This term which is constituted by the state was adopted by the Indian constitution replacing terms such as untouchables, or even Harijan, which was treated as the morally/culturally problematic term at least by those designated as Scheduled Caste. The tormentor has sought further language distortion by fracturing it into '*schaddu*'. (This is the distorted version devised by upper caste medical students doing their MBBS course in one of the colleges in Delhi. They devised this special language in order to humiliate Dalit doctors also studying for their medical degrees in the same college. This college is situated right in the heart of India's capital.) In this regard, it is also interesting to note that the social elite in Japanese society uses a sign language in order to establish the identification of Burakumin who are the object of humiliation (Zizek 2000: 189). The socially superior in Japanese society indicate four fingers at the Burakumin communicating to the latter that they are like four-legged animals. It is normally observed that the tormentor use words for communicating humiliation. In this regard it is interesting to note Baxi's understanding that it is also possible for the words to be humiliated. Thus, language also suffers humiliation.

Resistance is internal to humiliation. Since humiliation does not get defined unless it is claimed, it naturally involves the capacity to protest. A society or a group with socially dead people would not offer any space for resistance against humiliation. In such cases, people lack the minimum moral capacity to take risk. Risk is motivational and leads a person to make sacrifices in favour of higher goods like the right to appear in public without a sense of shame. Those who seek to exercise this civil right would always run the risk of inciting opposition from those who want to push these people to the margins. The Dalits of the villages in southern Tamil Nadu ran the risk and had to pay a heavy price. The humiliation, however, extracts a range of responses from its victims, from refusal to comply with the order of the dominant or the re-signification of what is humiliated to the taking to terrorism. This volume seeks to unfold the complex meaning and practices of humiliation. It does not impose the abstract framework on the empirical; in fact, the abstract emerges only from the concrete. The study of humiliation through its interdisciplinary thrust seeks to incorporate within itself concepts from the fields of history, sociology, psychology, and political theory. For example, the concept of humiliation can expand the meaning of other concepts such as justice, equality, and nationalism. Moreover, the attempts to theorize humiliation would help us understand the structures that underlie and renew the attitude of humiliation. The present volume is expected to generate among the readers a compelling sense of appreciation of the need for a decent and just society. It is also expected to question on normative grounds, those who are the source of humiliation. Humiliation studies in India could be built around a new conceptual language that could unfold for us a complex dimension of social reality that otherwise keeps escaping the attention of the established social and political theory in India.

NOTES

1. This is Kant's own confession, available on the opening page of Nicholas Dent's book on Rousseau; see Dent (2004).
2. See Taylor (1997: 225–57, 1985: 79) and chapter 11 of Walzer (1983). See also Barrington (1978: 69); Fraser and Honneth (2003); Habermas (1991: 39); Heller (1985: 233); Margalit (1996); Nussbaum (1993: chapter 2); Rorty (1979); Young (1990).
3. See Bhikhu Parekh in the same volume for crude forms of humiliation and Fanon (1967) for subtle forms.
4. Sanjay Palshikar in the same volume.
5. The karma theory has been outlined in the Manu Dharma Shastra.
6. Phule himself was thrown out from a marriage procession of a friend in Pune. In this regard it is also interesting to note what Phule has to say about the humiliation of the Dalit corporeal body. He says, 'the Brahmins used to cover their nose so as to communicate that the dalits' bodies are repulsive and polluting' Phadke (1991: 567).
7. The Apoha tradition has been part of Buddhist philosophy.
8. See Moor (1978: 69). Moor points out that the untouchables were reduced to 'walking corpse'. I have argued that they are reduced to the level of 'walking carcass'; V.S. Naipaul has pointed out that the untouchables were reduced to the identity of 'walking carrion'. Please see Naipaul (1988: 37).
9. *Ponga Pandit*, the satirical play in Chattisgrahi, written in 1932, and re-adopted and directed by Habib Tanveer.

SECTION I
FOREGROUNDING HUMILIATION AS CLAIM

1 Logic of Humiliation

Bhikhu Parekh

WHAT IS HUMILIATION?

Since humiliation is a highly complex and largely unexplored phenomenon, and is easily confused with discrimination, rejection, degradation, and other apparently similar but basically quite different phenomena, it would be useful to begin with a brief sample of its real life and paradigmatic cases.[1] Real life cases are important because hypothetical cases oversimplify situations and miss out their contexts and nuances. Paradigmatic cases, by which I mean those that the individuals involved as well as most of the rest would recognize as examples of humiliation, provide a relatively unambiguous starting point and a stable frame of reference. The situations cited below fall within this category and highlight different forms and features of humiliation.

1. A hostess was handsomely complimented by her guests on the quality of her food. Her husband remarked that they should compliment the Sainsbury's supermarket where she had bought it.

2. Unable to get his way, a fourteen-year-old boy shouted at his father in the presence of his friends, telling him what a horrible father he was, that he had no respect let alone love for him, and that he wished he had a different father.

3. A white feminist in France rushed up to a fully veiled Muslim woman and tore off her veil. Shouting curses at the institution of patriarchy, she asked her to rebel against it and stop behaving like a precious doll.

4. Mahatma Gandhi had a valid first class ticket to travel from Petermaritzburg to Johannesburg. Since the rules barred blacks and Asians from travelling first class, the ticket inspector asked him to get out of the carriage. When he refused, the inspector insulted and shouted at him and threw him and his luggage out of the carriage at the next station. Feeling bitter and demeaned, he spent the rest of the night shivering in a dark waiting room on the platform.

5. When a member of the conservative Bohra community in India challenged its authoritarian supreme leader, the latter ostracized him and ordered his followers to avoid all contact with him.[2] At his mother's funeral a few weeks later, no one turned up, not even his brothers and sisters, driving the devastated man into a long period of depression and self-pity.

6. When Indians all over India protested against the British government's repressive measures in 1919, General Dyer ordered his troops to fire at a peacefully assembled crowd in Jallianwalla Bagh, killing nearly four hundred people. Not content with this, he issued 'crawling orders', which required all Indians to crawl on all fours when passing through certain streets in that area. Indians were outraged at what they called national humiliation.

7. Iraqi soldiers in the Abu Ghraib prisons were stripped naked and photographed by the jeering US camp guards. They were spat at and urinated upon, and made to stand naked for days and slide on their stomachs. Some of them were stacked on top of each other in such a way that the genitals of those below touched the bottoms of those above them. Some were forced to masturbate in the presence of others while their guards, including a woman, photographed and videotaped them.

8. During the decades of racial segregation in the southern states of the United States, blacks were served at different counters and ate in separate quarters in restaurants. They sat on reserved rows in buses, paid at the front of the bus and entered it through the rear door, and were insulted and sometimes assaulted for failing to show whites adequate respect when passing them on the streets.

9. For centuries the untouchables in India were confined to segregated areas and prevented from coming into physical contact with upper caste Hindus. Even an accidental contact with them was considered polluting and required a ritual bath. In parts of south India they were required to make loud noises when passing through upper caste areas, so that the upper caste residents could quickly retreat

into their houses and avoid even their shadows. Untouchable women were not allowed to wear certain kinds of dress or even cover their breasts, this being an exclusively high caste privilege.

10. During the Soviet trials of political opponents in the 1930s, the latter were forced to make false confessions, to admit what they had earlier denied, and were publicly ridiculed before being imprisoned, sent to a concentration camp, or shot.

11. In the 1930s the Nazis compelled the Jews of Vienna to get on their knees and scrub the streets. In concentration camps, they stripped, abused and mocked the Jews, made them conform to every passing whim of the sadistic guards, and subjected them to all manner of indignity before sending them to the gas chambers.

Although the situations described above differ in several respects, they share one central feature, namely, an assault on the self-respect of those involved.[3] The latter are demeaned, belittled, devalued, mocked, made objects of ridicule or contempt, and diminished in their own and others' eyes. They have a certain view of themselves and the kind of minimum treatment that is due to them. When this is denied and others' treatment of them falls below their expectations, their self-respect is violated. An individual who lacks a sense of what is due to him, and the concomitant sense of self-respect, would not know what it is to be humiliated. And, conversely, if someone was humiliated and did not mind it in the least, we would wonder if he had any self-respect.

When an individual's self-respect is violated, he feels hurt or pained. The pain is not narrowly psychological in nature as in the case of frustrated desires, but moral in nature in the sense that it arises from the violation of what is due to him/her and diminishes him/her as a person. When individuals have been subjected to long periods of humiliation, they develop all kinds of defence mechanisms and take the assault on their self-respect in their stride. The fact that they do not feel hurt or complain does not mean that they do not feel humiliated. They know that their self-respect is violated and that they are devalued and treated with contempt, but choose not to let it get to them. Extreme situations arise when the wider social structure so crushes their spirit that they fail to develop even a weak sense of self-respect and accept their treatment as all they are worth. Since they lack self-respect, they do not feel humiliated. However, since the objective thrust of their treatment and often even the intention behind it is to prevent the development of, and crush any expression of, self-respect, the social structure could be said to have a humiliating impact on them. Humiliation is most effective when it is so deep and pervasive that it is no longer recognized for what it is, but that does not gainsay its reality.

Humiliation might, but need not, involve physical cruelty. The husband who remarks on his wife's cooking, the ticket inspector who threw Gandhi off the train, and the American guard who urinated on the Iraqi soldier are not necessarily cruel to their victims. Conversely, a man who starves another to death, tortures him and in these and other ways shows cruelty to him does not necessarily humiliate him. Humiliation need not involve the use of physical force either. It did in the case of Gandhi, the Jews, and the untouchables, but not the case of the hostess and the Bohra reformer. Humiliation, again, may and generally does involve insult but not always, and when it does, the insult it not enough to constitute humiliation. The Bohra leadership humiliated but did not insult the reformer. A bureaucrat who courteously and politely but relentlessly forces a welfare claimant to reveal intimate details of his private life, and leaves him in no doubt about what he thinks of him, humiliates but does not insult the latter. Conversely, if the ticket inspector had insulted Gandhi for daring to travel first class and left it at that, his behaviour would not have amounted to humiliation. One might insult and dismiss a tenacious beggar, but one does not thereby humiliate him. Although humiliation involves disrespect, the latter too is not enough to constitute humiliation. If I fail to get up from my seat when my guests arrive or leave, I show them disrespect but do not humiliate them, unless I damage their self-respect by suggesting that I did not get up because I regarded them as persons of no consequence or because I had not really meant to invite them.

Humiliation takes different forms and varies in degrees. One can humiliate others by words, gestures, and actions, and even by simple silence. Humiliation can be sexual as in the case of the Iraqi solders, or social as with the Bohra reformer, or political as when no one turns up at a pompous politician's meeting or when he receives a derisory vote in an election. Humiliation can be minor and casual as in the case of the host and his wife, most acute as with Nazi treatment of Jews, or fall somewhere in between as with many of the other examples cited above. It is important to bear these differences in mind because otherwise one either concentrates only on the most acute forms of humiliation and ignores the rest, or focuses on the latter and fails to appreciate fully the enormity of its most brutal forms. Humiliation can be simple or multilayered in nature, and simultaneously affect different persons in different ways. The host's remark about his wife's cooking in our earlier example is a case of one-dimensional humiliation, whereas the Serbian soldier raping a Bosnian Muslim woman in front of her husband and children inflicts a highly complex and multidimensional form of humiliation. In the latter case, the soldier humiliates the woman by raping her, humiliates her husband by mocking his inability to protect his wife, and humiliates both husband and wife even further by mocking them in front of their children.

Contrary to what is commonly argued, humiliation need not necessarily involve a third party. It implies going down in one's own eyes, or those of others, or often both. While the presence of others accentuates the feeling of humiliation, it is not essential. The boy in the case cited earlier humiliates his father even if no one else is present. Gandhi would have been humiliated even if there were no other passengers in the carriage and there was no danger of the incident acquiring wider publicity. Even when only two parties are involved, it is not necessary that there should be direct contact between them. If the boy in our example were to mumble to himself the humiliating remarks about his father, which the latter accidentally overhears, the father could and would feel humiliated.[4]

The objects of humiliation cover a wide spectrum. They obviously include individuals, but also groups. Jews and blacks have long been subjected to both humiliating treatments and stereotypes. In the aftermath of World War I, Germany was subjected to demands that were intended to humiliate it and which most self-respecting Germans did see in that way. After its invasion of Kuwait, Iraq was systematically humiliated by being required to meet increasingly new conditions to which no other country in a similar situation had been subject and which any self-respecting country was bound to find unacceptable. Colonized societies were often mocked, ridiculed, dismissed as worthless, and in these and other ways treated in a humiliating manner.

Sometimes those affected by a practice might disagree about whether or not it represents humiliation. We then need to probe its deeper meaning and significance by looking at its context, social role, and underlying assumptions. Take, for example, the judgement by the American Supreme Court in *Plessey v. Ferguson*.[5] The plaintiff argued that separate rail cars for blacks were inherently degrading and humiliating, a view denied by whites. The Supreme Court rejected the plaintiff's argument saying: 'We consider the underlying fallacy of the plaintiff's argument to consist in the assumption that the enforced separation of the two races stamps the coloured race with a badge of inferiority. If this be so, it is not by reason of anything found in the act, but solely because the coloured race chooses to put that construction on it.' The Supreme Court made two mistakes. It questioned the construction that blacks had put on separate cars. Even if they had put a more charitable construction, whites might not have and then the separate rail cars would be seen as a badge of white superiority and *mutatis mutandis* of black inferiority. Secondly, the Supreme Court did not ask why there were separate cars at all. The blacks clearly did not want them, only the whites did. Creating separate cars implied that only the views of the whites mattered, and that they decided not only where they sat but also where the blacks sat. Furthermore, the whites wanted the blacks to sit separately because they did not want to associate with them, and this was so because they regarded them as an inferior 'race' from whom a respectable distance had to be maintained.

Separate cars sent out the humiliating message that blacks were inferior, that close contact with them was undesirable, and that whites alone had the right to determine the nature and extent of this contact. If the rest of society had not been based on segregation, and separate cars had been introduced by mutual consent, the situation would have been different. Under the circumstances, the construction blacks put on this segregation was the only valid one. The Supreme Court was wrong to argue that the implication of black inferiority was a product of black imagination and not to be 'found in the act'. The meaning of an act is not inherent in it but derives from its context and underlying assumptions. Against the background of the wider society, both blacks and whites knew that separate cars signified black inferiority, which is why the former complained against them while the latter vigorously defended them.

Although degradation sometimes coincides with and makes its victims more vulnerable to humiliation, the two should not be confused.[6] Some practices involve both, such as the Nazi treatment of Jews and the Indian treatment of untouchables; others involve one but not the other. In the examples cited earlier, the husband humiliated but did not degrade his wife, and the ticket inspector too humiliated but did not degrade Gandhi. By contrast, pornography degrades the women involved and even perhaps, by association, all women, but it is not obvious that it also humiliates them. The practice of tossing dwarfs as far as possible with their consent and willing participation was rightly banned by the French and German courts on the ground

that it degraded them and violated their dignity. It is not obvious that it also humiliated them.
A practice then can be humiliating without being degrading, and vice versa. And when it is both, it is not one by virtue of being the other. Since they often go together and have many features in common, the distinction between them is neither easy to articulate nor can be located in a single, distinguishing characteristic. Broadly speaking, degradation consists in treating human beings in a manner that violates the prevailing moral consensus on the minimum that is due to them as human beings. Prevailing norms define the threshold, the base line, below which the treatment of human beings should not fall. If it does, it is said to degrade them, to fall below the requirements of their humanity or moral status. We consider prostitution degrading because we hold certain beliefs about the nature and significance of sexuality, the human body, and so on, and feel strongly that they should not be bought and sold. If we did not hold these beliefs, we would see prostitution as just another way of earning one's livelihood and find nothing degrading in it. Again, we believe that human beings have an intrinsic worth and should not be treated as things or objects of amusement, and find dwarf-throwing degrading. Whether or not the dwarfs themselves share this view is irrelevant. In actual fact, the dwarfs had disagreed with this view and had appealed against the ban which was upheld by the higher courts. The dwarfs shared the belief in human dignity, but not the view that throwing them around constituted a violation of it.

While a practice or a form of treatment is degrading irrespective of what the individuals involved think and feel about it, this is not the case with humiliation. Humiliation consists of disrespecting and demeaning others, damaging their self-respect, bringing them down in their eyes, and causing them hurt and pain. If a form of treatment does not do this, it cannot be said to humiliate those involved. This is why throwing dwarfs degrades but does not humiliate them. It is based on their consent, which is not coerced, and is often initiated by them; it does not belittle them in their eyes and damage their self-respect; and it does not cause them moral hurt or pain. This is also the case with the women involved in prostitution and pornography. By the norms of our society and even perhaps on more general grounds, they are degraded, but they are not humiliated unless they are made to do things that violate their self-respect and cause them hurt and pain. By contrast, in the example cited earlier, the white feminist humiliates the veiled Muslim woman because she violates her self-respect, belittles and demeans her, yet she does not degrade her or treat her as if she were subhuman or devoid of worth and value. In fact, she humiliates her precisely because she is outraged by what she takes to be her degradation and her failure to rebel against it.

Just as humiliation overlaps, but is not identical with, degradation, it also overlaps, but should not be confused with, humbling someone. The latter consists in deflating an individual's ego and taking her down a peg or two with a view to getting her to take a just view of her abilities and achievements. One might dent a talented but arrogant student's ego by setting her an impossibly demanding task or taking an excessively critical view of her work. This is designed to humble and not humiliate her because it neither displays disrespect/contempt for her nor seeks to undermine her self-respect.

Such a process of non-humiliating humbling forms part of the training for priesthood in many religions. Total surrender to the will of God requires the religious aspirants to annihilate all traces of pride, the greatest sin not only in Christianity but also in all other religions. Since it is not easily eliminated, all religions prescribe a programme of appropriate spiritual exercises. For centuries some Catholic orders, for example, required their novices to assemble at the end of the day to confess publicly whatever base or egoistical thoughts they had entertained during the day, and to report with brutal honesty whatever expressions of pride they had noticed in other novices with whom they were paired during the course of their training. Although these exercises sometimes came close to humiliation, they aimed not to humiliate but to cultivate deep humility. Their purpose was both to annihilate pride and to build the self-respect of the aspirants by getting them to appreciate that, while at one level they were insignificant, nothing but bundles of sinful passions, they were at the deepest level divine, made in God's image, and could, when free of pride, become worthy objects of the highest esteem.

In the light of our discussion, humiliation covers a wide spectrum. At one end, it is a casual phenomenon involving intentional or inadvertent put-down remarks and insensitive or arrogant treatment. At the other end, it involves forms of human relationships with humiliation built into their very structure. Although hurtful, the former are sometimes part of life, taken in one's stride, and generally leave no deep psychological and moral scars. The latter are far more complex and serious in their consequences and deserve closer examination.

INSTITUTIONALIZED HUMILIATION

Humiliation, I have argued, involves violating an individual's self-respect and demeaning or belittling her in her own and/or others' eyes. Organized or institutionalized humiliation exists when social institutions and practices embody disrespect for, and systematically violate the self-respect of, groups of individuals. An unequal society in which some enjoy considerable power over others and exercise it with relative impunity is obviously its ideal home. However, not all unequal societies involve institutionalized humiliation because much depends on the nature, extent, and basis of inequality.

Take, for example, the modern liberal bourgeois society. Although marked by deep economic, political, and other inequalities, institutionalized humiliation is largely marginal to it. The poor and the powerless are exploited, coerced, manipulated, and some are, from time to time, humiliated, but they are not subjected to systematic or what one might call a regime of humiliation. Inequalities are relatively fluid and allow for vertical mobility in principle and to some extent even in practice. Since one's place in life is contingent and not fixed forever, no major group has an interest in establishing a humiliating structure of practices lest it should itself one day be subjected to them. This makes it easier to agree on the moral minimum to which all are entitled. Welfare provisions that are to be found in liberal bourgeois societies ensure that all citizens enjoy the basic conditions of a reasonably decent life, and none has to put himself or herself in a humiliating situation in order to stay alive. The inequalities, further, are underpinned and limited by a collective commitment to the basic equality of all human beings. All citizens have equal worth and dignity, and none is more of a human being than another. An employee is subject to the power of his employer at the workplace, but that is not carried over into other areas of life where he remains his equal. And even at the workplace, there are strict limits on how he may be treated. The equality of respect, and civil, political and other rights, moderates the prevailing structure of inequality, and ensures that it does not cross certain limits.

The situation is quite different in societies where inequalities are differently grounded. They might be ascriptive, based on colour of skin, race, birth, ethnicity, etc., and hence unalterable, or they might be quasi-ascriptive, based on religion, language, etc., and alterable only by the greatest of efforts or at the cost of one's pride and self-respect. Inequalities here are frozen, congealed into a fixed hierarchy of status, and allow no or little vertical or even horizontal mobility.

They are interlocked and no amount of superior achievement in one area overcomes or compensates for basic inequality. Human worth is equated with social status and those of an inferior status are considered less human. They count for little and their views and feelings are treated as of no consequence. Since these societies are underpinned by a belief in the hierarchical gradation of humanity, humiliation is built into their very structure.

Societies based on slavery, racial segregation, hierarchical status, untouchability and the caste system are all examples of institutionalized humiliation. Although they differ in important respects, they all share certain features in common. In all of them identifiable groups of men and women are viewed and treated as inferior beings, deserving little, if any, respect. Social institutions and practices lay down what occupations they may pursue, where they may live, who they may marry, how they may address and be addressed by others, how they may interact with others, the kind of life they may lead, and the inflexible parameters within which they must operate.[7] Legal institutions deny them basic rights, and political institutions deny them a voice in the conduct of their common affairs. Indeed, every area of life proclaims their inferiority and marginality.

Humiliation in such a society in an integral part of its system of domination. Established practices and forms of relationship embody disrespect bordering on contempt for subordinate groups, and not only relentlessly assault their self-respect but even seek to prevent them from developing it. Since humiliation is deep, pervasive, routinized and woven into the language in which subordinated groups are talked about, such a society does not generally need to resort to blatant acts of humiliation except as periodic reminders of their inferior status. The dominated groups might sometimes be treated with kindness and even respect, but such acts are undertaken against the unchallenged background of the reality of humiliation, and based on the unspoken assumption that the recipients will not misconstrue them and seek to get above themselves.[8]

Societies based on institutionalized humiliation generally rely on four interrelated measures for their survival and stability. First, they need to persuade both the dominant and dominated groups that the prevailing social system is right and just. Although every social system needs a legitimizing ideology to secure consent, one based on humiliation needs it more than others because of the way it assaults the human sense of dignity. The ideology is most effective when it becomes the common sense of society, so that its members instinctively understand their social world in terms of its categories and cannot even imagine that it can be organized differently. This is achieved by embodying the dominant ideology in the major educational, cultural, and other institutions of society and transmitting it to succeeding generations by cultivating among them appropriate patterns of thought and behaviour.

Secondly, humiliation is most easily accepted when it is accompanied by degradation. Those living in degrading economic, social, and other conditions do not have the opportunity to develop their capacities, and are easily perceived and presented as legitimate objects of humiliation. They generally fail to develop their self-respect and tend to take a low view of themselves, which makes it easier for them to accept their humiliation. Degrading conditions of life also often so crush the human spirit and enervate their victims that they find it difficult to organize and challenge the prevailing social structure. For these and related reasons, a society based on humiliation uses all means at its disposal to keep the humiliated groups in conditions of poverty, squalor, long working hours, ill health, political isolation, and social marginalization.

Thirdly, a society based on humiliation requires an informal and diffused system of coercion administered routinely by the dominant group. The clear boundary that such a society draws between the dominant and subordinated groups needs to be diligently guarded and enforced by punishing the smallest real or imagined transgressions. No central agency can do this because of its obvious administrative and other limitations. The society therefore relies on the individual members of the dominant group to act as the guardians of the system, and authorizes them to administer chastisement, dismiss from jobs, ostracize, insult, and use such sanctions and coercive measures as they think appropriate to keep the subordinated groups in their place.

Finally, every society based on humiliation depends on the physical force of the state to sustain it. The dominant ideology does not always succeed in winning the hearts and minds of its members; the informal system of coercion needs the help of the well-armed state to give it credibility; and however degraded the dominated groups might be, there is always the danger that their anger, hatred, and bitterness might boil over. Although no system of humiliation can be maintained using physical force alone, it cannot do without it either. The state intimidates, arouses fear and awe, and expresses the society's determination to act decisively when threatened. Since a good deal of its work is done by other agencies, the state generally remains in the background, making its presence felt in periodic displays of strength, showcase trials, and exemplary punishment of carefully selected and dramatized cases of transgression.

Since the society based on humiliation is supported by these four strategies, a successful challenge to it requires co-ordinated action at all four levels. A systematic and persuasively articulated critique of the dominant ideology weakens its hold and creates spaces for individual and organized dissent. The economic and social struggle to improve the material conditions of the dominated groups builds up their self-confidence, widens their horizon, increases their range of opportunities, and throws up successful individuals whose achievements refute the assiduously fostered belief in their inherent inferiority. The struggle for basic human rights and the rule of law limits the exercise of arbitrary individual power, gives the dominated groups an effective redress against its excesses, nurtures their sense of human dignity and equality, and in these and others counters the informal system of coercion. Since this reduces the need for a regime of formal and informal sanctions, it reduces the coercive role of the state, expands the area of, and better protects individual liberties. This calls for democratic institutions, including universal franchise, free and fair elections, free press, civil liberties, and a vibrant civil society. Since these four struggles target different defences of the prevailing system, they reinforce each other and are all equally important.

FOSTERING SELF-RESPECT

I have argued that a society based on organized humiliation represents a systematic assault on the self-respect of its victims. A good society should, among other things, nurture the self-respect of its members and devise its institutions and practices accordingly. This raises several questions relating to the nature and basis of self-respect, what it entails, why it is important and how it can be fostered. Since Kant offers one of the first and most sophisticated accounts of the subject, I shall concentrate on him and develop my view through an internal critique of him.

For Kant, human beings are marked out from the rest of the natural world by virtue of their unique powers of reason and morality. Thanks to these, they are capable of rising above the automatic processes of the natural world and governing themselves by means of self-given laws. The capacity for freedom or self-determination is unique to them and is the basis of their dignity, infinite value, or worth. Their dignity is derived not from an external source but their own nature, and is intrinsic or inherent in them. Since they share a common human nature and are equally capable of freedom, Kant argues that they have equal dignity or worth. Moral conduct consists in acting in a manner that accords with the equal intrinsic worth of all human beings, and requires that the principles of one's action should be capable of universalization or being adopted by all without defeating their purpose. Kant discusses self-respect and respect for others within this framework. Human beings deserve respect because the powers of reason and morality deserve respect. 'All respect for a person is only respect for the law of which the person provides an example.'[9] Self-respect is the 'duty of man to himself', and is derived from the duty 'to respect human nature'. To respect oneself is to have an inner sense of one's absolute worth, to value oneself as a noumenal being and an end in himself.[10] The grounds on which one has a duty to respect oneself also entail a duty to respect others. One should value and respect them as beings of absolute worth, as one's moral equals, and should do nothing that humiliates them or detracts from their dignity. Kant is so anxious to avoid the slightest traces of humiliation that he wants help to be given to the needy in such a way that one not only does not let them feel 'humbled' as objects of charity but expresses one's gratitude to them for accepting the help.[11]

Although Kant's account of respect for others and oneself is coherent and basically correct, it is not without its difficulties. Kant's theory of respect has a quasi-religious orientation, and his view of respect borders on reverence. For him rational and moral powers are of supreme and infinite value, and human beings have value because they are their bearers. Just as human beings have value for a religious person because all human beings are made in the image of God and thus should be honoured as a way of honouring Him, for Kant, human beings derive their value from impersonal powers and should be respected as a way of showing respect to these powers. As he puts it, to respect a human being is to show 'reverence' for 'humanity' or 'human nature'. Kant's moral thought is underpinned by a religion of humanity of the kind popularized by some of the leaders of the French Revolution, which he admired and which influenced him deeply. For Kant, human beings have value and deserve respect not in their wholeness, that is their powers, needs, desires, limitations, and vulnerabilities, but only as embodiments of transcendental and quasi-divine powers.[12]

Kant reduces self-respect to species-respect in the sense that individuals are to respect themselves and others as exemplifications of the human species and not as unique individuals, because of their shared humanity and not their individualizing identity. Indeed, since it is the noumenal or transcendental self that is the object of respect, and since it is identical in all, Kant's doctrine has a deeply homogenizing thrust and cannot provide the basis of respect for individuality and difference.[13] Furthermore, as Kant understands it, self-respect is an intellectual and individual achievement, an insight of reason acquired by rising above one's contingent features and recognizing one's essentially rational and moral nature. He fails to appreciate the vital role of the social structure, one's treatment by others, the conditions in which one lives, etc., in the development of self-respect. Kant argues that human beings can temporarily forfeit their dignity, and the concomitant respect of others, by failing to act according to the moral law. This makes respect for oneself and others contingent on good behaviour, and weakens his case for inalienable human worth.[14]

In the light of our brief discussion of Kant, we need both to build on his account and go beyond it.[15] The individual is both a human being like all others and a distinct and unique person, a 'what' as well as a 'who'. Both these dimensions are the bases of respect for oneself and others. In one case respect is generic or species-based, in the other it is individuated or individual-specific. In the former, one respects others and oneself as human beings and values the shared human or species identity, in the latter, as unique individuals and values their individual identity and difference.

Individuals are human beings possessing certain distinctive capacities, by virtue of which they belong to an ontologically privileged species and deserve respect.[16] They are also distinct centres of self-consciousness, each unique in his or her experiences, history, background, talents, sensibilities, and ways of looking at the world. They pursue their own purposes, dream their dreams, understand and organize their lives in their own different ways, build their own worlds of social relations, cherish different ideals, and forge distinct identities in terms of which they define their self-respect. They also grow and are shaped by particular cultural, ethnic, religious, and political communities. Insofar as they identify with and define themselves in terms of some or all of these, their membership of them becomes an important part of their individual identity and self-respect. Their self-respect is attacked not only when they are attacked as human beings but also as Jews, Christians, women, blacks, or Frenchmen. This is why they might rightly say in certain situations that as 'self-respecting' Jews, Hindus, or Englishmen, they will not allow themselves to be treated in certain ways and their individual or communal identity to be mocked and belittled.[17]

Self-respect then has two dimensions, universal and particular, as a human being and as a distinct and unique person. Each has different implications. Self-respect as a human being implies that one values one's ontologically privileged status, asserts one's equality with others, and respects oneself enough to resist their attempts to treat one as their plaything. It also implies that one cherishes one's dignity, values oneself, and neither treats oneself nor allows others to treat one in a manner that violates the basic demands of the shared humanity. Self-respect as a unique individual implies that one defines oneself as a particular kind of person, as a bearer of a particular identity and shape's one's life and makes choices accordingly. One respects oneself not because one is a human being like others but rather because one has chosen to be and values being human in a particular way. And one demands respect from others not for one's shared humanity but for one's distinct identity. Self-respect as a unique individual is based on one's ability to live not so much by certain universal norms as by those implicit in one's identity.

Although self-respect as a human being and as a unique person are closely related, they are conceptually separate. When one fails to live up to the demands of one's self-chosen identity, say as a Christian, one might lose respect for oneself as a Christian without losing respect for oneself as a human being. The difference between the two is also evident in the way people respond when the two forms of self-respect are violated. When treated in a manner that outrages one's dignity, one would say, 'What do you think I am? An animal? A vegetable? I am a human being like you and will not be treated in this way'. When one's status as a distinct person is violated, one is more likely to rejoin, 'Who do you think I am? Your clone? A nobody? I am not you, not him, but me, with my own identity. Respect my difference and understand me in my terms'.

Respect for others is the obverse of respect for oneself. It too is two-dimensional, respecting people both as human beings and as certain kinds of persons. To respect people as human beings is to appreciate their common humanity, to acknowledge their equal worth, to give their interests and feelings equal weight, not to use them as a means to one's end and take advantage of their vulnerability, etc. To respect them as unique persons is to respect their identity, individuality, differences, the integrity of the world they have built for themselves, and accepting the obligation to understand them in their own terms. The two are conceptually distinct, for one might disapprove of and lack respect for the kind of identity they have given themselves while continuing to respect them as human beings.

Self-respect in both its forms it neither a natural endowment nor the achievement of an isolated individual but a collective achievement. Learning to see oneself as a human being possessing intrinsic worth is possible only under certain conditions. For centuries human beings defined themselves as members of a particular family, clan, caste, class, and religious, ethnic, cultural, and political community, not as human beings who transcend and are more than the sum of their social positions. Notwithstanding Kant's optimism, reason is historically and culturally conditioned and finds it extremely difficult to break the hold of the institutionalized categories of everyday life. The awareness of common humanity develops at a certain point in history, and is acquired by living in a society that proclaims and embodies it in its institutions and practices. As its members define themselves as human beings, and as the demands they make on each other are met, the consciousness of a shared humanity finds a basis in their daily lives and becomes an integral part of their self-understanding.

This is equally true of self-respect in the sense of respect for oneself as a distinct person. It is not a natural endowment or a solitary individual achievement but requires the right kind of social and cultural environment. Individuals learn to respect and value themselves as unique and self-determining persons when they are not only left free but encouraged to run their lives themselves, develop their individuality, and to cultivate and express their identity. Respect for oneself as a unique person requires institutionalized rights and liberties, widespread tolerance of and respect for difference and diversity, and opportunities to develop the capacity for self-determination. It also requires access to the basic conditions of the good life so that one does not live on the sufferance of others, and a participatory ethos in the major institutions of society so that one's sense of one's individuality is nurtured and affirmed. An oppressive, hierarchical and unjust society that subjects large masses of its members to degrading conditions and systematic humiliation frustrates a strong sense of the self, the necessary basis of self-respect. Like other human capacities, self-respect develops through exercise and does not emerge, and, if it does, it atrophies if the social conditions militate against it.

A strong and widespread sense of respect for oneself and others constitutes the indispensable basis of a good society. It cherishes human dignity and gives it a secure foundation by integrating it in the self-understanding and normal relations of its members. It enables human beings to rise to their full stature and avoids the deep frustrations, alienation, and human decay endemic under institutionalized humiliation. It ensures that people act in a desirable manner, not out of fear of the law or what others might do to them but because they respect themselves and others. They do not cut corners or become free riders when out of others' gaze and create a climate of deep mutual trust. Since this reduces the need for a regime of formal and informal sanctions, it reduces the coercive role of the state and expands the area of, and better protects, individual liberties. For these and other reasons a good society should aim to create the social, economic, political, and other conditions necessary for the development of a culture in which respect for both oneself and others are not only cultivated but seen as inseparable.[18]

NOTES

1. For one of the few systematic and stimulating discussions of it, see Margalit (1996). See also the symposium on it in *Social Research*, spring 1997, vol. 64, no. 1.
2. The Bohras are a small Muslim sect, originating in India.
3. Humiliation could be an isolated event or a condition of life when its impact is lasting and leads to deep ontological damage.
4. Quinton (1997: 81) argues that although humiliation need not be public, publicity is a 'normal requirement.'
5. See Ripstein (1997: 99–100) for a good discussion of this case.
6. Lukes (1997: 44) distinguishes humiliation from the various phenomena with which it is frequently confused.
7. In hierarchical societies a servant is expected to show servitude in all areas of life. He must not sit while the master is standing or speak unless spoken to, render him personal services, must not contradict or even disagree with him, and so on. His inferior status follows him like a shadow, and there is not a single area where he is his master's equal. In such a society the servant has no sense of self and is often an echo of his master. As for the master, his self is defined almost entirely in terms of his status, and any threat to its entitlements and privileges is seen as a threat to his self and his self-respect. A different kind of dialectic is at work here than the master-slave dialectic analysed by Hegel.
8. Although victims of humiliation are never without the power to retaliate, their power may be worth very little in practice. If the Jews in Vienna, or in the concentration camps, had refused to obey orders, they would have saved their self-respect but lost their lives.
9. Cited in Seidler (1986: 45).

10. Ibid.: 30 f.
11. Ibid.: 80.
12. Different moral and religious traditions conceptualize human beings differently and emphasize different fundamental responses to them. Some talk of 'valuing' them, others of 'cherishing', 'honouring', or 'loving' them. By and large, 'respect' is not a central category in any religious tradition, except perhaps some forms of Protestantism.
13. Sartre makes the point well when he says that Kant respects the individual as a human being but not as an individual in his unique identity. However, he is wrong to argue that this is characteristic of liberalism, and that the latter has a 'tinge of anti-Semitism' because it is 'hostile to the Jew to the extent that the latter thinks of himself as a Jew' rather than as a human being; cited in Seidler (1986: 54). It is worth noting that although the concept of human dignity has now become central to liberal thought, it is either absent or assigned a limited role in the writings of Hobbes, Bentham, and others.
14. Kant is not alone in thinking that respect is conditional. This view is also shared by the Stoics, Locke, Rousseau, Hegel, and many others. In the West, the idea of absolute and unconditional respect that is never forfeited first emerges with Christianity. Not all Christian thinkers however subscribed to it.
15. For a valuable discussion of respect that builds on and goes beyond Kant, see Raz (2002).
16. For a further discussion, see Parekh (2000).
17. Self-respect covers not only respect for oneself as a distinct person but also for all that one considers constitutive of one's identity, including one's ethnic, religious, and other communities.
18. One can think of unusual situations in which humiliation might seem to have a case. We all agree that brutal and murderous dictators, mass killers, perpetrators of genocide, those guilty of killing hundreds of children by adulterating their food, and serial, sadistic, and brutal rapists deserve the severest punishment. What kind of punishment measures up to the enormity of their deeds? It is sometimes argued that sentencing them to a dignified death on the gallows or to lifelong incarceration is too lenient, and that they should also be subjected to public ridicule, paraded through the streets, made to stand in public places with placards listing their actions, or should, in some other more acceptable way, be publicly humiliated. In this view such humiliation expresses the community's deepest outrage, publicly affirms its commitment to certain basic norms, and at least partially measures up to the enormity of the deeds involved. For reasons I cannot discuss here, we should not go down this route, but it would be wrong to ignore the perplexity posed by the moral asymmetry between such deeds and the normal forms of punishment.

2 Humiliation
Politics and the Cultural Psychology of the Limits of Human Degradation*
Ashis Nandy

Years ago, Giri Deshingkar, distinguished Sinologist and peace researcher, told me a story that may be, for all I know, apocryphal. When diplomatic negotiations took place after the Boxer Rebellion in 1900 between the defeated Chinese regime and the triumphant western powers, they ended in a humiliating treaty for China. However, the Chinese rulers looked at it differently. They had sawed off an imperceptible length from the legs of the chairs on which the western negotiators sat, so that they spoke to the Chinese from a lower height. The Chinese were convinced that they had decisively humiliated the western powers in the negotiations. The western diplomats, of course, knew nothing about this and, naturally, did not feel humiliated at all.

It is possible that, while thinking that they had triumphed over the imperial powers, the Chinese also knew they had lost. That awareness might have powered their politically impotent, self-congratulatory venture. I am also ignoring the quasi-therapeutic role the attempted humiliation might have played for the Chinese, facing traumatizing disgrace and national crisis. The European diplomats may not have been affected, but the attempt to humiliate them protected Chinese self-esteem. Human nature is a multilayered affair; people acknowledge

*This paper has grown out of a keynote address at the conference on Humiliation, organized by the Centre for the Study of Developing Societies, and Nirman Foundation, at Ranikhet, 7–9 September 2002. It was presented in its present form as a public lecture, at the invitation of the Institute of Postcolonial Studies on 27 August 2003 at Melbourne, Australia. At both places, the paper gained much from the comments of the listeners.

or respond to events at many levels. I am merely proposing, as a basic assumption of this essay, that humiliation is a form of human relations that can never be a one-way exchange. Unless the humiliated collaborate, by feeling humiliated, you cannot humiliate them, however hard you try. No humiliation is complete unless the humiliated oblige their tormentors by validating their desire to humiliate. The Boxer Treaty did not fully humiliate the Chinese and the Chinese did not humiliate the victorious powers either. Those trying to humiliate may get a kick from what they do, but unless there is consensual validation from the 'humiliated', humiliation remains a one-sided venture or takes place only in the eyes of a third party.

It follows, counter-intuitive though this may sound, that the humiliated, too, have some control over their tormentors. This control is not overt, given that in a game of humiliation the parties involved often have asymmetric power relations. Yet, sensitive ethnographers and litterateurs have frequently come close to acknowledging that, in India's caste system for instance, while the Savarnas apparently control the rest, the Dalits also have traditionally controlled the Savarnas through their power to pollute by touch or presence and through the Savarna's constant fear of pollution.[1] This dyadic relationship explains why, at moments of crisis or conflict involving the Dalits, so much of venom is released. Conflicts bring to the fore what is tacit in the caste relations and creates in the Savarnas a crippling fear of losing control. When Mohandas Gandhi insisted that anyone joining his ashrams had to first clean toilets, he was not practising, despite appearances, reverse humiliation as a penance. He was striking at the heart of the compact of humiliation that has tied the untouchable to the 'touchable'. He was redefining the idea of pollution. In 1973, the Government of Karnataka banned the practice of carrying night soil. If the government were sensitive to Gandhi's project, it would have made the ban applicable only to the Dalits.

Some are uncomfortable with the proposition that successful humiliation needs acknowledgement from the humiliated that they are being dishonoured. They believe that persons or groups may be so numbed by institutionalized, regular humiliation that their sensitivities are blunted and they do not feel humiliated. A third party has the right, they feel, to declare a situation as humiliating. Such an argument apparently has some validity; those who use it, usually have in mind the Dalit predicament, what V. Geetha calls 'the dark narcissism of untouchability'. However, appearances notwithstanding, the argument is absurd and anti-democratic. If some victims do not feel humiliated, others have the right to convince them of their situation. But that gives no one the right to declare, on behalf of someone else, that humiliation has taken place, that the victim has become too used to humiliation to sense it and, therefore, he or she could act or speak on behalf of victims. Let us not forget that the Hindu nationalists, too, argue, on behalf of all Hindus, that the Muslims have humiliated the Hindus for centuries and the Hindus who do not admit that have turned numb. Even when not invoking the ideas of numbing, the assumption of the right to talk on behalf of the humiliated has its hazards. During the Emergency in 1975–7, when civil rights were suspended in India, sycophantic bureaucrats and ruling party functionaries decided, on behalf of Prime Minister Indira Gandhi, that Gulzar's *Aandhi*, a film based on her complicated relationship with her husband, deserved to be banned because it was humiliating to the democratically elected prime minister.

This is a cure worse than disease, though in recent years it has acquired certain legitimacy, thanks to the intellectual climate created by the growing global concern with victims of trauma in general, and post-traumatic stress disorders in particular. 'Such is the preoccupation with trauma', says Vanessa Pupavac, 'that over the last decade, trauma victims have displaced famine victims in western imagination' (Pupavac 2002: 489). These diagnoses of victimization give social analysts the right to 'pathologize' not only individuals but also entire communities and declare them socially dead. When a psychiatrist declares a person as numbed by years of oppression or as overly sensitive to perceived humiliation due to deep feelings of inferiority, the diagnosis at least does not generally involve a summary trial of an essentialized collectivity.[2] The use of the idea of social death does.

The situation in India is complicated by a number of excellent and suggestive studies that show that sycophancy or ingratiation, one of the main indices of passive acceptance of humiliation, is often deployed as a Machiavellian tactic to control the powerful and to limit their options.[3] Specially when the institutional context is bleary or ill-defined, as inter-caste relations have become in recent times, and also in situations of resource scarcity (Pande 1980, 1981b, 1981c, 1986). Those who seem to accept or 'enjoy' humiliation do so, these studies suggest, not because they are reconciled to their lot, but because they consider it legitimate manipulative behaviour when confronting the powerful and think it a small price to pay, to neutralize or contain the dominant in a fluid politics of hierarchies and to have privileged access to power.

Finally, if we grant a third party the right to declare a situation humiliating, independently of the victim's point of view, what happens when an ethnic or religious community's claim does not mean to humiliate anyone by following age-old practices or conventions? Do we accept the claim at face value or grant others the right to proclaim the community dishonest or hypothetical? Conversely, when some groups claim to have been humiliated, do others have the right to deny those claims? Such questions are becoming important because globalization today is bringing communities into more serious contacts. The scope of unintended humiliation is growing. The dog-loving English have to now deal with dog-eating Koreans. Pork-loving Germans and Chinese cannot avoid pork-shunning Muslims and Jews. The chance of humiliating someone unintentionally has increased enormously.

However, if we accept humiliation as a reciprocal relationship, humiliation can be an interpreter's nightmare. Who humiliates whom, when and how? Thus, I confess that I have always felt uncomfortable with the American Blacks changing the name of their community according to their changing ideas of what is humiliating and what is not. They were first Negroes and many of them did not like the name because it was associated with the humiliation and indignity of slavery and, later, discrimination. They became Blacks and after a while some of them did not like that either because it ironed away ethnic distinctions. Since then they have become African Americans. I have always felt that this kind of response declares the locus of control to be outside oneself; the response is a reaction to what others think of one and an attempt to revise one's self-definition accordingly.

Yes, the term Negro was associated with slavery and with that term of contempt, 'Nigger'. But Negro also means black and it is still associated with the self-definition of Francophone Africans who have no option but to use the term, because it is the only one available to them in French. *Noire* just does not have the same ring as black. More importantly, the term Negro has been associated with much resistance, protest against oppression, and creativity against immense odds. It is associated with Leopold Senghor's idea of negritude; Paul Robeson's Negro spirituals; and W.E.B. Dubois' work on the African cultural heritage of the Negro and their cultures of survival and protest under slavery and afterwards, when slavery ended but discrimination and humiliation did not. 'Black' does not have that kind of association. The term African American is in some ways worse. It blurs the entire recent past of violence, torture, and exploitation through which Black Americans have passed and links them to their African heritage about which they know little. What I resent most is the tacit admission in such renaming that the memories of slavery and racism are more shameful for the Blacks than for the Whites. As if the Blacks had to more carefully and diligently erase their past than the Whites who practised slavery. The Whites have not changed their names or ethnic tags, though they carry the heavier historical baggage of slavery. No white has resented being called white, on the ground that name has been associated with oppression, exploitation, and genocide in the more populous parts of the world and can be used as a term of abuse. I cannot but suspect that the attempts of American Blacks to rename themselves are partly predicated on the belief that it is more honourable to be a master than a slave. At the same time, I am also vaguely aware that in a future society, after the collapse of racism, calling oneself a Negro may be considered an attempt to insult the White by recalling the days of slavery. Symbols of defiance do sometimes enshrine entire world views.

I

This brings me to my second proposition. While civilization as a process means the gradual abolition or dilution of master–slave relationships, it also means a growing awareness that it is more honourable to be a slave than a master, if not as a viable social or personal choice, at least as a normative and cognitive frame. (For wider acceptability, I am willing to rephrase the proposition and claim that it is less dishonourable to be a slave than a master.)

This is a position different from the one that asserts that it is as dishonourable to be a master as to be a slave. The first presumption—that the slave is morally and cognitively superior—allows a collectivity to 'work through' its past, as psychoanalysts describe the process, and opens up the possibility of wide-ranging creative use of the past. The latter—often prefaces reactive ethno-nationalism, built on defences such as projection, displacement, and identification with the aggressor— in practice a façade for the entrenched belief in the master's moral infirmity but cognitive superiority. Above all, it leads to a constant effort to beat the master at his own game.[4]

I have discussed this issue elsewhere in some detail (Nandy 1983, 1994). Let me confine myself here to its implication for communities trying to escape humiliation and protect their dignity.

Humiliation in South Asia is usually a story of separation and the pain of separation. But like the post-Boxer treaty negotiations in China, that story too has a built-in Roshomon affect.

Caste and religion are seen as the main source of separation in our part of the world. Most people hope that both will dissolve obligingly in an egalitarian, modern society, giving way to separations based on non-ascriptive, secular, social divisions that are, for some reason, presumed to be less painful and squalid. Yet, paradoxically, most serious battles waged against caste and religious bigotry has used caste and religion, and not secular social categories like class. These battles have weakened caste and religious bigotry socially, but also strengthened them as principles of political mobilization.[5] The dramatic rise of the numerically preponderant, lower castes in Indian public life has come through caste mobilization, with its attendant problems. It is only our self-serving, cultivated blindness that stops us from acknowledging that the same may be the case with religion, that we may have to cope with problems associated with religion by deploying religion itself as an input into the culture of politics and as a principle of political mobilization. Even a hardboiled, modern secularist like B.R. Ambedkar, to fight religion-based discrimination and exclusion, had to make a statement by converting to Buddhism, a religion neither immune to exclusion and chauvinism nor to caste-based discrimination, as the Sri Lankan experience shows. In our times, the Dalai Lama and Desmond Tutu have shown how such religion-based mobilization can be deployed in public life.

We would like to believe that all principles of separation humiliate. They may not. As an old, poor, Muslim riot victim living in Delhi's Jama Masjid area said many years ago in a television interview, 'previously we did not eat together, but our hearts met. Now we eat together but our hearts do not meet'. Nearness may not merely sour, but also implode. Let me go back to a story brought to my notice by Dipesh Chakrabarty, which I consider in many ways paradigmatic.[6] Unfortunately, the story is not widely known; to use it, I shall have to tell it again.

Jasimuddin was the best-known folk poet of Bengal of the twentieth century who was also a devout supporter of the Muslim League and the idea of a separate homeland for the Muslims. He came from a humble background and was a co-student of the famous radical film director Mrinal Sen in a school at Faridpur, now in Bangladesh. Mrinal's father spotted Jasimuddin's brilliance very early and young Jasimuddin began to visit the Sens and soon became virtually a member of the family. An indicator of the intimacy between the budding poet and the Sens was that Jasimuddin used to call Mrinal's mother 'Ma' and the Sens in turn called him by his pet name, Sadhu (literally, a world-renouncer). As communal politics began to warm up in the 1940s, Jasimuddin and Mrinal's father often entered into fierce debates, Mrinal's father supporting conventional nationalism, Jasimuddin its ethno-nationalist version.

One day, during the course of one such debate, Jasimuddin asked why the Sens, if they considered him a member of their family, made him eat at their place separately. This embarrassed everyone, for it was true. Mrinal's mother, with tears in her eyes, explained that it was the servants who objected to Jasimuddin's eating with the rest of the family. Indeed, they resisted washing the plates he used. She added that she had been washing up after Jasimuddin ate.

We have no clear picture of how the dialogue ended and of the fate of the relationship after the event. However, we can make a few guesses. First, the Hindu servants, themselves of uncertain social status in the family, were the ones who tried to protect their self-esteem by separating and humiliating Jasimuddin in this instance. They must have felt threatened by the closeness of a Muslim to the head of the domestic power structure and insisted on their right, as Hindus, to observe the principles of purity and pollution, to reaffirm a social hierarchy that was getting dangerously fuzzy. They were making a point by humiliating the new member of their employer's household who dared to call the mistress of house 'Ma', not the way servants in a Bengali household call their women employers so, but the way a surrogate son does. Indeed, one suspects that they were protecting themselves from humiliation by humiliating the new-found 'son' of the family and reducing him to his 'true' stature—a poor Muslim patronized by the family.

The result was that Mrinal's mother's moving gesture—an upper caste woman washing the plate of her son's Muslim friend, and humiliating herself vis-à-vis the servants to protect her adopted son from humiliation—did not get its due either from an angry young partisan of ethno-nationalism or from her own modern son. Jasimuddin *did* feel humiliated and even the self-abnegation of Mrinal's mother could not erase the hurt after a point. However, it is also clear from the story that Jasimuddin felt humiliated at least partly because he had come close and entered the circle of commensality and kinship and was expecting a different kind of behaviour from the family. It was not distance but nearness that created the problem in the first place.

Do separations, encrypted in principles of commensal taboos, automatically lead to humiliation, as Jasimuddin seemed to believe? Had he not felt humiliated, would it have been because he was numbed to the demands of ritual hierarchy and closed circles of the touchable? A part-answer lies in an interview Saba Khattak did in Pakistan with a woman victim of Partition for a collaborative project on mass violence (Khattak 2001). The victim firmly denied that the observations of rules of purity, impurity, pollution, and touch had anything to do with Hindu–Muslim tensions or the violence of Partition. Hindus did not eat with most Hindus in any case, she said. In another variation on the theme, Prafulla Sen, a refugee from the former East Pakistan, though he himself did not believe in caste-based checks on commensality, remembered with great fondness his Muslim friend's, Sirajuddin Ahmed's, father, who was once furious with his son for hosting Prafulla and breaking Prafulla's commensal taboos. The relationship between the two families had spanned two generations; Prafulla's late father too had been a friend of Sirajuddin's father. The latter, on hearing of the transgression, lamented: 'How will I show my face to your father after I die? How shall I tell him that my son helped your son to lose his religion?'[7]

One sees in these episodes three faces of humiliation in a political culture. In the last case, both sides accept separation in some areas of social life as almost a cultural 'eccentricity', an old but 'inviolable' religious practice of a community. The distance that humiliated Jasimuddin does not poison social relations in the other two cases. One is tempted to add that 'if one is not committed to a melting pot model and is ready to view public culture partly as an interplay of contending, incompatible cultures of communities that observe built-in limits on interaction, one has to be prepared to confront situations where some degree of tolerance will have to be exercised for rituals and practices that look hierarchical or humiliating from within a melting pot model. I remember my late friend Jaidev Sethi, an activist-scholar and Gandhian, telling me that he had to virtually starve when visiting his ancestral village in Pakistan after a gap of fifty years. No longer having Hindu neighbours, the villagers went by their memories and reduced Sethi, who did not know how to cook, to virtually tears by affectionately gifting him a huge mass of uncooked green vegetables and cereals. They expected the returning son of the village to observe caste taboos and cook his own food. They did not believe him when he said that he ate everything and was perfectly willing to eat at anyone's place.

Such tolerance presumes, however, two relatively autonomous, self-confident communities or persons, something that cannot be said in the case of Dalits, Saba Khattak's case strengthens the argument. In it, familiarity with other cultures assures the respondent that separation is not targeted towards the respondent or her community specifically. Separation becomes acceptable because already two generic, internally fragmented entities called 'Hindus' and 'Muslims' have emerged and one is able to say, as Khattak's respondent did, that 'they' treat their own kind the way they treat 'us'. In Jaismuddin's case, the closeness of the budding poet to the future film director's family gives separation a different meaning. The threshold of tolerance has been lowered because the two parties have redefined their communities. Both sides are modernized to the extent that they cannot have asymmetrical relationships with each other and hierarchy-tinged separation becomes a marker of humiliation.

I am emboldened to add that Jasimuddin's story is paradigmatic also in the sense that most modern social scientists can empathize with Jasimuddin's and Mrinal's point of view, not with the predicament of Jasimuddin's adopted mother or that of the servants. The 'strange', politically incorrect categories of those at the receiving end of a social order are an embarrassment and must be quickly forgotten, presumably for the benefit of the victims themselves. It is a bit like a consistent forgetfulness that I have found in the plethora of reports and studies that came out after the massacre of Sikhs in Delhi in 1984. No one mentions a recurrent theme in the testimonies of the Sikh victims talking of the complicity of the Indian National Congress and the Rajiv Gandhi regime in the pogrom: 'they got us beaten up and killed by the Bhangis (lowest among the untouchables)'. Some kind of humiliation, we implicitly recognize, no respectable victim should complain of.

Insensitivity to such situations is what makes the psychological measures of social distance so vacuous in countries like India. Scores of studies were done at one time on inter-caste and inter-religious relations here with such measures like the Bogardus Social Distance scale. All of them assume a graded relationship between different kinds of social interaction. (For instance, if I accept my daughter's marriage with your son, I am closer to you than if I am willing to only to dine with you.) In a complex, highly diverse traditional society, such simple, linear relationships do not obtain. Emory Bogardus would have been surprised to hear that in many South Asian communities, despite intermarriage, commensality may not be always possible. (Even in a modern setting, there is George Bernard Shaw's crypto-Biblical injunction, 'do not do unto others what you would that they do unto you. Their tastes may be different.' I have heard of at least one French family that is happy that their progeny has married into an Indian family, but has resisted eating at the home of their in-laws, lest they have to eat Indian food.)

This flux in the meaning of humiliation is well exemplified by one of the darkest periods in South Asia. The idea of pollution and purity acquired an entirely different meaning during the Partition riots when, by most conservative estimates, a hundred thousand women were abducted. Strangely, a very large proportion of the abductors married their victims in Punjab. All the abductors could have raped and killed their victims, as many of them did. Why did they have to marry their victims? How did communities and the families of the abductors accept the women from enemy communities in a caste society? Unlike Bengal, in Punjab abduction was a three-way traffic. All three religious groups—Hindu, Muslim, and Sikh—participated in the game and in all three religious groups, a large number of families, clans, and communities accepted the abducted women. In the course of a study, some of us have even identified villages and urban neighbourhoods where a majority of the elderly women, even today, are women abducted during Partition. Presumably, these women live with their trauma and memories of humiliation, but they live with them not as aliens or strangers but as insiders. How have the concepts of pollution and purity worked in these cases? One possibility is that, after humiliating their enemies by stealing their women, the abductors felt morally obliged to protect a semblance of the dignity of their victims by marrying them. Another is that marriage could establish 'honourable victory' or seal the social superiority or equality of the abductors. The concept of *rakshasa* or 'demonic marriage' in India's epic traditions might have supplied a framework of justification for such feelings. Perhaps, for some abductors, the humiliation of the enemy was not complete if they had only raped and abandoned their victims or remained anonymous rapists and killers. Losing one's own women or capturing other's women took place within a common frame of humiliation and counter-humiliation, defeat and victory. But these are guesses; we do not really know.

Compare this experience with the rapes committed during the 2002 riots in Gujarat where, in many cases, after raping a woman the rapist would set her on fire. Some of the killers justified themselves by saying that they were advised to prevent the multiplication of Muslims through unwanted pregnancies. The game in Gujarat was not humiliation, but annihilation. In the Bosnian genocide, too, rape was used as a well-organized technique of dishonouring and polluting the other and as a means of systematic deracination. As part of a jury in the women's Court against Racism set up in Durban in 2001, I heard testimonies on the chronic culture of rape under slavery in the United States (WCW 2002). One testimony based on the diaries, autobiographical records, notes, and letters of plantation slaves in the United States claimed that many women knew that their mothers and grandmothers had been raped, they themselves would be raped, and their daughters would be raped too. Rape was a part of normal life; it includes a component of amoral, nihilistic, destructive humiliation that was anti-life. In the same category fall the recent cases of two Dalits at Thinniyam, Tiruchi, Tamil Nadu state, who were forced by persons belonging to a non-Brahmanic, upwardly mobile Thevar community to eat human excreta and that of the Dalit domestic help who underwent the same treatment in eastern Nepal at the hands of a Chhetri couple.

Finally, to be aware of the instrumental use of the rhetoric of humiliation, one must be also aware of voluntary or invited humiliation as a technique of political mobilization and consolidation. Humiliation can be imagined and cultivated, in response to contemporary political and social needs. First, a record of humiliation can become a badge certifying one's identity and membership of an in-group. Violent nationalism has always carefully nurtured the feeling of humiliation, Nazism being its best-known example. However, there are less diabolical examples of invited humiliation being used as means of political and social mobility. Some Cochini Jewish immigrants in Israel talk of centuries of oppression in Kerala, whereas their own community in Cochin talks of two thousand years of non-discrimination and life of dignity. Indeed, the Cochin Jews are surprised and amused by the history of oppression that some Israeli Jews of Indian origin have concocted (Nandy 2002b). But in Israeli public culture, there is a rat race of communities in experienced oppression and humiliation; not having a record of ill treatment is a misfortune in that society. In that rat race, the European Jews have an edge, because their persecution over the centuries is one of the key imageries around which the self-definition of the Israeli nation-state is built.

When the creation of a feeling of humiliation is part of a political programme, it is not necessary to have any genuine record of oppression and violence. Ethno-nationalists know this. Hindu nationalism, for instance, talks of humiliation that has looked contrived, fictitious or a projection into the past of more recent feelings of inferiority vis-à-vis Islam and Christianity. Empirical evidence that suggests that no generic category called Hindus defined themselves as Hindus till the nineteenth century fails to cut ice. The sense of humiliation and feelings of inferiority in recent times is real, history serves as a projective test, and political propaganda works.

II

I have already mentioned the growing use of the technique of pathologization. That technique is quickly becoming a postcolonial version of the technique of infantilization. It is, therefore, important to remember that though the pathologies of humiliation attract public notice because of their incendiary potentials, humiliation can also open up new, creative possibilities. If the capacity to feel humiliated presumes minimum self-esteem, the capacity to withstand or stand up to humiliation, too, presumes ego strength, a sense of mastery over oneself and one's environment.[8] An incapacitating or crippling fear of humiliation may also indicate low self-esteem. This is the other side of Geetha's formulation that humiliation is fundamentally an experience which questions and 'recasts' one's relationship with oneself.

There are many instances when attempts to damage or narrow the target's sense of self have instead ended up expanding it. When a racist white conductor threw M.K. Gandhi out of a train compartment in Pietermaritzburg in South Africa, despite holding a first class ticket, the conductor did not know that he was gifting the world a new political weapon for the oppressed—militant non-violence. The humiliating encounter in a lonely, South African, railway station turned out to be a boon not only to the world but also to Gandhi himself. It woke him, as it were, from a stupor. Some forms of humiliation—such as the crawling order enforced in Punjab in the wake of Jalianwalabagh massacre in 1919—degraded and silenced the victims, but possibly also helped crystalize new forms of political awareness. Others directly create new formations. These consequences have as much to do with the nature of the humiliation as with the nature of the victim.

The experience of Pietermaritzburg may have also sensitized Gandhi to the pedagogic possibilities of milder forms of humiliation. During India's freedom struggle, many found Gandhi's dress disgraceful and his negotiation with the Viceroy on an equal footing humiliating. Winston

Churchill felt offended by the antics of 'the half-naked faqir'. Others found it provocative and humiliating, when, after the famous Salt March and the successful movement against the newly imposed salt tax, while negotiating with the viceroy, Gandhi took out and sprinkled some illegally made salt on the snacks he was served by the viceregal kitchen. It is doubtful whether it is possible to remove humiliation from human affairs. Someone somewhere is always going to feel humiliated. We shall probably have to console ourselves by acknowledging that sometimes some humiliations can be a means of renewal and re-education for both sides in an unequal partnership.

These creative potentialities are there because humiliation, when it is not an isolated case but a chronic ailment, is usually a political statement. Some form of playful counter-humiliation—often a non-destructive refusal to play assigned roles—becomes in such a context a counter-statement or rebellion. Humiliation breaks out in an epidemic form when the humiliated refuse to abide by well-established, institutionalized rules. Humiliation then becomes a means of reasserting the old hierarchies increasingly under stress. That is the crux of the Dalit problem in India today. The humiliation of Dalits accomplishes what in other situations is achieved through mass murder.

Humiliation becomes a substitute for genocide, partly because, unlike the American Indian, a good Dalit has never been a dead Dalit. Though outcastes, Dalits remain within the caste system by being a collection of service castes. If they do not supply these services, others would have to step in, or one would have to opt for self-service. In either case, the result is a quick loss of social status. Humiliation is a means of avoiding that status loss and the resulting humiliation. This leads to strange anomalies. While doing a study of Partition violence of 1946–8, we discovered how the Karachi elite and the Pakistan's political leadership had to cajole the Hindu Dalits of Karachi to stay on in the city while ethnic cleansing was taking place all over northern India. In fact, when after the destruction of the Babri mosque in 1992 some targeted the Karachi Dalits, they stopped work immediately and quickly reduced the city to a stinking slum. They were provided armed security in no time. In a caste society, fears of pollution can supersede fanaticism.[9]

In the classical Hegelian master–slave relationship, one can build upon Octave Manoni and affirm that the slave, to survive, cannot but be sensitive to the moods, foibles, and personality dynamics of the master. The master, on the other hand, can to an extent afford to objectify his possession; he does not have to internalize the slave. This splits the slave into two. One part of his or her personality wants to equal the master, to do to the master and to others what has been done to him as a slave. Gandhi in his 'Hind Swaraj' identifies it as the eagerness to acquire the tiger's nature without the tiger (Gandhi 1963). Building upon the original psychoanalytic construct, we can call it identification with a 'remembered' aggressor, an ego defence that can be seen in full play in today's Israel and in the cosmology of Hindutva.

In this identification with the aggressor, there is often an attempt to undo history, real or imaginary, by re-enacting it with oneself on the winning side. This is accompanied by a search for scapegoats, by humiliating whom one can undo the past. Yet, even when such re-enacting and scapegoating succeed, one cannot forget or overcome the past and move on, because one has, in the meanwhile, redefined oneself and given a central place in one's self to the repeated attempts to re-invoke and undo the past through violence; these attempts become the means of holding together one's fragile self-definition. Even successful genocidal revenge, directed against real or imaginary enemies, cannot square the balance. For without the triad of scapegoating, undoing, and acting out, such a personality faces collapse.

Valentine Daniel describes how, in the process of combating evangelism, to counter the claims of the Christian missionaries, every religion has internalized in the last hundred years the categories and the self-definitions of European Christianity and the European meaning of religion, turning the twentieth century into a cultural triumph of western Christianity (Daniel 2000). To face and fight humiliation and acquire respectability, according to European concepts of respectability, every major religion in the South has sought to redefine itself to conform to a standardized definition of religion.

Daniel's formulation prompts one to question the idea of respectability itself, because, in this instance, respectability means respect from within the Hegelian master's world itself. Such respectability inextricably ties the victims of humiliation to the 'tiger's nature', and, in the long run, creates new targets of humiliation. Perhaps the real counterpoint to humiliation is not respect, unless we mean by it self-respect of the kind that goes with what psychologists call ego strength, that too of an order that can survive experiences of humiliation. The real counterpoint to humiliation is probably empathy. Unfortunately, empathy is neither a political category nor can it be inculcated through institutional means. In everyday politics, it is probably safer to presume that the 'normal' counterpoint to humiliation is the absence of humiliation. This is particularly true in societies where communities are not dead and people expect, from fellow citizens belonging to other communities, not brotherly love but some degree of distant tolerance (Nandy 2002b). This emphasis on the idea of self-respect is not incidental. In India at least, when one talks of humiliation one invariably has in mind the Dalits. And when the Dalits talk of humiliation, there is always the presence of a de-recognized psychological variable: hostility towards one's own culture and vocation inculcated in the Dalits over generations. Hence, no rhetoric of recovery of indigenous cultures or protection of artisan skill goes far among them. The Dalit commitment to modernity may be fuzzy and uninformed, but it is usually total. The modernist social reformers have endorsed this social image by constantly describing Dalits along only two dimensions: they are poor and they are oppressed. As if the Dalit communities did not have their gods, caste puranas, legends, cuisines, and systems of knowledge. As if empowering their culture was to disempower the Dalits. It was against this flattening of the image of the Dalits that the likes of D.R. Nagaraj protest (Nagaraj 1994).

To return to our core metaphor, there is the other part of the slave's personality that fights the master by refusing to internalize him, even while acknowledging the master's humanity. As if the slave recognized, as a key to his or her survival, that in the long run it was better to be slave than master. That is the ultimate meaning of rebellion and the guarantee of destruction of the master–slave relationship, not the glib talk of equality and justice.

Thus we come back to square one and to the proposition that the growth of the awareness that the slave represents is not merely moral but also one of cognitive superiority over the master. The master has more reason to refashion his identity than the slave has. This is what I mean when I confessed my discomfort with African Americans changing their name because of the history of slavery.

However, I should not end this essay without taking note of a basic contradiction in the master's personality. It arises from the basic incompatibility between humiliation and what Aimé Cesairé calls 'thingification' (Cesairé 1972). Institutionalized slavery requires 'thingification'. One has to objectify a human being to efficiently use him or her like a machine or a domesticated animal; one has to redefine the slave as only a factor in production. But then, one cannot humiliate things or animal because, as I have argued already, the victims must grasp their humiliation for humiliation to succeed. Humiliation is a human situation. It can never be extra- or trans-human. To humiliate someone, you have to grant your target human sensitivity. You also have to be willing to be a captive to the will of the humiliated. In this respect, humiliation is a bit like torture. One is a successful torturer only when one's victim begs for forgiveness and screams for mercy thereby satisfying the torturer's sense of power, control, or sadism and thus endorsing his sense of mastery over himself. But think of the torturer whose victim laughs at him and denies his ability to inflict pain, thus gradually reducing the torturer to a frustrated, desperate and even humiliated being, struggling to maintain his dignity.[10]

Humiliation can destroy people only by bringing them closer and inducing them to share categories and establish common criteria. Humiliation cannot survive without some degree of consensual validation. Humiliation dissolves when the dyadic bonding—and the culture that scaffolds it—is disowned by at least one of the two sides.

Notes

1. There are of course subtler fears that plague the oppressor in any system of dominance. V. Geetha talks of accusations of witchcraft against Dalit women as another instance of oppression. It can be read as another admission of oppression by the oppressive and their haunting fear of retributive justice. See V. Geetha in this volume.

2. Though even such trials are now no longer rare. Entire populations are sometimes declared politically 'incompetent' because of a history of violence and trauma. See the suggestive paper of Pupavac (2002); for the larger issues involved, see also Herman (1995).

3. For example, Pande (1980: 15–17) and Pande (1981a); Pande and Rastogi (1979); Tripathi (1981). See also Bohra and Pande (1984).

4. The ways in which the memories of British colonialism in South and Southeast Asia are deployed are an example. As a general rule, countries, regions, and communities that are more self-confident and less plagued by memories of real or imagined humiliation, like persons with robust ego strength, need lesser symbolic reparations and ritual and/or compulsive 'undoing' of the past. Even their nationalism reflects the lighter burden of the memories they carry. There is a difference between a nationalism built on an underlying strain of anti-imperialism, and is heir to an anti-colonial movement, and a nationalism that seeks constant national and cultural security by bending or distorting the entire machinery of the state and the entire culture of politics. Mohandas Karamchand Gandhi, officially remembered in India mainly as a nationalist leader, was sensitive to this issue. Nationalism,

to be authentically anti-imperialist, had to be non-violent, he openly claimed, for armed nationalism was the other name of imperialism. See Gandhi (1967: 369). What remained unsaid was that non-violence was the natural political stance of the psychologically healthy, not of political eccentrics having a poor grasp on the reality around them. To opt for violence as the 'proven' technology of the master is to admit defeat even when the master has been formally defeated.

5. In the case of caste, D.L. Sheth has attempted an insightful stocktaking that explores the long-term consequences of the process. See Sheth (1999).

6. Chakrabarty (1996). Elsewhere, I have discussed the reasons for homing on this story. See Nandy (2002a).

7. Anindita Mukhopadhyay, Interview with Prafulla Sen, Delhi, 1977.

8. See Geetha in this volume.

9. Unpublished case study presented by Suchitra Subramanyam Sheth at the Conference on Life history Construction and Mass Violence, organized by the project on Reconstructing Lives, Centre for the Study of Developing Societies at Udaipur, 25–29 July 2000.

10. In Romain Gary's novel, *The Dance of Genghis Cohn*, the anti-hero, former SS officer Schatz, is possessed by the ghost of Genghis Cohn, a Jewish comedian, who became Schatz's victim when an inmate of Auschwitz. Cohn remains, even in death, defiant and insolent. He haunts Schatz by displaying his only, apparently impotent, comic defiance. See Gary (1978).

3 Humiliation and Justice

Upendra Baxi

PREATORY REMARKS

The relationship between 'justice' and 'humiliation' remains largely untheorized. Many a fact may account for this and the range of concerns is enormously complicated. Neither notion carries any excess of self-evident meanings. Practices of humiliation and injustice vary within societies and across cultures. Such practices are often said to be embedded in distinctive religious world views which also provide articulation of their justification. Humiliation is not usually constructed as political or structural injustice. While thus violated individuals or groups fully know that humiliating treatment towards them is always inherently unjust, they often do not have at hand well-worked-out approaches to justice or the individual or collective strength to resist it. The languages of contemporary international human rights (in so far as they concern themselves with humiliation) are thought to impose obligations of conduct and result on the side of state actors, leaving unaddressed practices of humiliation at various sites in civil society, including here as well the market or more generally the spheres of production, exchange, distribution, and consumption. Further, I believe that our present initiative ought to be an aspect of the nascent cross-cultural humiliation studies and it would be an egregious error to pioneer distinctive forms of Indian understanding without some advertence to these. Contemporary humiliation studies allow/authorize no linear acts of summation. This chapter does not offer any theory of justice and humiliation. Rather, it speaks to our responsibility for analytical clarity, descriptive realism, and social commitment, as providing the first steps towards such a task.

CONCEPTUAL CONCERNS: THE ANALYTIC OF HUMILIATION

Base Meaning

No doubt, much of our time may be devoted in identifying the appropriate sense of the term of 'humiliation'. The appropriateness will, of course, be context dependent, even when we concede that all social relations are shot through by the probability (or rather possibility) of humiliation, even its base sense of denying equality of deference to the other. The pioneering efforts at deploying the Hartling 'Humiliation Inventory' by Evelin Gerda Linder (2001a) employed a rating of 1 to 5 for questions capture many meanings measuring 'being teased', 'bullied', 'scorned', 'excluded', 'laughed at', 'cruelly criticized', 'treated as invisible', 'discounted as person made to feel small and insignificant', 'unfairly denied access to some activity, opportunity, or service called names or referred to in some derogatory terms', or viewed by others as 'inadequate' or 'incompetent'. She found, understandably, this inventory 'premature' for a cross-cultural study of humiliation, in genocidal contexts such as Rwanda and Somalia. And to this one may now of course add the contexts of the 'war on terror' (Linder 2001a). This inventory presents a staggering vast range of phenomena attracting the rubric of 'humiliation'. Yet, it also makes significant sense for any endeavour to construct an analytic of humiliation, both in an agentive sense (intentional infliction) and experiential sense (of being humbled/humiliated/violated), these ingredients do not miss the mark. These also correspond preciously to the commonsense understanding and experience of humiliation.

Construction of humiliation also requires us to revisit not just some 'standard suspects' such as notions of pride, honour, shame, dignity, degradation, deference, decorum, aggression, violation, and violence but also some new ones such as generosity and meanness in public life (Mills 1997) and 'corporate Darwinism' (Moore 1997) in this era of hyperglobalization. At the outset then we realize that humiliation is not a freestanding notion, indeed the meaning we chose to invest in associated notions will condition, even determine, our understanding of humiliation.

The analytic of humiliation thus framed concerns the well-celebrated difference between the 'politics of recognition' as distinct from the 'politics of redistribution' elaborated variously by Nancy Fraser (2000;

2003). In this decidedly post-Marxian perspective, the logics of cultural harms (mal- /mis-recognition) caused by humiliation may not be redressed merely, over even primarily, via material redistribution. This is scarcely a site to more fully attend to this inaugural discourse; however, in passing, it remains pertinent to note that neither Fraser, her theoretical allies, or critics, remain conversant with the germinal contribution of B.R. Ambedkar who differently privileged 'politics of redistribution' over the Gandhian (almost Fraser-like) insistence on the primacy of overcoming cultural harms done to Indian untouchables, now named as 'Dalits' (Baxi 1995). This observation directs attention relocating Fraser-type discourses in terms of the global South understandings and approaches to the relationship between humiliation and injustice, and not just at the levels of meta-theory.

I believe that even in our post-Marxian moments it remains important to acknowledge the significance of Marx (in the companionship of classical Marxians, as opposed to the contemporary 'Marxists'). 'Exploitation' is a category embedded in capitalist relations of production.[1] One way of reading Marx is to say that exploitation equals humiliation plus injustice. The life of every worker in early capitalist mode of production (the scientific Marx specifically says in his preface to the *Capital* that he specifically wishes to limit his analysis to the early phases of the industrial revolution) is an endless narrative of humiliating degradation and economic immiseration. How further other modes of production may be studied (from the Asiatic to now Post-Fordist, flexible accumulation, and even 'post modern' mode of production should form an arena of anxious concern for justice/humiliation studies. Further, it is now a commonplace of thought that gender- and race-based exploitation, and forms of environmental racism (Wester and Lawson 2001) emerge as a distinctive specific form of exploitation, which Marx did not perhaps fully foresee. Yet, in Marxian social theory, repudiation of ownership in the means of production provided both a necessary and sufficient condition for the construction of a social order, or *socious*, cleansed of residues of exploitation (both thought of comprising practices of humiliation and injustice), thus maximizing the virtues of fraternity (common dignity of all socialist beings). In practice, quite some distinctive socialist forms of humiliation and injustice emerge. Theory and history of ideas, ideals, and ideologies often do not converge, a fact as much true of Marxian legacy as any other liberal inheritances.

Even so, we learn from the Marxian analyses, first, that each form of exploitation involves acts of structural imposition of experiences of degradation, pain, and suffering, entailed in humiliation. Second, for Marx it always remained important to dy-mystify exploitation as primarily a cultural category. How far some contemporary categories of humiliation (as, for example, developed by Linder and on a different register by Fraser) amount to humiliation as exploitation thus remains an open issue for any Marx-based humiliation studies, far away from the habitus of vulgar Marxism rubbishing of mechanistic economic determinism that Marx never practised. Third, and in particular, humiliation studies need to foreground the logic of specificity, whether the specificity of the political, economic, cultural, even civilizational, entailed in theory of production.[2]

Etymology: Conventional and Critical

As always, recourse to etymology helps. We now know (thanks especially to Miller 1993: 175) that prior to 1757, humiliation remained connected (in English language) to humility and 'to making humble'. Its equivalence with the act, performance, event, or experience of mortification, comparing, lowering, or depressing 'the dignity or self respect' of the other emerges only in the middle of the eighteenth century.

But this recourse to conventional etymology (that is, forms that trace usages of Euroamerican words, which, in turn, endow them with a range of dictionary/encyclopedia controlled meanings for almost everyone on the Planet Earth) fixates discourse on the social experience of Euroamerican word as constituting the world. In this sense, the discourse occurs as a kind of *worlding* decision. By critical etymology, I here invite not just attention to origins (or lack) of corresponding words, and usages in languages other than Euro-American. It is unfortunately nowadays considered inaugurally brilliant to ask whether non-Euroamerican cultures had words corresponding, for example, to 'law', (and 'rule of law'), 'human rights', 'justice', 'republic', and 'democracy'. This 'brilliance' itself masks several forms of Eurocentrism that South humiliation studies at the very least need to more fully understand, if only because sociolinguistic practices often express epistemic domination. Lest we were to get carried away by this indictment, we need to recall that the vernacular languages also encode functional equivalents of epistemic domination. Think, for example, of the Hindu canonical texts which extol the notion of humility in the much elaborated terms like *punya, satkarma, sadahchar, sistachar, namrta, vinamtra.* These specifically extol humility and willingness to accept hierarchy as pious virtues and further relate to *Dharmic purushartha* in the Great cosmic chain of Karmic being.

To read all this from the lenses of conventional etymology is to expose acts of epistemic violence. The very first task thus posed by (what I here name as) critical etymology is the search for *words of the humiliated* that correspond to the above-mentioned six terms. The critique and reconstruction of these virtues in varieties of discourses (such as the Bhakti movements, Buddhism, and Sufi hermeneutics) may provide a starting point here. Practices of critical etymology begin when we pair, word by word, the vocabulary of the dominant (the humiliator) with that of the dominated (the humiliated).

Ranajit Guha offers precisely this kind of demonstration in his *Elementary Aspects of Peasant Insurgency*. He guides us to the ways in which the *Manusmriti* creates 'negative class consciousness' (1983: 23–8) and how as a semiological coding system it 'sanctifies a range of verbal and non-verbal signs of deference and distance, into which is embedded a whole way of constructing social reality of dominate and subalternity' (ibid.: 35–76). He brings to full view how insurgency consists in rebel speech that performs 'perspective reversal' (ibid.: 36) by 'massive and systematic violation of these words, gestures and symbols, which had the relations of power in colonial society as their significanta' (ibid.: 39). His further work (1997) demonstrates how the Hindu canonical texts and imperial law and policy weave together a complex mosaic of dominance without hegemony and aspects of resistance to it.

It is only when such labours of critical etymology are surely in place that any significant movement towards locating comparable and comparative understanding of 'humiliation' begins to make sense. For Indian humiliation studies, the bridge or the chasm appears acutely in the confrontational discourse of the Mahatma (Mohandas Gandhi) and the Aristotle of the Dalits. (B.R. Ambedkar, who deployed a wider category—*atisudras*—to refer to the historically perenduring social and economic proletariat of the colonial and postcolonial India.) Secularization of humiliation remained their uncommon project, long before the Euroamerican political theory addressed this very task. The Mahatma rather astutely reconstructed the potential of the Hindu religious syncretism form and redirected it towards the secularization of humiliation and injustice; the Aristotle of Atisudras proceeded radically otherwise, notably via the rejection of the Brahminic forms of Hinduism and ultimately embracing, in a gifted feat, radically reconstructed Buddhist theology. Ambedkar further composes the Indian Constitution that seeks to strike at the very roots of the radical evil of humiliation/exploitation/injustice encoded in millennial historic wrongs and in making ample constitutional reparative justice provision reversing these.

Indian humiliation/injustice studies may serve the intendment of cross-cultural exploration only via the similar practices of agonal political, for example, embodied in Nelson Mandela and Martin Luther King, Jr unfortunately, the current state of art even fails this enterprise. Prescinding this, I wish to underscore a simple point: at the threshold of any arrival at critical etymology of the future 'Indian' humiliation studies lies a series of narrative concerns about the ways in which 'we' construct orders of memory orders also celebrating human rightlessness.

Forms of Humiliation

Equally central to our discourse is the issue of identification of forms or types of humiliation. On this plane, notions of intention and of effect, agency and structure, history and culture, shape our ideas and experience of humiliation. Distinct disciplinary traditions also give rise to different ways of understanding humiliation. Even more crucial will be the focus on practices of ideology that sustain and enforce notions of self and society, freedom and coercion, human rights and defining counters of legitimate governance and levels of visibility/invisibility of acts, events and experiences of humiliation. Humiliation then is indeed a conceptual 'minefield' (Linder 2001: 52–61). Linder offers a haunting typology (in the context of exploring psychology of humiliation in Rawanda) of 'honour humiliation' a social form where 'masters rule over underlings and everybody is convinced that this is how things ought to be...' The construct of the notional 'everybody' is precisely what subaltern students of humiliation ought to challenge. Precisely because of this, her typology remains of compelling interests from postcolonial theory, Dalit feminist, and subaltern perspective.

The first form is named as 'conquest humiliation' where a 'master' subjugates 'formally equal neighbors as inferiors'. The second is 'reinforcement humiliation', the use of hierarchy by 'master' to 'keep it in place'. The third form 'regulation humiliation is, used to push an already low ranking "underling" even further down'. A fourth form signifies the exclusion of a 'party from the hierarchy altogether' in the Rwanda context (2001).

These categories, evolved in pursuit of specific empirical studies remain valuable for Indian humiliation studies, more so were we to add more complex understanding of the emergence of societal norms (Margalit 1997), supplemented by the rather interesting work concerning 'indignation entrepreneurship' (Margalit and Sunstein 2002). Indignation entrepreneurship is a construct that enables us to understand the experience of humiliation in relation to social resistance and renovation. Margalit and Sunstein pose the general problems in terms of situation where 'on reasonable assumption change seems quite impossible' and yet it occurs; they suggest that this occurrence may be grasped through the figure of indignation entrepreneurship. This emerges when the disadvantaged convert moral indignation (senses of injustice) in ways that 'lead them to disrupt an otherwise stable situation by sacrificing their material interests for the sake of increased equality' (2002: 3). This analysis is important for Indian humiliation studies at least for three principal reasons. First, it helps mapping variance: 'moral indignation, and the willingness to act on it, will vary across adversely affected populations'. Second, even so, 'the [anti-humiliation] rebels face some serious collective action problem'. Third, not to be entirely ignored remain the logics, and paralogics, of the law as well as the constitution (considered here as legislation, administration, interpretation, and enforcement) play in struggle against humiliation. Indignation entrepreneurship may evoke the 'expressive function' of legal normativity; the law also 'can help... to dissipate pluralistic ignorance', 'fuel and legitimate indignation, and offer some hope for change in the future'. Further, disadvantaged groups' may enlist the law to offer the opposite signals and to produce contrary effects'.

Important as all this remains, Linder's distinction between 'trauma without humiliation' and 'humiliation as the core of trauma' urges us to revisit the germinal distinction between situation of *misfortune and of injustice* (Shklar 1990). Perhaps, we may say that trauma without humiliation occurs when social horrors[3] are presented and regarded as misfortunes. However, it remains the province and function of indignation entrepreneurs to seek to develop the capacity to problematize situations of misfortunes as acts and performances of injustice. Yet, Linder remains right in bringing to our attention the psychohistorical, psychogenetic grasp of routinization of trauma as core of humiliation,[4] a great deal of careful analysis is needed by those seeking to understand humiliation in Indian contexts. To this, we now briefly turn.

An Indian Excursus

The institutions and practices of untouchability, in all its different histories and geographies, combine all the four forms of humiliation. The constitution of India (especially through Article 17 that abolishes 'untouchability' as an integral aspect of human right to equality) may be construed as outlawing the millennial form of conquest humiliation. The history of emergence of constitutionality as a declaration of normative belligerency against millennial humiliation afflicting the dalits needs to be explored in terms of ways of pioneering indignation entrepreneurship, especially, and ironically, symbolized by B.R. Ambedkar.

Truth to say, the Indian experience of the variously described constitutional policies and practices of affirmative action, compensatory and reverse discrimination, constitutes simultaneously the regimes of 'regulation' and 'reinforcement' humiliation as well as many (sub, even anti, Ambedkar like) practices of indignation entrepreneurship (see, for example, Baxi 1995 and the literature cited there). This is an important realm for future exploration. Clearly, these policies are not designed to further depress the historically disadvantaged classes (though this preposition stands persuasively contested by radical forms of Dalit critique). But both the manner in which the policies are crafted and administered illustrate some latent effects (dysfunctional potential) that produce the very effect of 'regulation and reinforcement' humiliation. The extent to which this happens remains the matter for close empirical examination in terms of experience of regulatory humiliation suffered routinely by affected individuals and communities. Some reconstruction of this category here becomes imperative. The experience of many a affirmative action programme is indeed humiliating, even when it may be said that the overall impact, across generations, may not be accurately framed in terms of 'regulator' and 'reinforcement humiliation'.

I here only point to a few aspects worthy of empirically informed research examples, necessarily bereft (for reasons of space) of available bibliographic references. First, the plight of scavengers and sweeper communities, and more specially of women in these communities, among the broad masses of 'untouchables', remains open to the precise description in terms suggested by notions of regulation and reinforcement humiliation. Sixty plus years of Indian constitutionalism have not notably affected their working or social conditions. Nor are there on view any eminent emergences of 'indignation entrepreneurs' among these, or within the wider dalit or activist communities. Second, affirmative action programmes, epitomized by the crises over implementation of the Mandal Commission report, and the subsequent adjudicatory policy, and administrative discourse, reveal the difficulties of constructing, let alone accomplishing, conscientious exclusivity. By this I designate the problems of crafting and implementation of policies that reach out meaningfully to meet the dire existential needs of the most 'backward' of the constitutionally christened 'socially' and 'educationally backward classes and other backward classes'. They remain the ramparts of the worst off peoples in an ocean of the forever worst off communities. (Indeed, constitutional euphemisms provide an interesting site for Indian humiliation studies.)

Third, the patterns of social violence remain an integral aspect of regulation humiliation. Indian constitutionalism and legal order have, no doubt, fashioned new normative means to designate this problematic, whether by the Civil Rights Protection Act replacing the earlier deficient Untouchability Offence Act), the Atrocities Act of 1989 and the Bonded Labour Legislation). Indifferent implementation of these legislative policies surely counts as regulation humiliation, both in terms of lived experience and historic effect.

Fourth, the experience of regulatory and reinforcement humiliation stands constantly enacted in social attitudes, idioms, and approaches surrounding forms of administration of affirmative action programmes.[5]

Fifth, much the same may be said concerning of Indian constitutionalism the unique system of legislative reservations, now an integral dimension. All I need to say on this count is that many Ambedkarites and neo-Ambedkarites (myself thus included) critique the forms and practices of ethnic feudalism that this ordering now entails. Put simply, even simplistically, for the present purpose, the system of electoral reservations itself entails the experience of humiliation in the sense that it continually shapes social identities that count merely as representational tokens (Baxi 1984; Galanter 1984; Mendelsohn and Vicziany 1998). These tokens constitute primarily the plebiscite *bazaars* of entrenched *'vote banks'*, bereft of any serious prospect of promoting structural transformation. The resultant forms of rather abject ethnoclientism (that is the zamindari type relations that subsist between the individuals belonging to the Scheduled Castes and Scheduled Tribes and their 'political' leaders and representatives) tend to further inhibit generation of indignation entrepreneurship. In any event the varieties of humiliation experiences entail the labours of production of new typologies of humiliations.

EROTIC HUMILIATION

Most generally put, concerns here wrestle with the issue of patriarchy in knowledge/theory production. In what ways the patriarchical cultures encode acts, intentionalities, structures, events, performances, and impacts that constitute humiliation for women? I note a few fields thus constituted by patriarchies, summated here as *erotic humiliation*.

The 'great' corpus of the Dharamsastras richly and canonically elaborating the regimes of purity/pollution encodes many a mode of eroticizing dominance. Its *dandniti* does not view, for example, a Brahmin (high caste) sexual congress with dalit women as much of transgression, to be as severely penalized as low caste sexual relations with upper castes. We find similar processes at work in the domain of *apad*-Dharma (the Dharmic discourse in *extremis*). The *Manusmriti* exemplifies the fear and trembling of the crisis of sexuality by providing a most fierce regime of sanctions for illicit liaison between a *shiysa* and *gurupatni* though it remains relatively inarticulate concerning sexual transgression by the Guru. The Sastric injunctions thus, in many places, eroticize humiliation.

The investiture of God-like charismatic status for religious preceptor/ Guru figurations constitute many culturally sanctioned forms of sexual submission/dedication that invite understanding by Indian humiliation studies. The Devdasi system, for example, furnishes a most resilient field for such investigation. The idea that a Guru-figure is by definition, as it were, beyond average 'lust' sustains sexual offerings by the devotees with the rather malodorous bhaktic surrender. Instrumental aspect of sexual surrender by women are not also unknown (as when 'altruistic' socially enforced sexual coupling with a Guru is seen as a 'pious' solution for infertility). The notion, in any event, that sexual submission is the highest form of devotion (and occasional offspring constitute a *Maha Prasad*, a kind of mystical oblation) spiritualizes rape culture. Only with the rise of militant feminist consciousness in past two decades, prosecutions for Guru-led—sexual transgressions have begun to occur and this brings to view merely a dot on the tip of the iceberg of practices of erotic humiliation.[6] In any event, much of the Indian secularism discourse thus remains sexist at its core by its silence concerning codes of spiritualized erotic humiliation.

Secularized forms of erotic humiliation have, in comparison, achieved a far greater social visibility in a post-*Mathura* India,[7] (especially in terms of domestic violence, principally dowry and sati) and sexual harassment in public places, as well as sexual exploitation of labouring women (domestic 'servants' contract and bonded/attached labour, and transgender peoples). These enormously significant movements assume a form of partnership among assorted indignation entrepreneurs such as activist justices, media persons, and communities of human rights advocacy. Indian humiliation studies can, in the present opinion, enhance all this by practices of reading Indian constitutionalism as enacting hitherto unscripted human right against sexually humiliating practices.

Even so some multinational-corporation TRIPS/WTO imbued industries now constitute new markets in erotic humiliation, multimedia practices of such humiliation are also on a high growth curve in hyper-globalizing India. I single out here specially the Internet genre of erotic humiliation, sites that constitute variegated species of soft porn. Indeed, erotic humiliation is an integral part of contemporary processes of globalization. It remains important for Indian humiliation studies to further pursue:

1. *Mediatization* of sexual exploitation in Indian mass journalism and the Bollywood culture industries.
2. *Naturalizing* sexual harassment, in its myriad contemporary Indian forms.
3. *Promotion* of markets for internal and global sex tourism.
4. *Justifying* cyber-pornography, as an integral aspect of human right to free speech and expression, unfortunately (in my view) making globally accessible, as a postmodern aspect of women's autonomy and pursuit of women's rights (the iconic figure here being the porn star, whom I shall not here name, who represented her triumph over 'patriarchy' by a 'heroic' exploit of having, in one night, sexual union with 151 male partnership in the full cinematic gaze, now open to view to all across the world by push of digital button, accompanied of course by a credit card! (Incidentally, the proliferation of the device of plastic money in promoting organized market of erotic humiliation should surely interest postmodernist pioneers of humiliation studies.)

Very summarily put here: How then may we seek to understand agency and structure in the diverse forms of erotic humiliation? How may Indian humiliation studies essay a critique of global markets of erotic humiliation without yielding a centimetre to the moral militias of the extreme right, or sacrificing women's right to life and livelihood in their own preferred ways?

TORTURE AS HUMILIATION

Indian political and social theory provides, on the whole, little evidence of concern with the practices and institutions of torture, and its diverse histories. I do not here attend to aetiology of high social and political theory (an important task in itself) but I do wish to maintain that humiliation studies worth the name may not replicate this not-so-benign neglect. Contemporary international human rights values, norms, and standards, especially through the 1984 United Nations Convention against Torture and Other Cruel, inhuman, Degrading Treatment or Punishment, provide clear enough starting points for humiliation studies. Clearly, this discourse provides many a benchmark for measuring the processes and practices of humiliation.

What constitutes 'cruel, inhuman, degrading treatment and punishment' remains open to vast contention from several perspectives. Feminists critique readily and rightly enough demonstrate the scope of the Convention that limits itself to acts that only implicate 'public officials acting in official capacity' on the ground that this all over again reproduces the nefarious public/private distinction that 'obscures injuries...typically sustained by women'. Such an approach also excludes humiliating violence inflicted on women and children through 'widespread and apparently random terror campaigns by both governments and guerrilla groups in times of civil unrest or armed conflicts' (Charlesworth 1991; Power 2002). For Indian students of humiliation Maheshweta Devi's *Draupadi* (1997) ought to serve, in this context, as an inaugural text.

From a social anthropology perspective, Talal Asad (1987) remains an insightful preceptor. We may transfer his message on the plane of humiliation studies in terms of its valorization in Western colonial discourse in which '[P]ain endured in the movement of becoming 'fully human'...was seen as necessary because social or moral reasons justified why it must be suffered' (p. 205). He demonstrates how the very idea of cruelty and degradation becomes and remains 'unstable, mainly because the aspirations and practices to which it is attached are themselves contradictory or changing' (p. 304). Asad also alerts us to the possibility, and the social fact (even in a strict Durkheimain sense) that 'cruelty can be experienced and addressed in ways other than violation of rights—for example, as a failure of specific virtues or as an expression of particular vices' (p. 304). Bringing back cosmologies thus complicates (as earlier noted) the analytic of humiliation, even as this performance remains welcome as marking an interlocution of the fractured universality of contemporary human rights language, logics, and paralogics (Baxi 2009).

As concerns humiliation, these reflections point to at least two dimensions. First (and we extend the analysis to postcolonial experience as well), we stand confronted by the distinction between *necessary* (from whatever standpoint) and *surplus* acts of humiliation. For example, the quotidian practices of macroeconomic development policy regimes (for example, large dams and now orders of Special Economic Zone) accustom us to think that orders of humiliation and injustice that displace vast impoverished masses constitute 'developmental' necessities, 'ensuring' the eventual future amelioration of those thus fully humiliated and subjugated.

Thus arises a formation, in the second or third 'best' conception of social world, of naming justifying the excess of the political economy 'developmentalism fully detracting from the values, standards, and norms of contemporary human rights as ironically also said to be serving some new futures of human rights! All this complicates the humiliation talk via manifold intersections that produce the 'modern' human subject, caught equally between forms of 'tradition' and 'modernity' under the sway of progressive/regressive. Eurocentric languages and projects and the 'body in pain' (Scary 1987) as the very site on which the many modern and postmodern 'truths' of politics and resistance stand inscribed/produced. Practices of humiliation thus seem to be ineluctable for the processes of social, human transformation. Social movement and human rights activist praxes, however, invite attention to humiliation as constituting injustice when these produce the 'radical evil' of what Hannah Arendt named as *human rightlessness* (2000: 43–4), whether under the auspices of state or social power.

However, and even so, the experience of humiliation ought to reconstitute the standard recourse to the figure of Dalits, so as to include at least the following constituencies:

1. The physically disabled (or differentially abled) for whom the experience of assumes horrendously diverse form of stigmatization and exclusion, a social form that must be regarded as reconstitute of practices of torture.[8]
2. The disabled 'entrusted' to psychiatric care custodial institutions as well as others like juvenile institutions, women's remand homes,

and the like, that render them for all purpose socially invisible (to the point even of death, as the Tamil Nadu expose testify; the 'insane' at Erwadi were charred to death as they were in chains when a fire broke out, despite all Supreme Court rulings prohibiting chaining).

3. The practices of medical experimentation without a shade of informed consent in state and now increasingly private managed, custodial institutions.

4. The constitution of the 'afterworlds' of victims of the recalcitrant third degree policing and legal administration methods and means (I refrain from citing here the exponentially growing literature).

5. Those violated by the production of politics of catastrophic practices of 'communal' (of which Gujarat 2002 furnishes a horrendous archetype (see Baxi 2002, and the literature therein cited).

The contemporary practices of Indian state formation, to reiterate, reconstitute and recreate new forms of dalitness, which Indian humiliation studies need to more fully cognize. Our best guide here, I suggest, stands offered by those who here—and—now, and also across generations, experience the practices of humiliation, shaming and sorrowing, grief and bereavement, deprivation, destitution, disadvantage, and desolation hitherto unnamable strangers to our erudite lexicon. Whatever we may choose the name as 'humiliation,' it exists in lived spaces of individual biographies and collective histories of social hurt and harm. These spaces configure the spatial politics, embodiments of *lived* and *live* human/social struggle. It is a notable social fact that the life under conditions of domination in also (as Michel Foucault constantly sought to remind us) is as well, and also, a life of insurrection against the established orders of imposed humiliation.[9]

The Law and Humiliation

The relation between the law and humiliation, already thus far noted, is, exceedingly complex. At the level of constitutions and progressive legislation, the state law may provide precious roles for indignation entrepreneurship. Enunciation of human rights values, standards and norms (and their expansive interpretation by an activists judiciary remain extremely valuable in naming and outlawing millennial practices of humiliation.[10]

At the same time, the state law and its administration also result in 'regulation' and 'reinforcement' humiliation. Dalits form the bulk of the people at the receiving end of state sanctioned torture-like treatment and punishment. A gravely disproportionate number of dalits constitute both the convicted and undertrial populace. Prison conditions and other custodial institutions daily outrage their dignity. Even the state legal aid programmes at times treat their unmet legal needs with manifest contempt. Dalit women working as contract labour, and engaged in other forms of disorganized labour (I use this expression rather than the complicit phrase 'unorganized labour') remain subject to systematic sexual molestation and assault. In all these, and related, domains the state law, its managers and agents, practise and promote imposition and experience of humiliation, which it also aggravates by protecting the humiliator. The ultimate form of humiliation they experience is the systematic conversion of human *rights* into *favours* and *concessions*, to be made expediently available as an aspect of administrative and political largess.[11]

Despite constitutionally enunciated people's rights, dalit communities have no effective right to dignity and livelihood, after fifty plus years of the Indian constitutionalism. And, for all practical purposes, they remain *subjects*, not *citizens*. The collapse of normative Indian legal order is only a part of the problem. The vitality and resilience of the law conceived here also as people's law (Baxi 1982; Dhagamwar 2002) adds to the repertoire of humiliation. Institutions, agencies, and practices of popular justice, especially the caste (*biradari* and *jati*), tribal/indigenous, and religion-based panchayats systematically make use of shaming punishments (often even with fatal impact) that impose destructive humiliation beyond redress. The terminal impact of shaming sanctions falls most heavily on women in terms of governance of sexuality. The staid, but for that reason no less crucial, discourse concerning Uniform Civil Code seldom addresses this dimension. The inhuman costs of Indian jural pluralism remain largely unconcerned with the human and social costs of values and practices of toleration.

Theorizing humiliation in the Indian juridical context must also remain alert to the discourse concerning shaming sanctions, as an aspect of retributive approaches to punishment (see, for example, Kahan 1996; Posner 2000; Massaro 1997; Markel 2001; Nussbaum 2004). Sooner or later the justification of shame sanctions is bound to excite attention of mimic Indian law reformers.

Activist communities are also likely to espouse the 'greater' effectivity of such sanctions in relation to sexual harassment, a criminal assault.

Even I find somewhat persuaded by the West Coast (San Francisco) forms of legality subjecting 'men convicted of soliciting prostitutes to sit through lectures by former prostitutes who describe the unfortunate conditions of life on the streets.' (Markel 2001: 2176), I can almost hear echoes of Indian (and South) juristic excitement at this discovery of a whole new continent of social sanctions, which in some ways 'proves' the importance of shame over guilt cultures. At the same time, aggravated cacophony of the 'virtues' of non-European modes of punishment, on the register of juridical/jural humiliation production, must remain a cause of considerable concern.

The 'Word of the Humiliated' and the 'Humiliation of the Word'

In conclusion, I turn to a wholly new problematic, constituted by what may be called *spiritual, exegetical studies* that explore the relationship between the Word and World, as register that situates our understanding of humiliation in terms of the transformative relationship between, on the one hand sacred text and the ways of pious exegesis and, on the other, the state of art of contemporary human and social sciences.

Jacques Ellul in *The Humiliation of the Word* (1985)[12] provides a stunning message: 'Anyone wishing to save the humanity today must first of all save the word,' underscoring 'the tragic crisis of language, in which words can no longer attain the level of speech.' He remains concerned, but transcends, the canonical Word.

Ellul's great work needs to be understood, beyond the canonical word, as a critique of devaluation of language in general, caused in part by practices of politics and of technology that induce an irreversible word—denying techno-scientific mindset. In this zodiac, 'Everyone holds in contempt' the use of language by the politician because by now it is well known that 'this language does not *commit him to anything*' (italics added). A similar 'emptiness' of words is replicated by the techniques of mass media and the Internet (where indeed the 'word becomes an image', 'changed into a thing, into space, and something visible') marked by both 'the emptiness of the word spoken by an anonymous speaker who is not committed to his word' and 'the triumphant evidence for the efficacy of the action.' Indignation entrepreneurs thus have to inhabit a world inhibiting words emptied of any sort of authentic commitment towards public action.

This 'scorn', 'contempt', even 'fury', for ordinary languages also marks vandalized expropriation of language for unsurpassed domination and hegemony. Thus, the humiliation of the word is also at the same time constitutive of humiliation of all that we proclaim the 'essence of being, and remaining, human'. Ellul dramatizes the resultant human situation evocatively thus:

Who amongst us has not talked with developers and builders and been struck by their irritation when we speak of term like 'quality of life', not in vague terms but saying exactly what the expression means.' You are a humanist', they respond. Such a response communicates clearly how Language is despised. When an expression such as 'quality of life' or environmental protections' catches on, they say 'of course!' They take over the expression and apply it to 'develop' land, to destroy genuinely human life and landscape, or to change the environment. 'Why not?' These are just words, and therefore nothing. They are just popular expressions. Let us put serious ideas into practice, such as growth and development. And when you show that such 'expressions' have vast content and value, and they involve basic choices, these people reject what you say. 'Practical matters are completely different from your talk,' they say. They refuse to be directed by our words or references to values. And under thin, icy politeness of the chief engineer or the Highway Commission, his scorn for the philosopher and the humanist immediately shows: 'Go ahead and play with words: we'll chose a few for decoration; but leave the practical matters to us.'

The humiliation of the word as narrated by Ellul also extends beyond the theft/appropriation of the languages of the humiliated. It refers to the domain of erudite knowledge production, especially of the 'word of humiliated' by varieties of structuralisms/post-structuralisms. I can here do no more than to invite your attention, in swift different strokes, to his deconstruction of deconstruction, resisting 'contempt', even 'hatred' for the word.[13] Resiling against the humiliation of the word, Ellul (1985) asks us to think:

In reality, the word is revolutionary in itself. Just as it was the agent of humanity's formulation in the midst of animals, so the word is the agent of great refusal. *Only* the word revolutionary, and only language can lead us to the realization of human hope. This is because of the language's relationship to truth. The ruling class has to fight an enormous battle to prevent this mole's undermining the status quo. They need to have a purpose, in order to castrate the word, to domesticate and circumscribe it—to sap its strength—to make language a simple neutral instrument.

The Alpha and the Omega of the Indian Dalit humiliation studies consist precisely in the practice of resistance against the 'castration' of the very word 'humiliation'. The word and the idea of humiliation has to serve as the agent of the Great Refusal, the force that symbolizes the Dalit right to be, and to remain, human, *as historically and for the future defined by them*.

NOTES

1. Roemer (1986) has identified five types of exploitation thus: *Structural exploitation* (workers may not withdraw their per capita share in production even when capitalist may as a result be worse off), *Capital theory exploitation* (*workers* are denied any significant decision power in production decision), *Dominance exploitation* (workers are forced/coerced to sell their labour power at disadvantage), *Corporeal exploitation* (workers are robbed off their time since labour power cannot be disassociated from the labourer and remain exposed to disease, disability, and death at the site of production), *Authority exploitation* (regimes of control at the workplace remain despotic, limits to authority of the employer remain undefined or ill-defined in the contract of sale and purchase of labour power).

2. This is surely important as bringing a certain methodological rigour and commitment. I realized this on a fuller reading of Roy Bhaskar's critique of Richard Rorty (1991) and the many-splendoured conversation between Judith Butler, Ernesto Laclau, and Slavoj Žižek (2000).

3. Such as varieties of social apartheid, violation of women's rights as human rights, continual abrogation of human rights of the First nations people, and the plight of victims of mass disasters produced (from Bhopal to Ogoniland and beyond) caused by intransigent corporate 'governance' (Baxi 2009).

4. Linder further directs our attention to everyday but still exceptional forms of subaltern resistance (2001: 66). Rohintoon Mistry's epic novel, archiving humiliation, *A Fine Balance* (1995) in any event ought to furnish us an inaugural point of departure.

5. There are several ways in which this occurs and I base these observations of my personal experience as a University administrator, without any further reference to the sparse writing on the subject. Students belonging to the Scheduled Castes category are not always treated with respect accorded to 'meritorious' students; they are marked apart as already 'weak' students lacking the threshold competence, and when the medium of university education is the English language, they suffer many a privation.

   'Minority' colleges in Delhi University successfully (and even with the blessings of the Supreme Court of India) resisted my attempt to centralized admission procedures for the Scheduled Castes and

Scheduled Tribes students, deciding instead to fill the quota by their own 'pick and choose' method. Further, most universities and colleges consider their social responsibilities best discharged by enrolling them via a preferential quota; programmes of special assistance are rare; as a result augmenting consistent failure rates in examinations and eventual drop-out rates as well. Students labelled as belonging to 'other backward classes' were named during the violent Mandal agitation on the Delhi University campus as *'sarkari damands'*, the government's in-laws!

I have had the unfortunate experience as the Vice-Chancellor of Delhi University of living through the first months of the violent campus discourse of the Mandal policy. The best and the brightest of my colleagues critiqued my principled espousal of Mandal as marking the destruction of university-based integrity of knowledge production! Very few scheduled castes students receive, upon due completion of studies, equality of consideration for tenured academic jobs. Overall, even the best students emerge as millennially, marked communities. Very little space remains available for the creation of campuses as *caring communities*, given the intense forms of politicization of discourse concerning historically disadvantaged students. Even the then Prime Minister of India, Viswanath Pratap Singh, recalled piquantly my administrative style as contributing to the downfall of his government!

6. Because the agents of the law remain socialized in the legitimacy of erotic humiliation, these initiative carry an uncertain promise of enforcement. And it is only when homophobia is perforated that we may have access to narratives of child abuse and non-consensual homosexual conduct imposed by Godpersons in contemporary India.

7. Since not just the public but even activist memory is short, I need to explain that the experience refers to in the text is to the Mathura rape case, discourse concerning which was initiated by an Open Letter to the Chief Justice of India by four law academic, an intervention historically responsible for installing custodial rape on the agendum of Indian women's movements.

8. To provide just a vignette from my experience, visually disabled students in Indian campuses are with typical cruelty left to their own devices. Most university libraries offer a minuscule, if any, Braille collection, I dedicated much of my tenure as Vice Chancellor of Delhi University (1990–4) to creating a sensibility towards the needs of such students. The most meritorious among them, including Gold Medalists, were systematically denied not just tenure but even temporary teaching assignments, when collegial persuasion failed, I led the university towards 3 per cent quota system in recruitment for all physically 'disabled' candidates. I overcame the normative resistance only at the cost of behavioural interansigence! It saddens me beyond measure,

even as I compose this contribution, that this community has now to wage an uphill battle to activate the Supreme Court of India to enforce its own decision legitimating this reservation.

Perhaps the most poignant of my experience relates to a spastic young person who was disallowed a centennial prestigious minority Delhi University College the services of an amanuensis on the ground of possibility of unfair academic practices! I had to bear all the weight of my office to resolve the situation. Unfortunately, not many Vice Chancellors of Indian universities find time to 'entertain' such priorities!

9. Indian humiliation studies have much to learn from narratives of resistance to forms of macro-fascism of power (traced variously by works such as Ranajit Guha's *Elementary Form of Peasant Insurgence*, James Scott's *The Weapons of the Weak*, and David Harvey's *Spaces of Hope*). They also need, in this genre, to combine the corpus of Ambedkar with Hannah Arendt, both of who were deeply concerned with the tragic reproduction of *rightless people*.

10. The Indian Civil Rights Act (earlier called the Untouchability Offences Act), for example, makes it a serious offence to use derogatory caste names and to justify untouchability practices in any manner. Similarly, the Scheduled Caste and Tribes Atrocities Act of 1989, makes the practices of caste-based aggression and violence a serious offence. The voluminous complaint that these provisions are being 'misused' by dalits indeed provides an important index of their invocation of these provisions in real life.

11. In my studies of compensation for victims of collective violence (up to the 1980s) a dalit women sexually assaulted or even raped was eligible for compensation of Rs 250, even in comparatively 'advanced' states like Maharashtra! Should they be affected by natural, industrial, or political disasters (the latter known to us a' communal' riots') the compensation they receive remains meagre and remains available after many experiences of humiliation protestation before the *Babucracy* (to evoke Arthur Kostler's contrapuntal term for *Bapucracy*). As project Affected People, they tend to be regarded in the Hindutva fullness of the acronym PAP, literally meaning sinful people, rather than those sinned in the name of development. Examples of this indifference can be easily multiplied.

12. Not having access to the print edition, I rely here on its internet version (http://www.religion-online, visited 20 August 2002). The quotes here are mainly derived from chapter 4. The poignant irony of this recourse scarcely affects my profound admiration!

13. *First*, contemporary linguistic/semiotics tells us: 'There is no meaning. Everything in the text is educed to structural relationship. This amounts to negating the word that escapes the scientific method.'

Second, 'on the one hand, language is seen as arbitrary, on the other hand, the signifier is overvalued. Both coincide in their contempt for language,' *Third*, and as a consequence, the signifier becomes the interesting reality. What it signifies and the relationship of the sign to values or thought is no longer considered important.' The 'only things that concern us are the processes of transmission, the mechanism of circulation, the organization of the signifier, and its structure.' *Fourth*, 'language, communication and relationship all become machines' (the reference in particular is to the 'merry venture of Deluze and Guttari in demolishing the signifier). *Fifth*, and in various combinatory modes, the result that stands produced is this: 'the word conveys nothing, says nothing, and the speaker is nothing but a machine gone haywire—or that was never working in the first place.'

4 Understanding Humiliation

Sanjay Palshikar[†]

He had spoken of his own past violence. But he was calm now...
'What does Ambedkar mean to the Dalits?'
'There was a time when we were treated like animals. Now we live like
human beings. It's all because of Ambedkar.'

(Namdeo Dhasal in conversation with V.S. Naipaul)

To be humiliated is to be rendered inferior or deficient in some
respect by others in a deliberate and destructive way. It is therefore
a deeply distressing experience. It is something one cannot get over
easily, and those who have to face it everyday see in it a constant threat to
their sense of self-worth. Ordinarily, 'humiliation' is taken to be an
unwelcome assault on human dignity. Such an assault can be condemned
by a bystander as well as by those subjected to it. However, it may be
important to distinguish the first-person perspective from a third-person
perspective since it is likely to yield different insights.

In calling the assault *unwelcome*, I am excluding from consideration a
number of closely related interactions, which, for all their resemblances
with the sort of things I am planning to analyse, differ in certain crucial
respects. First, let us look at what is termed sadomasochism. Talal Asad
(1998: 300) cites from a sadomasochist handbook the characteristics of
such a relationship: these include a dominant–submissive relationship,

[†]I had a stimulating discussion with Sasheej Hegde during the early stages
of my thinking on this theme. I have found Bishnu Mohapatra's 'Understanding
Indignities' (1998) quite useful. I also found Gopal Guru's comments on an
earlier draft of this paper helpful. My thanks to all of them. An earlier version
of this article appeared in the *Economic & Political Weekly*.

giving and receiving of pain that is pleasurable to both the parties, and a conscious humbling of one partner by the other. While this is an immensely complex phenomenon, what is clear is that the humiliation involved in it is either welcome to the persons involved, or, they do not categorically and consistently reject the relationship as an unwanted one. Since I am using the expression 'unwelcome assaults' in a fairly straightforward, unequivocal sense, sadomasochistic humbling falls outside the scope of my discussion.

I also exclude the operations of what Foucault (1979: 170–8) calls 'normalising judgements'. These are part of the disciplinary techniques of 'correct training', forming individuals out of the 'moving, confused, useless multitudes of bodies'. The shame induced during training is systematic and aimed at making skilled but docile individuals. Shame can also result when we hear what the authoritative voice inside us is saying. An admonition, a rebuke, a reprimand, or a reproach is distressful to the extent that the authority which is its source is external, has not yet been fully internalized, and is still being battled with (hence the experience of humiliation), even though one has either accepted it as an authority or one feels powerless to defy it. Once the place of external authority is taken by one's own reason, it is the *introspective reflections* on one's follies and failings that generate shame. Recall Rousseau's lament: 'How humiliating are these reflections to humanity, and how mortified by them our pride should be!' (1973: 14). This transition from the first to the second, from receiving a scolding to introspection, for example, is the objective of what is variously called upbringing, transition to adulthood, moral development. A similar process is on in some religious orders where the novices being prepared for spirituality are sometimes upbraided by their master. My reason for excluding all these from my discussion is that in none of these instances is distress seen as caused by the unjustified actions of other human beings, and hence something that can be or ought to be rejected.

I am also going to keep instances of alleged abasement out of my discussion. First, there are those notoriously controversial instances where a person does not agree with others' evaluation of his or her acts. Take beauty contests and fashion parades for example. Miss Universe 2002, Oksana Fedorova, a Russian policewoman, saw nothing wrong 'in exchanging her crisp, blue uniform for a minimal bikini'. She said: 'I don't think it's humiliation for women. It's good to show off your beauty.' A similar problem arises vis-à-vis devotional prostrating, either before god, a god-like person, or a great leader, which is described by those outside that experience as self-humiliation. The devotees themselves would regard the attitude of 'abject or self-effacing humility' to be a virtue. Usually in such cases critics of unwarranted humility appeal to criteria that do not depend upon the subject–agent's corroboration and this applies to the critics of beauty pageants too. Somewhat more complex are the instances of debasing oneself, often in a public and symbolic way, as a form of protest. A couple of years ago, newspapers reported that a legislator in Andhra Pradesh had publicly tonsured his head in protest against water shortage. Several farmers from his constituency also participated in the protest. During the anti-Mandal agitation, there were reports of upper-caste youth taking to shoe polishing at busy intersections in some cities, and, ironically, the same form of protest was used more recently by leaders of a Dalit caste in Andhra Pradesh demanding categorization within the Scheduled Castes (SCs).

I have two reasons for excluding cases where someone allegedly brings humiliation upon himself or herself. First, it is not the aim of this article to derive norms legislating individual behaviour from some fixed and abstract notion of human dignity. Moreover, since these are instances of alleged *self*-humiliation, we can make better sense of them if we first understand what humiliation is. Our immediate response to the question 'what is humiliation?' is to either give a psychological description or to resort to normative philosophy. While I do not want to reject out of hand either the dimension of feelings or the attempt to arrive at a notion of human dignity, I think it will be far more economical and at least as illuminating to take 'humiliation' to be a *claim* or claims of certain kinds and explore the structure of these claims, their logical or conceptual conditions, and their role in the reproduction of relations of power.

It might be thought that even with these qualifications, the net is still cast too wide. After all, we know that in the world of social plasticity[1] which we have come to inhabit, the language of 'humiliation' is available to anyone who wishes to use it. So you have Jayalalitha complaining that the central government insulted her and the people of Tamil Nadu by not inviting her to the new President's swearing-in ceremony; or, Lalu Prasad Yadav saying that the Indian Airlines authorities harassed, embarrassed, and humiliated his wife and Bihar's chief minister, Rabri Devi, by asking her to vacate her seat for some Bharatiya Janata Party (BJP) leaders travelling by the same flight.[2] The events of 9/11 were described by K. Subramaniam as America's humiliation, whereas

Habermas, speaking a month after the event, stressed the feeling of humiliation in the Islamic countries.[3]

Such examples can be multiplied. Evidently, people are not humiliated just because they say they are. But, for the direction in which I wish to take this enquiry, the question whether someone is *really* humiliated is not important. Asking that would be just another way of looking for the essence or objective description of humiliation, something I think we can bypass. I would instead like us to attend to the vocabulary deployed, the sort of claims made, when someone complains of humiliation. While it is true that nobody is so powerful that they can never be humiliated, we understand intuitively that the mighty and the weak do not get humiliated the same way. In the case of the elites, it happens in the context of insisting on a protocol, demanding a privilege, drawing distinctions. Correspondingly, the experience and the response to that experience are also different. A sudden and momentary reversal of relations of hierarchy produces the experience of humiliation for them. It is as if there has been an irretrievable loss, which explains the rage often disproportionate to the event. The excess in response is meant to drown the memory of the perceived insult and inscribe in its place a hateful assertion that the hierarchical social world is not easy to change. A close reading of the vocabulary deployed shows that the powerful speak of slight, offence, rudeness, temerity, whereas the subalterns complain of callousness, neglect, and inhuman treatment. Having fewer resources to immediately undo the damage to their self-respect, they ask for kindness, compassion, etc. Their discourse thus opens up more historical possibilities. But before looking at these possibilities, we need to spend some more time looking at the 'humiliation' of the powerful and its connection with distinctions and privileges.

In her study of the making of social categories in colonial Bengal, Anindita Mukhopadhyay cites the nineteenth-century Bhadralok complaining about being ill-treated in jails. In a petition to the authorities they say:

...the prisoners are given boiled gourd, or occasionally boiled rice is given to them for breakfast. Such nasty and unnutritious food is not fit for the prisoners who have to work hard...the dress of the prisoners scarcely covers their nakedness.... Prisoners are sent in a batch to satisfy the call of nature. This destroys their sense of modesty.... There are no paid *mehter*s [sweepers] in the jail. Hindu and Mussulman prisoners are employed to serve as *mehter*s. (Mukhopadhyay 2006: 116)

The Bhadralok prisoners are suggesting that even prisoners have self-respect and that some of the ways in which they are being treated are clearly inappropriate. This self-respect is however contingent on regarding sweepers' job as too lowly for them. The Bhadralok prisoners are also anxious to draw a distinction between themselves and the habitual offenders from the lower orders, as Mukhopadhyay shows in her work. This becomes all the more urgent when, in the course of the freedom struggle, several Bhadralok men are incarcerated for political offences, and the category of political prisoners emerges.

The language of humiliation plays an important part in making distinctions and fashioning categories and this is true even of those living in the most wretched conditions. George Orwell's *Down and Out in Paris and London* is full of instances of hopelessly poor, broken men (and in one telling example, a woman) clutching at scraps of respectability by finding someone to despise and shun. Boris, the Russian immigrant, finds it insufferable that he, a former captain of the old Russian army, has to live on the reluctant generosity of a 'veritable' Jew; the ex-Etonian at a poor-house refers to other inmates as 'low types...very low types'; and the only woman tramp that the author comes across considers it beneath her to speak to fellow (male) tramps and of course makes no secret of it.

There is a related but significantly different use of 'humiliation'. This use is deployed when the relationship between the subalterns and the elites is fluid, the terms of dominance and servitude ever changing. Such situations are more like a tug-of-war, a question of holding the line between the provisionally accepted and the *as yet unacceptable*. Whenever the line threatens to shift to the disadvantage of the subalterns, they invoke the language of humiliation. If, for example, there has been a practice of a particular community leading an annual local procession, or receiving gifts on an auspicious occasion, any violation of the practice is likely to invite the charge of insult. This may seem to be ironic since, to start with, the practice may have had the function of reproducing their inferior status. The irony resolves itself if we see such claims and complaints regarding privilege and offence as relative to a situation, which may seem at least temporarily unalterable to the subalterns.

It is often noticed how solidarities and friendships lessen the hurt caused by insults. Being alone, encircled by jeering contempt, can be debilitating. The presence of those who share the hurt with you can turn the traumatic situation into a battle and that is the first move from solitary and purely psychological suffering to collective action. (In the closing sequence of Vittorio De Sicca's *Bicycle Thief*, Antonio's son Bruno holds his hand and silently shares his father's hurt and shame; but this—the intensely personal moment—is where the film ends.) Organizations, political parties, and ideologies can bring together the half forgotten daily ignominies and organize public memory around a coherent and relatively stable account of the 'humiliating' conditions. But, for this politics to be truly liberating, a simple narrative of humiliation is not enough. The equivocation of belonging and yet not belonging represents a dilemma: to assert one's credentials within the order or reject the order, to accept the criteria of excellence or to defy them. This dilemma cannot be resolved unless it is realized that in complaining against a state of affairs, one may be unwittingly accepting the premises of that order. So the use of the vocabulary of humiliation demands certain clarity. Accounts of humiliation suggest that the acute discomfort of such experience is caused by this: someone who is insulted would leave the insulting situation, with or without retrieving his honour. But if he cannot, he must continue to suffer like someone who can't leave a party he realizes he is not welcome at. Someone is rejected as inferior, and he has to suffer the cruel equivocation, partly of his making, of having to live up to impossible standards and also being impelled to question those standards. This can be a stifling experience, an experience of being tied down, bound, cornered, *placed*. The only way in which one can be unshackled from this confining spatiality is by bringing into play the *temporality* of 'humiliation'. For, every complaint or protest about being humiliated involves a narration or a project. To clarify this further, let me identify three forms of 'humiliation' distinguished from one another in terms of the way each of them organizes temporality.

The full and exact meaning of humiliation, whether taken as an episode or a form of life, derives from what its opposite is presumed to be. The force or the point of the complaint depends on whether the purported humiliation is understood to be a negation of, say, one's manhood, or, one's majesty, or, simply, one's worth as a person. Whether the opposite is seen to be manhood or human dignity makes a world of difference to how we *describe* the event. More specifically, the subject–agent's response to the perceived humiliation is conceptually tied to the perception of what is it that has been violated. 'Affront to manliness' is obviously different from 'inhuman treatment'. It is in this sense that every complaint of humiliation implicitly operates with a pair of opposites. The opposite of whatever one is forcibly made out to be is either already present in the institutions and practices of the society, or, it is posited as a goal to be realized. For example, either there is a pre-existing practice of, say, honour, or self-respect, and its loss is construed as humiliation; or, alternatively, a project to win respect, honour, or glory enables one to characterize the situation that has prevailed so far as humiliating. In this, 'humiliation' is like 'alienation' which can either be used to tell a story of lost unity—a simple past to present movement—or to bring historically possible future into an evaluative relationship with the present.[4] As a result of this theoretical manoeuvre, the present begins to look morally wrong or deficient. Thus 'humiliation', like 'alienation', can work as a normative fulcrum of the critique of the present order.

Humiliation in war and sport is predicated upon already existing notions of manhood and glory (note the frequent, and apparently unproblematic, use in sports columns of the expression, 'humiliating defeat'); whereas a self-respect movement, like the one started by Periyar in Tamil Nadu in the early twentieth century, seeks to *create practically* conditions which will render felicitous its utterances about the humiliating present. This is then interestingly different from the naming of a ship, or the Christian wedding, where the speech community and the conditions of felicitous utterances are already given.[5]

It is tempting to take 'humiliation-as-loss' to be typical of the elite's experience and 'humiliation-in-retrospect' as that of the subalterns. But the classification may be too neat, for at least two reasons. The obvious one is that even the subalterns tell stories of a munificent and honourable past, a kind of golden period, which they were defrauded of. Here 'humiliation' is part of a project of retrieval. The other reason why such a classification won't do is that a loss can be, and in real life often is, a loss relative to some situation. Under the force of practical necessity we make peace with less than ideal circumstances and when even these start worsening because of somebody's deliberate actions, and the rudiments of dignity are snatched away, we complain as bitterly of humiliation as we would have had we been the most privileged and the most powerful. Human beings hold on or carve out dignity under even the most trying and degrading circumstances. (Recall Coetzee's poignant account of this in his *Disgrace*.) It is therefore impossible to tidy up the stories of better past and better future as belonging to the elite and the subalterns respectively.

Besides these two ways of talking about one's humiliation, there is a third possibility in which one claims to be humiliated, or gives an account of it, on the unreflected basis of an order of values, but later comes to reject that order, and reconstitutes the grounds of the claim.

This is famously exemplified in Gandhi. He began by thinking of the British rule in India as an affront to our manhood, and considered various ways of overcoming the lack of manly vigour in himself, to start with; over time, he came to see the empire as ill-treating its loyal subjects, and later went beyond even this basis of criticism. Here, we see notions of fairness and justice replacing the culture of masculinity and reformulating the account of humiliation on a new basis. There is a similar thing happening with Ambedkar's turning to Buddhism. Soon after declaring in 1935 his resolve to leave the Hindu fold, Ambedkar made a speech in the Mahar Conference. Conversion is not for the slaves, he said. It is part of the struggle against the caste Hindus. The oppressed needed three kinds of strength to win this struggle: manpower, finance, and mental strength. Regarding the last, he said the oppressed had come to accept without any complaint all manner of insults. There was neither 'retort nor revolt'. 'Confidence, vigour and ambition' had vanished, and the oppressed had become 'helpless, unenergetic and pale'. There was an 'atmosphere of defeatism and pessimism'. He ended the speech by saying that one of the reasons he was asking his followers to convert was to gain strength: 'convert to become strong'. Even two decades later, he remained pre-occupied with these ideas and the themes of strength and spiritedness surfaced even in his historic speech at Nagpur the day after he finally converted to Buddhism. He spoke appreciatively of the combativeness of the Muslims, and he also quoted Sant Ramdas to the effect that lack of enthusiasm or spiritedness leads to the disease of mind and body. But there was something else he wanted to tell his followers: 'lead such a life that you will command respect'.[6] This idea of character suggests that the notion of strength had undergone a subtle change: it was a willingness to fight for one's honour honed and tempered by righteousness and fortitude. In writing *The Buddha and His Dhamma*, Ambedkar can be seen to be moving away not only from the unqualified acceptance of the bourgeois values of liberty and equality to the new ground of *mitrata* and *karuna*, but also from a simple notion of aggressiveness to power born out of probity, determination, and temperance.

Loss, conquest, and redefinition: these three forms of 'humiliation', resulting from the interpretative and practical activity of the subalterns, can thus be seen as three alternatives in collective self-formation, three trajectories contingent upon successful political action. To get a grasp of the implications of this point, let me bring in another dimension here.

Let us pause for a moment to ask whether humiliation is a form of power, like exploitation[7] or manipulation. It seems to me to be more accurate to recognize it as an element present in all exercises of power, a communicative dimension accompanying this or that form of power. To say this is different from saying that all forms of power require communication as a condition of their possibility, which they of course do: blackmail is not conceivable without some threat being conveyed, giving or distorting information is necessary for manipulation, and exploitation needs institutional arrangements embodying a distributive mechanism. Communication is not a condition of humiliation; humiliation is itself communication. In protesting against an insult as well as in insulting, something is being said to the other. And this communicative exchange is possible because of a shared language. This language is the prevailing order of norms and values which in the first place makes it possible to humiliate and be humiliated. We should perhaps distinguish two distinct but related levels here—the level of the more or less conscious subscribing to the order and the more insidious and elusive operations of power whose effects are *inscribed* in the bodies of the dominated (Bourdieu 2000). What a given instance of humiliation does is that it mobilizes that order communicatively and constrains you to suffer the consequences of being constituted by that order. But there is also another side to it. When, for example, a farm labourer is dragged through the streets on charges of petty theft, our habitual, taken-for-granted hierarchies come to the surface and get exposed to attention. When a powerful person ill-treats someone beneath him, he is reiterating that order, but he is also risking widespread reflection on that order. Humiliation is a critical point in a power relationship, the cusp region as it were, something that brings sharpness to the exercise of power and helps reproduce those relations of power, but it can also lead to their ultimate dissolution. It is a potentially disruptive element of power.

To push the argument further along, however, humiliation is not disruptive of the given relations of power alone, but has corrosive effects for the underlying normative order as well. The claim, 'I am humiliated', is only half a claim, or no claim at all. There is nothing in it to suggest what is to follow by way of the subject–agent's response. It is open to them to want to avenge, and thus seek the experience of manhood, or question the way they are being treated on the basis of the widely acknowledged but inconsistently applied criteria of decency, civility, etc., or, in a radically creative response, critique the present order and make good the claim regarding humiliation on an entirely new vision of social relations. In short, if 'humiliation' is a claim which is made complete only by incorporating in it the proposed response to the alleged humiliation, then those who are making that claim must face a situation of *choice* and attain the clarity required for making the choice. It is then that 'humiliation' becomes more than a language used to make sense of a disagreeable situation.

Revenge, retribution,[8] and forgiveness are the main historically evolved responses to 'humiliation'. I argued earlier that 'humiliation' is essentially a communicative interaction, that in protesting as well as in insulting we are saying something. It is a deeply ambivalent 'saying', fraught with opposite possibilities. Whether we stay on or exit from the 'community' depends on the outcome of this interaction. It will be illuminating here to look at what John Dewey (Ball 1995: 85) said about communication: 'There is more than a verbal tie between words common, community, and communication. Men live in a community in virtue of the things which they have in common; and communication is the way in which they come to possess things in common'. If this is true, then 'humiliation' is a trial or a testing period through which our belonging to the same commonness goes. The outcome of this test determines whether we remain together and on what terms, whether we reconstitute our commonness or whether we reflectively 'recollect' the bases of our common life. The interaction that is 'humiliation' may turn out to be ironic in that it may be communication about snapping all communication, about breaking away, or, less cataclysmically, about refusing to regard the other as worthy of a dialogue. If this is what 'humiliation' can be about, then it is incongruous to regard retaliation as the only response possible normatively. It means that the situation is not seen as confronting us with a momentous choice, it means that the history-making potential of 'humiliation' is not explored.

Violent retaliation has indeed been a most preferred response in many cultures and its appeal endures today in cultures of masculinity. But there are reasons that question our taking such a response to be obvious. Since violence is, literally speaking, destruction, or attempted destruction of something regarded by somebody as inviolate (Scruton 1983), in the context of what we are discussing here, it may be permissible to run the ideas of violence and retaliatory humiliation together.[9] Violence, to say the least, is a complex matter. But let us consider, for the moment, one kind of violence. Violence as a dialogue with oneself, is a cleansing act (to recall Sartre in his Preface to Franz Fanon's *The Wretched of the Earth*), it is something that cures the oppressed of their ingrained feelings of inferiority. It is man 're-creating himself', if only *monologically*. But 'humiliation' is also about re-evaluating the present, transforming it, *through one's interaction* with one's humiliator, and not simply a matter of 'bursting into history' (Sartre) as male adults. In humiliating the humiliator, one is either playing God, or, less audaciously, desperately seeking to erase the ontological status of the acts perpetrated by the humiliator. But this may unwittingly result in the confirmation of the underlying order of evaluations which made these mutual humiliations possible in the first place. The second reason for being sceptical about violent response is more general. If the Hobbesian State of Nature is the logical extreme of mutual violence, then the corollary is that it is impossible to normatively universalize violence. For, if you visualize a situation where everyone uses it, or can in principle use it, against everyone else, then everyone will be ultimately left to live a solitary life where nothing common is possible. But a *norm* is essentially something common and shared, and hence violence as a universal norm will end up eventually destroying itself, and logically it will not even get going. In case of violence understood as mutual humbling, however, we also witness the opposite consequence, namely, strengthening of values, of glory and pride for example, which make humiliation possible at all. Perhaps it is wrong to speak of strengthening here; what takes place is a rigidification of our values. They become opaque and resist reflection. Violent retaliation therefore produces a contradictory situation of reinforcing some values while weakening the conditions of normativity as such. But while arguing that therefore a response other than violent retaliation may have more justification to it than mutual humbling, we should also realize that the moral shock or revulsion induced by an act of violence often obscures a certain deeply held urge behind such an act: the urge to start afresh. The person killing his humiliator, for example, is hoping to stop the flow of history and start a new story.

What about forgiveness? It has been observed that 'forgiveness commonly requires that the victim have a change of heart or express a commitment to eradicating his resentment to the wrongdoer. Consequently, forgiveness may be too demanding or too intrusive for politics'.[10] More seriously, 'demanding' forgiveness may be seen as a way of short-circuiting justice, especially if the wrongdoer's acknowledgement of the wrong done to the victim is not seen as a precondition of forgiveness. This discussion brings to mind the South African experiment of the Truth and Reconciliation Commission (TRC), though it dealt mainly with instances of alleged *mutual cruelty* and not with cases of humiliation. Apart from the obviously Christian theological texture of the notion of reconciliation deployed by the Commission, the TRC has been criticized on the ground that the institutionally mediated reconciliation imposes a temporality often out of synchrony with the different time spans of the victims' mourning and healing even as it constructs a collective self for them and invites them to participate in its magnanimity (Hamber and Wilson 2002: 35–53).

This quick look at some of the relevant issues does not even remotely do justice to the complex legal, conceptual, and moral matters involved. Nor is it intended to help us conclude in favour of any option. It is meant to drive home the point that precisely because of the *linguistic form* of 'humiliation', that is, because it is a complaint about a violent deployment of certain constitutive values, in making such a complaint one is in principle leading oneself and one's adversary to a situation where all these issues have to be faced. The least, I think, that can be said is that there are choices here with widely different possibilities.

The choice is necessary but it is also important to realize that it is not always made *discursively*, and sometimes not made at all. A collective action that exposes the very fabric of the society to conscientious scrutiny and has the power to invite everyone to soul-searching is one of those momentous happenings of which written history consists. And such history is not made everyday. In everyday life the oppressed have much smaller but no less urgent battles to fight, compromises to make. And yet, in the midst of tactical servility, manipulation, sporadic outbursts, and precarious victories, the oppressed remember—and revere—their leaders and through these remembrances keep hope and faith in the idea of heroic choices alive. Naipaul (1998) has captured this well in his account of the long line of people that he saw on his arrival in Bombay: freshly bathed, and peaceable 'even in the sun and the brown smoke of exhausts' from the vehicles, they were on their way to a suburb where Ambedkar *jayanti* was being celebrated. Such celebrations are a regular, and one might even say ritualistic occasions, neither overtly political, nor in the realm of the heroic. But between the heroic and the ordinary of the politics of the oppressed, there is a thread of resilience, of not giving up hope, even if one has to muddle through the uncertainties and banalities of manipulative politics punctuated by quasi-religious anniversary celebrations. Naipaul calls it 'rejecting rejection' (p. 119). No account of humiliation will be complete without appreciating the significance of this rejection of rejection.[11]

NOTES

1. I borrow this expression from Kaviraj (2001: 238).
2. Illustrations taken from news reports appearing in the Hyderabad edition of *The Hindu*. The Lalu Prasad Yadav/Rabri Devi example is taken from the Bombay edition of *The Times of India*.
3. '...the prospect of spiritual freedom, which finds its political expression in the separation of church and state, has been impeded there [i.e., in the Islamic countries] by feelings of humiliation.' From the acceptance speech by Habermas at Frankfurt on the occasion of being awarded the Peace Prize by the Association of German Publishers and Booksellers, on 14 October 2001.
4. Bertell Ollman does well to see in Marx' theory of alienation an *internal* relation between the present and the future. He says: 'alienation can only be grasped as the absence of unalienation, each state serving as a point of reference for the other'. But, apparently under the influence of fact-value dichotomy, he obscures this insight by treating the theory of alienation as not evaluative. He states his position better when he says that when present and future, like disease and health, are *internally* related, there is no *external* standard being invoked to judge the present. See Ollman (1976: 131–2).
5. The allusion here is to J.L. Austin's concept of 'performative utterances'. See Austin (1976), especially the first lecture.
6. The excerpts cited here are from Vasant Moon's translation of the two speeches included in Grover (1992).
7. Robert Goodin (1987: 181–2) has pointed out that exploitation is primarily a modal category, not a scalar one, though we do speak of degrees of exploitation. I think this applies to 'humiliation' too.
8. Arindam Chakrabarty (2005: 33) distinguishes between revenge and retribution as follows:

   Retributive punishment comes from neutral legal authorities. Revenge is contemplated by the affected victim... The purpose, even of retributive punishment, can be reforming the wrongdoer. The purpose of revenge is simply to show that the victim can also hit aback... While punishment belittles and shames the wrongdoer, revenge... glorifies and valourizes him.

   And finally, pointing out that revenge, unlike retribution, involves 'mimicry of violence', Chakrabarty says, 'The imitative nature of revenge sharply distinguishes it from jusitce. Justice does not normally copy the crime it curbs.' I thank Mangesh Kulkarni for making available to me a copy of this article.
9. The important difference of course is that in humiliation as violence there cannot be complete annihilation of the other; something of the other must survive to experience the agony of humiliation.

10. For these and related philosophical issues see Peter Digeser (1998: 700–24). See also, Jacques Derrida (2001) on the unconditional nature of forgiveness.

11. In an interview with Gowri Ramnarayan (*The Hindu*, 22 August 2004), Homi Bhabha makes an interesting point when he says that we know a lot about victors and victims, but, 'survival is an in-between state that we all share. The fabric tears everyday, you stitch it back, and carry on'. I am, however, not sure if we can be said to be surviving without any stories of victories and losses, however small, in our daily lives. The important thing is that there is no finality to these accounts, no happy or tragic endings.

SECTION II
CONTEXTUALIZING HUMILIATION

5 Bereft of Being
The Humiliations of Untouchability
V. Geetha

ABOUT HUMILIATION

Fundamentally, humiliation is an experience that interrogates and recasts one's relationship to oneself. Whether endured as an occurrence where one's pride and self-esteem have been bruised, or suffered as a condition that is degrading and wounding, humiliation is felt, held, and savoured in the very gut of our existence, in the core of our being. It exacts from us a range of responses: from the vengeful to the stoic. When subject to a consistent dishonouring, wounded pride flares into counter-hatred and goes on to hurt and pain those responsible for the wounding in the first place. But when one's corporeal and spiritual existence is itself considered evidence of one's lowness, when being (as in the self) is disallowed the knowledge of its integrity, its claims to self-respect, then a profound crisis besets the self—a crisis which the American philosopher Cornel West describes very aptly as 'an ontological wounding'.

I am not concerned here with the first kind of humiliation but with the second: at one level, to degrade, hurt, and render passive another person or another society is clearly an expression of power, but such acts of degradation and violation are seldom that alone. Often, they exist in excess of what the exercise of power demands, the deploying of authority requires. These are acts that appear intent on making the human body—a certain sort of human body—bear witness against itself; which wound the being at its constitutive core. They also appear to demonstrate the workings of a perverse will—one that is so profoundly negative that it can only define itself through the destruction of another being.

Kate Millet has eloquently described how such a perversion achieves its intent. In her essay on *Closet Land*, a film on torture set in an unnamed South American country, she refers to the power that is invested in the figure of the torturer, that connoisseur of abasement and humiliation:

> There is a great narcissism about the figure of the interrogator: the victim exists to indulge it, to assist him in exploring the dark depths of his soul, an avocation, the subtle 'philosophic' dimensions of his profession. The knowledge of evil is one of the fringe benefits of the experience of state power, soldiery, masculine pursuits in general: women and children function as sounding boards here, foils, mirrors, means of comparison.... Only through abusing his victim can he catch sight of his own goal...(Millet 1994: 189–90)

It seems to me that this dark narcissism and the cold, cruel pain it demands and relishes are central to the practices of untouchability.

ON UNTOUCHABILITY

Untouchability, as most of us know, is both a condition of existence, as well as a violent expression of power. To B.R. Ambedkar, this system embodied the principle of 'graded inequality' and to E.V. Ramasamy Periyar, untouchability was a norm that informed the caste system, at every level of its hierarchical existence. For both these lifelong students of the *varna-jati* order, untouchability was the most important and expressive instance of an unjust, inhuman order.

In an order, which holds that human beings are not, indeed, cannot be coeval with each other—I use the word 'coeval' in the sense the anthropologist Johannes Fabian uses it in *Time and the Other*—untouchables are important. Their existence connotes an enhanced negativity, for they *are* the taboo against a coeval existence—they are physically set apart and their bodies are called to bear witness to the salience of a system that requires their continuous humiliation. The fact of their being set apart is thus an ontological condition, the very ground of their existence as human beings.

The unjust nature of the caste order may be variously understood—in terms of the imperatives of production and reproduction, discipline and punishment, sexual control and regulation. Yet, none of these helps us comprehend the grit and grime of actual practices of untouchability—the segregation of living spaces, the taboos against sharing water points, burial grounds, temples, the ban on adornment, the consigning of an entire group of people to deadening labour, the haunting of their existence by the fear of punishment, should they fudge norms, cross limits. This punishment is as soul-wounding as it is gratuitous: the forcible eating of excreta, punishment by fire-branding, the rape and mutilation of bodies. Whatever its structural correlates, untouchability is essentially an experience of wounding, of wilful hurt, through which the outcaste body becomes a stranger to itself, and is ever ready to fall off the edge, give into anomie and fragmentation.

Untouchability however is not an act of dramatic horror—it exists most powerfully in the everyday, is at home in the quotidian, and sustained and legitimized by a tortuous semantics of tactility. Several hundred pages have been devoted to understanding the basis of touch and recoil that characterizes the caste order: anthropologists and sociologists have enthusiastically committed themselves to examining this semantics, and have thereby served, unwittingly, in some cases, to further reify it. This semantics is particularly cunning in the manner in which it ensures its own continued reproduction—the untouchables who have the greatest stake in challenging it are subject to its merciless logic, and reproduce amongst themselves the vicious logic of graded inequality.

To understand the experience of untouchability for the essential metaphysical horror it is, and the everyday crime that it enables, we need to understand untouchability both as a layered experience, and as an evil that is stunning in its banality.

The Curse of Labour

At one level untouchability is a form of extreme alienation where the labourer—the Dalit is invariably a labourer—is dissociated not only from the products of her own creation, but also from her own labouring body. Complicated norms of tactility mandate that the low-born alone should labour at difficult and hazardous tasks, since their bodies, being constitutively impure, are held to be suited to these and not other vocations. The untouchable body thus becomes a distinctive labouring body, whose work, unlike the work of the peasant and the artisan, does not secrete either material or symbolic value. For, according to the stunningly circular logic of the caste order, the untouchable's labour, her vocation, by simply being of her body and being, is doomed to irrelevance. This body in which the untouchable lives but does not inhabit is her prison-house: even if she changes her vocation—through negotiation and struggle—her corporeal being precedes her. Forced to live out of a body that is its own ruin, the Dalit suffers a state of permanent dissociation.

This sense of alienation from her body and its productive worth is further accentuated by iterative acts of humiliation which separate the

Dalit from her fellow beings in an everyday existential sense: food taboos, taboos on the use of water, certain sorts of clothes, the association with refuse and death, all of which are rationalized as custom and valorized as the writ of god or destiny serve to fix her in her hurt, and worse, grind her down into the dust which is held to be her natural habitat.

This logic of lowness and labour exists in contrast to counter-logic of highness and intellect. Brahmins, born into an exalted status, are meant to perform only acts of the mind, and these, in turn, become them, sanctified as it were by their bodily purity. These two contrasting logics bear a curious relationship. Born to labour, Dalits cannot claim the right of knowing; and being denied that right they cannot know of or escape their condition of being labourers. Brahmins on the other hand are the natural custodians of learning, but the knowledge they produce is like a fetish, a mysterious thing which escapes—and transmutes—the labour, which is instrumental in creating the conditions of knowledge in the first place. This transmuted knowledge returns to haunt the Dalit with its fictions of origins, purity, and pollution, which, in turn, help to naturalize the exclusion of Dalits from the commonweal and render them bereft of rights to those common courtesies, laws of conviviality and mutuality which mark our relationships with each other. At the same time, they elide the Dalits' centrality to our productive life, to our existential imaginings.

These fictions of the caste imagination do not merely damn the Dalit, like racial myths damn the black-skinned. Rather they construct the Dalit as an expendable negative other, who is also wholly necessary. Like Kate Millet's torturer whose existence is linked to that of his victim, the caste imagination needs the untouchable, his continuous humiliation being the condition of our social order. However hierarchical, caste society assigns a functional place to various jatis in its dizzying taxonomy. The Dalit alone is excluded—denied forever the joys and poignancies of any sort of fraternity.

Ambedkar understood the venality of this relationship in all its tragedy—the most humiliating aspect of Dalit life must certainly be this, that the life, however lived, represents the very antithesis of a common core of existence. To underscore the inherent tragedy that is the Dalit's situation, he movingly evokes instances of comradeship that mark a common life. He quotes the apostle Paul: 'Of one blood are all nations of men. There is neither Jew nor Greek, neither bond nor free, neither male nor female; for yet all are one in Christ Jesus.' Even more evocatively, he quotes the Pilgrim Fathers who landed in what was then the new world and extended a thanksgiving to each other: 'We are knit together as a body in the most sacred covenant of the Lord...by virtue of which we hold ourselves tied to all care of each others' good and of the whole' (Ambedkar 1987: 97).

Here we have a critique that is powerful and damning because it captures the angst of those who are denied the poetry of a fraternal existence. Here there is neither a divine nor mortal covenant that binds an untouchable to his fellow beings. On the other hand, as Ambedkar never failed to point out, both men and their gods have connived in the practice of untouchability:

The Hindu social order is based on the doctrine that men are created from different parts of the divinity and therefore the view expressed by Paul or the Pilgrim Fathers has no place in it. The Brahmin is no brother to the Kshatriya because the former is born from the mouth of the divinity while the latter is from the arms. The Kshatriya is no brother to the Vaishya because the former is born from the arms and the latter from his thighs. As no one is brother to the other, no one is the keeper of the other.

The doctrine that the different classes were created from the different parts of the Divine body has generated the belief that must be divine will that they should remain separate and distinct. (Ambedkar 1987: 100)

The Hindu instinct to remain separate, to 'never overlook a difference if it does exist', 'to recognize it and blazon it forth' is sustained not by belief alone, as we know. As far as the untouchables are concerned their separation is assured not merely by rules of work, but by norms of pleasure as well.

THE IMPOSSIBILITY OF LOVE

The separation of castes and their mutual antipathy are made possible through a complex sexual discourse: who shall touch who legitimately, who shall marry who are matters that are intimately discussed and dealt with in a range of literature: from the *Manusmriti* to *Kamasutra* on one hand, to matrimonial advertisements and legal arguments on the other. Love in a caste society is thus an intensely regulated phenomenon, perhaps also because these regulations have been and are continuously violated, with the violations serving as incitements to further law-making.

For, in spite of the taboos against touch, untouchable women are routinely sexually violated. In spite of their often asserted superiority of birth, upper caste men *feel* the need to assert their virility through sexual crimes that shame untouchable men. There is present here a great anxiety that entails one's promiscuous nature and prowess—an anxiety that betrays its own vulnerability. The converse too happens: upper caste women do fall in love with untouchable men, in spite of all the fictions of lowness, and untouchable women do woo away young men from the upper castes.

In these circumstances caste society has to normalize the sexual rapacity of upper caste men, and protect the chastity of upper caste women as well as punish the erring desire of untouchable men and contain the irrepressible sexual otherness of untouchable women. Law and punishment are used to good effect to achieve either intent, but as much as law, it is myth—as legend, folktale, scriptural story—that sustains our sexual fictions. I wish to discuss here a well-honed tale that is known across regions in the southern and western parts of India.

This is a tale that is associated with the life of Parashurama—in Brahmanical literature—and with Renuka, and is as diverse as the traditions of regional and folk literature. I wish to recount two dominant versions, one of which is to be found in the former and the other characteristic of the latter. However, neither version is free of the influences of the other.

Version (a): Parashurama's mother Renuka, celebrated for her chastity, allows herself to be observed and admired by a passing monarch who lusts for her. Her body is jolted by her crime: being the object of a man's lust. Her husband, the Rishi Jamadagni, realizes that his wife has been possessed for a while by an unclean thought. (In some versions, she is not watched, but watches: she is amused by a group of sporting *gandharvas* whose love-play she witnesses while fetching water. Her momentary indulgent appreciation of their amours besmirches her chaste imagination and her husband gets to find out.) Angered by her disloyalty (sic), he orders his son to behead his mother. Anxious not to disobey his father, who is also his teacher (guru), Parashurama brings his axe down on Renuka's head. But once the deed is done, he is so distraught that he begs for his mother to be brought back to life. Jamadagni relents and whispers a chant in his ears that will enable him to fix the cast-off head to its body. Unfortunately, at around the same time, an untouchable woman had been killed by having her head lopped off—for crimes of promiscuity—and Parashurama fixes his mother's head to her unclean body. Renuka, now resurrected, realizes that she is a monstrous creature and to expiate her impossible state of being takes refuge in the untouchable colony. She also seeks to absolve herself of her sinful existence by tending those struck by the pox; eventually she comes to be associated with the goddess of the pox, who brings the dreaded malady on as also relieving one of it, and comes to be known as Mariamma.

There are other heretical variants of this essentially Brahmanical tale, where Renuka is not beheaded but runs away from her angry son. In her hour of distress, an untouchable woman—also cursed for her impure bodily ways—embraces her, thereby polluting her being. Parashurama in his rage cuts away both their heads and then of course joins them back, but attaches, as we have seen, the wrong head to the wrong body. The woman with the Brahmin's head and the untouchable body becomes Mariamma, and the one with the untouchable's head and the Brahmin body becomes Ellamma. Both of them are lower caste village goddesses—of heat, the pox, and fertility.

Version (b): In this version, a Brahmin girl is abandoned by her family because she attains puberty before marriage. A Shudra family raises her. A *madiga* young man falls in love with her, but realizes that he cannot marry her, unless he masquerades as a Brahmin. He succeeds so well in his deception that she becomes his wife, and even has children by him. Meanwhile, he continues to follow his caste vocation—he stitches leather sandals without his wife's knowledge. One day his sons, curious to know what their father did everyday, away from home, follow him and see him busy at his task. Fascinated by his skills, they return home and try to do the same, using grass and leaves. Their mother is horrified and scolds them, whereupon they tell her that they are merely following their father's vocation. She is disgusted and angry—angry at her husband's deception and disgusted by his untouchable status.

Her anger causes her body to grow, grow in fury, in righteousness, till she is ready to avenge the wrong done to her. Her tongue lolling out of her mouth, hungry for the blood and flesh of the man who had cheated her, she roams the forests and the hills before she finds him. He tries to hide behind a buffalo grazing in the field, but she spies him out and slits his throat. Panting, she drinks his blood and then tears his flesh apart. Her great powers make her a goddess—the goddess Mari—who every year demands the sacrifice of animal flesh as an appeasement for the trick played on her.

In version (a) a king's lust is displaced onto the body of a woman— Renuka has to wear the marks of her intended seduction, thereby owning responsibility for it. The status of her desire is ambiguous, if we are to put the two versions of the tale together, but it is unimportant whether she actually allowed the passing monarch to eye her, or was taken in by that display of *gandharva* love. It is enough for the caste order to contemplate the possibility of her straying into an unchaste thought. The point is to make an example of an erring woman, one who dares to entertain desire, either on her own, or is made the object of it. This point is made simply, elegantly, by a clever turning of the plot: the erring woman is relegated to the realm of unredeemed pollution. It is another matter that in some versions she is embraced by an outcaste woman in her state of dishonour, a fact the tale hurriedly recounts, and passes on to note that for their sins, both Renuka and the outcaste woman are beheaded. Later, when Parashurama yearns for his mother, he is allowed to resurrect her, but not as herself. She has to, even after death, wear her lowness—thus she is raised from the dead as a curious and disgusting hybrid, chaste in the head and promiscuous in her body. That is, even if she were to live, she can only do so as a woman whose bodily being is inherently suspect.

In this tale, the king of course is absolved of moral intent and responsibility, and importantly, cautionary strictures with respect to the sexuality of upper caste women which are endowed with the force of law and dictum through a thoroughly cynical recall of the horrors of untouchability. That is, untouchability is the ultimate in punishment—a fact that the caste order recognizes—and to humiliate and indict illicit desire, the errant being is relegated to the ghetto of the untouchable. Further, female desire, however one understands it, as seductive or seducing, is held to be constitutively wrong—it cannot fulfil itself, being always already errant. Ironically, it turns out to be untouchable!

Renuka and her untouchable alter ego are in many ways interchangeable—an upper caste woman who desires beyond the bounds of chaste matrimony is deemed to be untouchable, an untouchable woman whose promiscuity has earned her punishment acquires a Brahmin body, but it is essentially a sinning body, being of a woman who dared entertain an unchaste thought.

In version (b) we find another logic at work. An untouchable man marries a Brahmin woman, through cunning and deceit. Clearly he cannot woo her as himself. And when she finds out, she turns ferocious and consumes him. He is literally torn apart, and his blood drunk. Here, the so-called sexual hunger of the upper caste woman—a favourite theme in Brahmanical texts, and the basis for the caste order's obsession with the chastity of the caste Hindu woman—is transformed to represent divine anger, which punishes the untouchable's misplaced love. In one stroke, her desire is rendered irrelevant, being subject to a mutation, and his love is turned against him—his body is mutilated for harbouring such a roughish thought.

Here we have instances of extremely subtle humiliation. There is shame in violation, yes, but the ennui and fragmentation that attends an experience of complete otherness, where one's body, in one instance, becomes literally untouchable and therefore the site of erring monstrous emotions that are held to be clearly beyond the pale of human desire, and in another instance is tortured and punished by the very desire it had experienced—these represent destinies which await love that dares to stray beyond the bounds of touch. They signify the hurt that scars a living sensuous core, which strikes at the heart of a very fundamental yearning to be loved.

These and several other tales demonstrate the monstrosity of sexual congress between an untouchable and a person from another caste and in doing so help to reproduce—across generations—the untouchable body as an alien. It is another matter that transgressions happen and the untouchable does not receive these tales kindly or that she rebels and negotiates received meanings on her own terms, but these do not disrupt the manner in which we notate intimacy and love in caste society.

UNTOUCHABLE ANGST

The seriousness with which caste society views crimes of love has meant that the untouchable reckons with the fact of his disconsolate aloneness. Deemed unfit for love by any but his or her own kind, the untouchable body is further pushed into and under its own skin. This state of being or (non-being) breeds a consciousness that has to constantly militate against its ontological status. However, the latter is kept in place by a whole plethora of practices which remind the untouchable that he is not merely an irreconcilable other but a negative being, that is, his otherness does not have any resonance of its own, but exists as the refuse of the caste order.

It is significant that the untouchable is associated in different ways with waste, trash, refuse: when in bonded servitude as agricultural labourers, Dalits have to make do with leftover grain, or food. As manual scavengers, they are the custodians of what the body rejects, of what is expelled to maintain the physical world in a state of health. As washer people, birth attendants who clean up the mess of being born, as removers of dead animals, carriers of the dead, caretakers of burial and cremation grounds—in each of these instances, the stigma of pollution which attaches to the untouchable is, most cruelly, one which he bears for the well-being of a commonweal that has no use for him. He takes on, literally and figuratively, the weight of what is ejected after use and thereby becomes himself an object that can be expended. (In the case of production, a slightly different logic is at work, as we have seen—his labour is utilized to optimal ends, but he is not allowed a knowledge of it, instead, he is persuaded to view his own labouring body as a site of dirt.) Ironically, the dirt that becomes an untouchable and renders him unworthy of touch is not his. This simple but often disregarded fact shows up the artifice of untouchability, its elaborate fictions and the sophistry they embody.

Interestingly enough, the caste order's obsession with notions of purity and pollution have not yielded a science of waste or led to viable sanitation practices, and this, again, has to do with the utter dispensability of the untouchable's body. (Gandhi attempted to work through a politics of waste, which was also simultaneously an ethics that desired to indict untouchability—a venture that was both ingenuous as well as problematic. This is a point that I cannot argue here.)

As long as it is present, in all its corporeality, caste Hindus will displace onto it their anxiety over refuse, thereby constructing a charmed circle of fictional purity around themselves. This is the informing angst of untouchability, that it defines being, a certain sort of being, as waste, as that which cannot be pertinent to itself.

The Impossibility of History

Considered its own ruin, the untouchable body is further scarred by its anomalous existence in time. The untouchable is bounded by her body, by its irrefutable presence, that to enquire into the origin of pollution or purity remains an act of stretching, of transgression. Such transgressions do occur but are often ineffable, fragmentary, and epiphanic—and they happen in and through deportments of the body, in possession, in trance, in performance. But these modes of bodily being are contingent as well as liminal, and by their very terms cannot effectively intrude on the time of the 'now'; on the other hand, they are not entirely lost to posterity. For instance, performances do inflect the text on which they are based and liminal moments very subtly leave their mark on everyday time. This is evident even in the Mariamma tale, where the transfigured women become goddesses—placed beyond the pale of mortal lives, yet profoundly present in them. But it is also true that the disjuncture affected by the body in revolt cannot be sustained as difference—and though recoverable as memory, the contingent remains a gesture within the hermetic realm of rituals and conventions. In the modern period, though, the contingent acquired a new status. For groups such as the untouchables, ontology became transformed into history, and instead of being located in the passivity of birth came to reside in the restlessness of the quest—a quest for personhood, comradeship, community. In some instances, as with the Tamil Dalit Buddhist Iyothee Thass, this quest translated into a search for a past that the untouchables could make their own and which showed their lives and identities to be governed by circumstance and conjuncture and not by the 'fact' of 'low birth'. However opaque and dense this past seemed, the adventure to recover it was important for the Dalit imagination, especially since, as D.D. Kosambi noted, the caste order in the present day could only survive through a negation of history and progress, through 'an exaggerated conservatism' that wrote the contingent into a text, claiming for both a timeless antiquity (Kosambi 2002: 775).

THE BODY OF KNOWLEDGE

This brings me to the second of my concerns: what is the imagination that sustains and reproduces this social order? The Brahmanical imagination has been discussed and debated in several political and social forums of the anti-caste movements. Its will to power, to supremacy, its winning flexibility, its hegemonic intent—all these have been systematically analysed and criticized by the Tamil Self-respect movement. Ambedkar has described with great precision and savage irony the Hindu social order. He has shown how pitiless it is about the inhumanity it has sanctioned and argued that this is because injustice and hierarchy have been consecrated as acts of god:

All these (religions) have sacred codes. They consecrate beliefs and rites and make them sacred. But they do not prescribe, nor do they consecrate a particular form of social structure—the relationship between man and man in a concrete form—and make it sacred inviolate. The Hindus are singular in this respect. This is what has given the Hindu social order its abiding strength to defy the ravages of time...(Ambedkar 1987: 129)

The word of god lends authority and urgency to claims that otherwise are deconstructed by history. The wrongness of the caste order is impossible to dispel as an idea because it is tantamount to dispelling god, a fact that both Ramasamy Periyar and Ambedkar understood in different ways. Writing of the power vested in state-appointed judicial functionaries in republics of the faithful, Kate Millet notes:

All decisions in theocratic circumstances are magnified, cut in stone. Even the smallest factions and disputes are intensified and enlarged when viewed in the prism of the eternal; a multiplication of power and significance takes place merely by the timeless dimension of the sacred. Everything now has the greatest possible import, implication, resonance. Crime becomes sin and in so becoming changes its nature utterly.... Everywhere under theocracy the ephemeral becomes the eternal, petty event augments, distorts, aggrandizes itself. Authority may be deceptive fraudulent but now under religious auspices as hard to refute as any imponderable. (Millet 1994: 287)

One may want to argue that Hindu society is not theocratic in the sense implied here (Millet is writing of Ayatollah Khomeini's Iran), but the implications for those who are denied a dignified existence by divine will are the same. It is because the everyday is viewed in the 'prism of the eternal' that transgressions that are essentially quotidian—like a Dalit carrying an umbrella, or wearing trousers—become charged with immense significance and invite the wrath of the caste Hindus. Every act that is out of step with what has been ordained for the untouchables becomes a crime in the eyes of the sacred: how else can one explain the measureless cruelty of forcing a Dalit to eat excreta? The burning of homes and people, should they rebel? It is not only caste Hindu pride that is at stake in these instances, but a sense of the self that requires a constant reaffirmation of the time-honoured divine right of an entire society to the labour, body, and life of the untouchable.

The sacred as we have it in Hindu caste society is a peculiar phenomenon—it is not an attribute of an immutable, vengeful god, but a dispersed ideal embodied in a complicated set of discourses and practices whose divine character is contingent on the sophistry of the upper castes, especially Brahmins. This sophistry works in interesting ways: it deflects the power of the contingent moment by invoking an eternal past that neutralizes it, or it affirms in a logical and philosophical sense a transcendence that obviates an engagement with the here and now. Thus in the early twentieth century, when Tamil Brahmins were confronted with democratic claims, they argued that the caste system as it existed in the present hour was but a perversion of an original, always already good, ideal. Some amongst them noted that caste divisions were irrelevant since Hindu society had always sought to reconcile these profane divisions to a transcendent atman that is common to all, both king and commoner, Brahmin and Shudra.

Invariably, then, when the untouchable questions the sacrality of the caste order he commits himself to history: he or she interferes with the logic of transcendence with her claim of the moment, in circumstances given to her by the present. This is why there is a lonely asceticism to those who insist on the importance of history—a loneliness that Dr Ambedkar only understood too well as he went about his intellectual labours, seeking to redeem the untouchable present from the grip of ahistorical time. This loneliness beset Iyothee Thass as well, as he contended with a stubborn Tamil past and tried to wrest meanings from it for the present, beckoning as it were an imagined past into the future.

Conclusion

This description of the conditions of existence of an untouchable is only part of the story. Untouchables, individually and collectively, have struggled to sustain their self-respect, dignity, and sense of purpose in the face of a generalized anomie. The modern notion of rights has provided them with a means to challenge and protest issues of humiliation—this is something that we see from the late colonial period onwards. At about the same time, missionary activity and the conversions it enabled suggested the possibility of a different sort of existence: the metaphor of bread and blood, of the body and spirit of Christ that is transferred from the priest to the faithful through the mediation of the host proved profoundly influential in suggesting a new brotherhood in Christ, however fraught with older caste animosities and tensions. Later on, the politics of self-respect, of a recovered history and the struggles of labour pointed to other possibilities, where the issue was not so much a recovery of self, as a radical remaking of it.

None of these moments in our recent history that have militated against the ontological hurt endured by untouchables has been definitive, yet each one of them has proved epiphanic—in the comradeship they enabled, the celebrations of reviled knowledge that they gave rise to, and the performances of a derided self they encouraged.

6 Untouchability, Filth, and the Public Domain

Valerian Rodrigues

The emergence of the public domain is a remarkable development under the complex processes of modernity. While the idea of the *common* is found in many societies worth the name, the public domain is a distinctive development of modern times. It is the domain claimed by the public as its own; where the writ of the public runs and which the public, through a broad consensus, resists from being appropriated by private interests. There could not have been such a domain without the precipitation of a public, bound together in a common identity and sharing a set of interests in common. Besides, the public domain marks itself off from the private at least in a minimal way and with regard to some relations, although such a demarcation may be expressed in numerous ways. The public domain is different from being merely a shared bond. In this regard, Sudipta Kaviraj formulates the following distinction:

In order to minimally function, all societies would need some notion of the common, and most would have some ideas about what a common space would be like—what it would look like, how it could be used, indeed, how it could be known that a particular space was common. The idea of the public is a particular configuration of commonness that emerged in the capitalist-democratic West in the course of the eighteenth century. It has some associations, particularly ones like universal access and *offentlichkeit* (openness), which might not be expected to exist universally in ideas of common space. (Kaviraj 1997a: 86)

The public domain is the social space with an evocative and assertive presence of the public. When the public is evacuated from it, its emptiness stares you in the face as do the streets of Mumbai or Kolkata on a day of total *bundh*; it takes on a macabre look when armed troops or lathi-wielding gangs patrol it.

The public here is not merely an assorted aggregation of discrete identities, ranked orders, and statuses. It upholds at least some interests as common and considers them essential to live a life of worth for each one of its members. Beyond it the public domain may be deeply marked by variegated forms of differences, which may even appropriate the common through their distinctiveness. The public domain cannot but be made of culture-bearing members bound together in concrete identities, many of them holding steadfastly to their affiliations while others revamping the same in their interaction in the public domain. However, unlike mere aggregation of identities their being present in the public domain characteristically marks their orientations, fields of operation, and even prospects. A lot of baggage often seen as essential to an identity may come to be shed over time while claiming the self-same identity.

In the public domain, people, mainly as citizens, meet, interact, and beget associational ties. Such a bonding is not possible without foregrounding an essential equality among associated human beings, qua human. They may be marked with diverse labels but they are all entitled to be considered as equals in spite of all and together with their distinct identities. While class positions affect one's access to and availability of resources and opportunities, the deliberative and moral orientations of the public domain, in a way, profoundly qualify the inequalities arising from such class locations. The goods that one seeks in the public domain are autonomous from one's position in the family and kindred relations.

It is not that the working of the public domain is always non-contentious and relationships between the different forces present are peacefully negotiated. The public domain is often jolted by a wide variety of forces jostling for their say and positioning. At times, the nature of the public domain itself and its ability to keep its promises may be under question. It may be accused by a wide variety of social forces and interests as overtly and covertly protecting certain interests or identities. It may afford a narrow say to some and a more pronounced one to others with regard to access and participation.

The emergence of the public domain denotes a value shift: It signals that the public is significant; its presence should be reckoned and provided for. The very notion of the public ascribes a distinctive agency to the public. Its arrival denotes reconstruction of physical and social space as it involves remaking the social map afresh. The gathering of the public and its wielding together cannot be possible without the acknowledgement of some kind of equality across all who gather together and to that extent undermine traditional hierarchies, ranked orders, and fragmentation. Equality of status in the public domain is an important claim. Such claims to equality have made the distinction between the private and public domains fuzzy, sometimes allowing the latter to make deep forays into the former, making room for all kinds of subversion.[1] Conversely, inequality may reinforce itself by laying stress on the private as against the public, suggesting one set of norms to the former and another set to the latter.

The idea of the public domain came to mark social space, and urban space, in particular, as it came to shape social, cultural, and political life under conditions of modernity. It specified the relations between the public and the private, religious and the secular domains. The public domain had an intimate relationship to the reconstitution of the notions of citizenship, rule of law, and democratic polity. The conception of universal citizenship is closely bound with the rise of the public domain and gets sustained by it. The conception of universal citizenship is closely bound with the rise of public domain and its suntenance while it was confined and restricted earlier.[2] Rule of law as regulating and governing public life can be postulated only on the basis of the rise of a social terrain such as the public. The public provided the basic minimum solidarity to sustain an inclusive democratic polity.

In fact, concepts like the public sphere and civil society and the reality they invoke can only be understood by foregrounding the public domain. Public sphere is the site of critical public discussion on matters of general interest removed from the regulatory control of state. However, sometimes the public domain is used synonymously with the public sphere. As Bhargava says:

By 'public sphere' I mean a common space, in principle accessible to all, which anyone may enter with views on the common good realized wholly or partially: a *maidan*, a coffee house, an exhibition hall, the *paan* shop on the road side, the sweet shop in the locality as also the discursive and representational space available in newspapers, magazines, journals, radio, television and now the internet. (Bhargava 2005: 15)

The public sphere has a specific affinity with politics, particularly in relation to the state. If we distinguish civil society from the public sphere,[3] civil society will largely mean 'an arena of society constituted outside...public power, a region of society where people have come together and formed associations outside the purview of the state....

Civil society consists of more or less voluntary associations outside the state' (Bhargava 2005: 14). Such associations may not be accessible to everyone nor directly concern everyone. On the other hand, by public sphere is meant 'a common space, in principle accessible to all, which anyone may enter with views on the common good realised wholly or partially' (ibid.: 15). It is a social space, inclusive of all, where everyone can pronounce the good of everyone. Those who participate in the public sphere do not directly exercise political power although they maintain an enduring engagement with it (ibid.: 16).

Nationalism rallied the masses to the public domain. With it social space assumed a very different meaning. Respect and honour came to be increasingly associated with the public domain. The masses were called out to the streets to assert their presence. Power came to be legitimized in this space and its effectiveness came to be reflected there more than anywhere else. Earlier, the rulers constituted 'the public' and its articulation was dependent on them.[4] Nationalism reversed in a way rulers' presence before the public and made public authority to rest on the will of the nation. Ultimately, legislative majorities depended upon the extent to which they could command this space. It eventually came to be linked to the idea of democracy and to the networks of informational and deliberative bonding suggested by Habermas in the concept of the Public Sphere.

Previously, the people outside the ruler's presence met, at the most, in the bazaar although the rulers devised a number of ways to control the bazaar itself. The bazaar was not ennobled and conferred with the respectability that was associated with the rulers and their durbar. What was common was profoundly caught in the prevailing social relations. Access and the extent and degree of access to the common depended on one's status and station in life. The status of the bazaar as something shared in common was highly problematic. Even if it was vital to the reproduction of social life it was little acknowledged. The bazaar, the grey zone, full of insinuations, from which the respectable kept their distance, came to increasingly dictate the terms eventually. Market became the new bazaar and it was closely linked to the public domain, the new site of power and authority.

A new sense of public duty to which all citizens were invited, and in many respects were bound, took root alongside the public domain. Public duty was essentially a duty in relation to upholding, reproducing, and enlarging the public domain. It was not a sense of duty integrally bound with social roles that one is condemned to play out. It was a reflective consideration that invoked personal agency, centrally and reflectively. There was present in it a degree of absence of restraint in making one's options. Public duty therefore was a reflective consideration deeply bound with the free self.

The public domain could not be constituted without the virtues essential to its making. It had to measure up to the requirements of the reproduction of public. Therefore, a certain quality in the public amenities, such as physical space, hygiene, sanitation, roads, lighting, safety and security, a market in basic goods, transport, etc. were essential requirements. But they were not adequate. The public domain set standards and advanced criteria for quality of life. It brought home what is to be valued and laid down the benchmarks. In a way it attempted to set standards for life in the private arena as well often leading to conflicts between privately held beliefs and practices.

The national movement in India invested heavily in the public domain. The respect and dignity one commanded in the public domain came to profoundly qualify the respect in which one was held in society. The emerging public domain in India had its impact on social relations, much at variance with other societies particularly in the West. Social agents related themselves to shared practices and institutions very differently. Access to institutions and practices reproduced highly differentiated, and, often, ranked belonging. They had little congruence with the values of equality and participation.

One of the grounds for the colonial derision of India was the widespread dirt and squalor. Catherine Mayo's work, which greatly incensed public opinion in India, highlighted this side of India, as were several tracts before and after. The British constructed India as made of 'crowds, dirt and disease' and that Indians were blind 'to the unwholesome aspects of their public places' (Chakrabarty 2004: 65). In fact this derision has persisted over time and is repeated even to this day. V.S. Naipaul, in *India: A Million Mutinies Now* and in his earlier *An Area of Darkness* (Naipaul 1990, 1964), draws attention to it and, in a way, connects it to the lack of distinction between the 'private and public' domains in India: 'People washed, changed, slept and even urinated and defecated in the open' (Naipaul 1990: 1). For Naipaul, 'Filthy drains...crowded and noisy lanes, people, birds, goats, dogs and fowls all worked together to produce the effect of a nightmare' (Chakrabarty 2004: 67).

Scholars such as Dipesh Chakrabarty find that a language of this kind is deeply caught in 'the language of modernity, of civic consciousness, and public health and even of certain ideas of beauty related to the management of public space and interests, an order of aesthetics from which the ideals of public health and hygiene cannot be separated' (Chakrabarty 2004: 66). He finds that it is the language not only of 'imperialist officials' but of 'modernist nationalists' as well. Even Gandhi is not an exception. He notes Gandhi's profound concern on this issue deploring the 'absence of a citizen culture' and desire to inculcate 'a sense of civic life and public interest' (ibid.: 68). Both imperialists and nationalists, he feels, wanted to make the bazaar 'benign, regulated places, clean and healthy incapable of producing either disease or disorder' (ibid.: 77); for the dirt and disorderliness of the bazaar threatened politically and medically (ibid.: 76). The British were concerned with the health of the Europeans, and especially of the British Indian Army and of the modern Indian state and its capitalism.

For Chakrabarty, the persistence of filth in public denotes that the kind of separation of the public domain from the private that both 'imperialists and nationalists' desired has not found much of a reception in India. He argues, 'as we all know, Indian history bears a constant testimony to a gap that persists well into the present day between the modernist desires inherent in imperialist/nationalist projects of social reform and popular practices. The complaint about popular blindness in India toward dirt and disease has not lost any of its force' (Chakrabarty 2004: 68). He feels that by rejecting the modernist distinction between the private and public the modern project has been profoundly challenged in India.

Chakrabarty feels that those who have engaged with issues related to citizen culture in India bring to bear on the scene the attitude of an outsider, 'who does not inhabit the conceptual or theoretical framework of the actor whom he or she observes'.[5] This 'observing position' he terms as modernist and accuses social sciences as wanting 'to build citizen cultures' by condemning 'the non-bourgeois subaltern citizen' (Chakrabarty 2004: 69). While his concern for inclusion of 'subaltern citizen' is well taken, his equation between 'observing position' = 'modernity' = 'social science' is not merely simplistic and banal but absurd as his own writings easily come within such an epistemological framework. He could not have written what he has done without taking such an observer stance. What is much more deplorable is the way he defends public life wrapped up in dirt by providing a cultural turn to the same. The dirty bazaar or the street becomes passè by invoking the yardstick of the clean and the dirty differently from their mappings by modernity. He skirts the normative concerns bound with the public domain by resorting to an anthropological and clinical turn, deeply caught in an unmarked universality which he is otherwise very critical of.[6] In the process he defends both essentialism and cultural stereotyping.

Reading from Mary Douglas, Chakrabarty feels that dirt is associated with 'a place that is designated as outside' that connects itself to the widespread belief that it is outsiders who despoil (Chakrabarty 2004: 69); 'Outsider carries substance that threaten one's well-being' (ibid.: 70). This outside is marked off from 'a hygiene space', the inside, closely associated in India, according to Chakrabarty, with the mistress of the household. The bazaar is the paradigmatic form of the outside. It is 'that unenclosed, exposed and interstitial outside that acts as the meeting point of several communities' and is not governed by a single set of communal rules (ibid.: 72). In the bazaar one comes across strangers; it is a place against which one needs protection. In the bazaar the codes of familiarity and trust are violated. However, the very character of its forbiddenness, he feels, makes the roaming of the streets of the neighbourhood a pleasurable activity. 'It is the space that produces both malevolence and exchange between communities and hence, needs to be tamed through the continual and contextual deployment of a certain dichotomy between the inside and outside'.[7] For Chakrabarty, the bazaar has remained the same. He does not see the metamorphosis of the bazaar in the modern public domain that we sketched earlier.

The refusal to sanitize the bazaar, the public domain, even today is seen by Chakrabarty as an affront of the masses to the insinuations of modernity. People have not heeded the nationalists' call 'to discipline, public health and public order. Can one read this as a refusal to become citizens of an ideal, bourgeois order?' There is no exchange of 'old pleasures' offered by the bazaar which threatened the soul for the new ones of capital. Even the threat posed to capital cannot set aside the dalliance of the bazaar and its attempts to roll the private and the public into a common rapture. Therefore, state action favouring 'public health or interest, will often take the form of a violent, intrusive, external force in the lives of people'.[8] It is not self-evident, he feels, that certain rituals of public life should be acceptable to people, to non-bourgeois peasant citizens, inhabiting the bazaar as against bourgeois modern position. To add weight to his sociological considerations, he doubts whether certain pursuits of the 'bourgeois order' such as 'long life, good health, more money, small families and modern science etc.' could be considered as universal concerns at all (Chakrabarty 2004: 79).

There are many problems in this position, which are not exhausted by popular affront to modernity and bourgeois order manifest in squalor in public places, even if it is true. Chakrabarty easily equates the modern with the bourgeois and, in a way, undermines the positive features of what it has meant to the lower orders to be included in the public domain. But the purpose here is not to combat the relationship between sanitation and modernity that he constructs, but the relationship between the inside and outside, home and bazaar, which he proposes, and the consequences it has in upholding the continued prevalence of untouchability in our public domain.

The extent to which the cultural universe of significant sections of the people was mapped by the relation and opposition between the inside and outside, home and bazaar, is seriously in doubt. The extent of resistance the bazaar or the public domain has offered towards its sanitization, and the reasons thereof, is a matter for empirical enquiry rather than for unfounded assertions.[9] There is little to suggest that the whole of the normative domain marked by Chakrabarty for the bourgeois order is characteristic of it, even if we accept that such an order, under conditions of bourgeois dominance, comes to be heavily shaped by it. However, our purpose here is not to subject Chakravarty's categories to an internal critique but to reject these categories and deploy in their place a set of alternative explanations of why the public domain or the modern bazaar in India continues to live in a great deal of filth and does not regard washing itself clean as an essential condition for its long-term reproduction. The absence of cleanliness in the public domain often results in creating sanitized islands begetting hierarchies and ranked orders of different kinds.

Chakrabarty does not give a thought to the idea that the bazaar might be considered as the site of the impure precisely because it is the site of the intermixture of castes. The outsider in the bazaar is dangerous precisely because his caste and the location of his caste identity in the system of castes is not easily predictable and even though one may anticipate it one might be helpless to do anything about it. The bazaar cannot be wholly insulated from the threat of intermixture no matter what kind of caution one deploys. Further, the bazaar has to necessarily deploy a number of labouring men for all kinds of services including scavenging and any kind of contact with such men and women would be highly polluting. The bazaar has a natural insurgency towards equality. Therefore, Brahmanical regimes such as that of the Peshawas enacted several injunctions ensuring that the untouchables announced their presence and thereby did not pollute the social space of interaction and intermixture and convert it into a potential public domain (Deshpande 2002: 66). In other words, the bazaar supposedly harboured within itself the debased and the unclean, and for the health of the rest it was important to quarantine their physical presence, marking them off and, in a way, denying them the status of being human as the rest.

Chakrabarty argues that caste was profoundly context-bound in India before the British: 'Caste society operated as a non-standardized system, and rules guiding caste transactions would have required a sensitivity to context' (Chakrabarty 2004: 83). The British attempted to fix and officialize collective identities such as caste and religion in the very process of creating the public sphere made of 'a free press, voluntary associations, avenues for uncensored debate and inquiring in the public interest' (ibid.: 83), and the state with its techniques of measurement was transforming fuzzy identities into enumerated ones.[10] While one may not have a problem with the context-bound nature of the caste system in India prior to the arrival of the British, it is important to note that significant aspects of social life in India too, prior to the arrival of the British, were context-bound and it was not merely caste. Caste organization reflected social life. But an institution called untouchability existed broadly all over India although what constituted the precise attributes of untouchability might have varied widely across regions and even localities.[11]

Chakrabarty does not pay heed to the existence of social dirt vividly present in the institution of untouchability and social life resting on purity and pollution inscribed in the caste system. Does the refusal to heed the voice of sanitation that Chakrabarty highlights have much to do with the continued existence of social dirt and the resistance offered by the public domain, the modern bazaar, to include the untouchables and the polluting in a common, shared space? Is the continued existence of squalor and dirt in the public domain in India an expression of the refusal of the dominant classes to include the lower orders, and, therefore, a statement on the nature of 'its bourgeoisie' rather than a protest of the lower orders? Is not the existence of the 'dirty' public domain a judgement on the refusal of its 'modern' and 'capitalist' counterparts to clean themselves up which would have enabled them to include the lower orders as equals in the public domain? Is not this refusal a statement on our public domain, which has not succeeded in inscribing the principle of equality in institutions resting on it? Can we build a robust public domain, bourgeois or non-bourgeois without doing away with social dirt? Should decency be the first claim on a civilization, any civilization for that matter, worth its name?

Chakrabarty presents the *outside* and *inside* as determinate entities, in an essentialized way, and does not see that they are highly differentiated realities. Even in the bazaar there are those who are the outsiders, who live at the margins of the bazaar, as in the Indian villages where there are those who live outside the village. While the bazaar is not wholesome, those who are immediately outside the bazaar are positively dirty. In fact, the latter and dirt are identical. Their association with the bazaar is their association with dirt. They have to clean toilets, cart dead animals, and perform all those social callings that are closely connected with dirt, both physical and ritual. One of the extreme forms of such a calling is scavenging, which is still quite widespread in India.[12] The impurity associated with the bazaar, which marks an occasional visitor, can be washed, both physically and ritually, but those who are part of the dirt have to live with it.

The impure were kept out of the social space of the bazaar through several direct regulatory mechanisms as was the case under the Peshwa regime[13] or through context-bound rituals as was the case in different parts of India. But the injunctions were more or less effective through a division of labour and the cultural modes deployed to reproduce the same. Therefore, there was hardly any equalitarian or republican upsurge in pre-British towns in India, something that Phule highlights in his own distinctive way (Deshpande 2002: 141–56). The British concern for the sanitization of the bazaar may have been to make it safe for colonial modernity, but the victims of the non-bourgeois subaltern orders were also asserting their claim to be human when a small space for asserting their rights came to be opened up under colonial modernity, not because it was interested in the 'subaltern' but because colonial rule invoked certain principles, and once invoked they had their inevitable consequences (Bhattacharya 2005).

The house too was not merely the site of love, nurture, care, and culture with its intergenerational composition made of the old, the young, and children. It was also highly graded and its spaces, social and gendered, were deeply caught in purity and pollution. While the bazaar, or the outside, could pollute the man, the woman could be polluted by her own body and insulated from social intercourse, during menstrual cycles, childbirth, and death of her husband. Access to the household was limited to the outsiders and was graded depending upon one's position in the hierarchy. In fact, the processes governing transaction of relations within and in between the household and the bazaar were akin and there was a hierarchy of accesses, although sometimes contexts and the interests of those higher in the hierarchy may justify exceptions to the rule. But in large parts of India the untouchables were not allowed to step in beyond the threshold of the house.[14] They were outsiders and this was so because they were both polluted and polluting. It was their permanent stable condition (Ambedkar 1989: 19–26). Their impurity could not be done away with except in the next life although trespassing liminal zones by household servants always took place and there were numerous rituals of restoration.

The outside domain that was subject to intermixture at all levels was constantly open to the threat of impurity and the most impure was the furthest end of this domain associated with filth. The furthest end of the bazaar and the furthest end of the village were in a way alike, both being the habitation of the untouchables. But unlike in the village, in the bazaar the social and ritual distance between the furthest and the nearest was very intimate and close. But wherever they may be, in the bazaar or the village, the untouchables were associated with filth in the real sense or in a ritual or symbolic sense. The great movements of the untouchables demanded that the filth be overthrown and the modern state in India evolve mechanisms wherein some do not have to undertake the task of cleaning the lavatories of others as the irrevocable code of their lives.

In India, therefore, when filth in the public domain came to be decried, by interventions such as those of Gandhi, the structures and social relations that reproduced filth too came to be decried. It was argued that to make the public domain clean it is not enough that streets be clean, but that everyone be involved in keeping the streets clean; it should not be a specific preoccupation of the untouchables, and the service of cleaning itself has to be invested with dignity.[15] When Gandhi started his public career in Champaran one of the things he requested the volunteers to do was to keep the streets clean, which they in the search of the heroic found quite humiliating, and this eventually resulted in many of them deserting the place (Misra 1963). Gandhi understood vividly the connection between untouchability and filth although the methods that he employed to attack both were woefully inadequate. One could probably argue that his invocation of a clean public domain was overruled by his associates precisely because it militated against, what they felt as integrally bound with, one's culture and religion and not, as Chakrabarty sees, due to its embeddedness in modernity. In fact, when Gandhi was arguing for the removal of untouchability he was also pleading for a clean public domain! He invoked the fundamental equality of human beings which entitled them to human communion.

The unclean public domain has remained with us primarily because there has been an inadequate response to the issue of untouchability.[16] Those who analysed dirt in India as a social relation initially were not social scientists with their positivist perspectives but thinkers such as Ambedkar and Phule. They drew our attention to the filth that untouchables had been converted into. Further, they ascribed to the removal of dirt a universality which is truly human and not bourgeois or modern. Therefore a clean public domain may be a bourgeoisie prerequisite but in contexts like in India it is also a human prerequisite. If the central human desideratum is being recognized and included within the community, the untouchables condemned to dirt are excluded from such recognition and inclusion. In fact, their being associated with dirt and the consequent rejection of any association with them is deeply humiliating. It is the rejection of human beings as human, 'that is, treating people as if they were not human beings but merely things, tools, animals, sub-humans, or inferior humans'. They are subjected to 'a constant threat of living a life unworthy of human beings' (Margalit 1996: 120–1). In the attempts to dissociate untouchables from dirt and vice versa, and to make dirt removal a universal disposition, we have a feeble acknowledgement of their being human. But in India, dirt was not associated with any occupation but is in fact considered the permanent attribute of entire communities. Therefore the claim to self-respect cannot but be a collective claim. Gandhi recognized this and explored several strategies in this regard. He called upon the upper castes to clean up dirt and had a long duel with his wife when she refused to clean the toilets used by the untouchable inmates of the ashram, and tried to imbue the occupation of the *bhangi* with respect even wishing that he should be born a *bhangi*. He tried to compare the *bhangi* with the mother who cleans up the child. But the contradiction that he ran into is by trying to preserve institutions, which, in their historical evolution, if not necessarily in terms of their religious tenets, had come to be intimately interwoven with the reproduction of untouchability.

One of the great experiments that India has tried out, particularly after independence, for the removal of untouchability, is to extend preferential treatment to untouchables under a regime of equal rights and liberties. These preferential measures while being extensive are far too thin at those points where they are likely to benefit a large number of members of the community. However, there is no doubt that these measures have benefited directly and often indirectly millions of members of untouchable castes and communities. While these policies have been resisted, and sometimes reluctantly conceded to, there has not been much of an opposition to employment prospects directly related to sanitation conceded to members of Dalit castes under preferential policies (Galanter 1984: 84–118). There are a surfeit number of people in the sanitation services who are former *bhangis* or those hailing from similar castes. With the privatization of services in several cities in India there is a great deal of privatization/outsourcing of sanitary services. A large number of people employed by these private agencies to undertake sanitary jobs are invariably Dalits, particularly Dalit women, or those who have become de-caste in the context of urban mobility, that if they wish to survive there is nothing else left for them to do. Refusal therefore to heed to the call of public sanitation is not a protest against bourgeoisie civility and the hold of cultural values but the hold of untouchability in India and its association with dirt. An attack on dirt calls for an attack on the social value of untouchability. Such a call need not necessarily be an argument for the open embrace of modernity as Gandhi's attack on untouchability was not.

It is therefore strange that Sudipta Kaviraj feels that the continued reproduction of filth in the public domain, particularly in sites such as public parks, 'shows in an everyday form the contest between a bourgeois order of the middle class and those who flout its rules' (Kaviraj 1997a: 83). He does not link it to the uprooting of people from their hearth and home, and the migration that is taking place which primarily affects the poor and the Dalits. For him it shows the refusal of the masses to be disciplined by modernity particularly a modernity which cannot keep its promises.

The very survival of dirt which Chakrabarty celebrates as containing and checkmating the triumph of modernity in India is a demonstration of the continued existence of untouchability in India. It is not the refusal of the masses to be disciplined by modernity, as Kaviraj suggests, that stands in sharp relief in contemporary India but the failure of the secular state to extend the project to the filth in spite of those in the filth crying out to be salvaged from it.

NOTES

1. Sudipta Kaviraj gives an account of the way the poor came to appropriate large spaces of the Deshpriya Public Park in South Calcutta from the 1960s onwards. See Kaviraj (1997a: 83–113 v).

2. Medieval thinkers such as Marsilio of Padua, who threw up a more inclusive notion of citizenship, theorized partly on the basis of their experience in city-states with an assertive and articulate public presence.

3. There are many who accept either one or the other, depending upon what goes into the making of these concepts.

4. A number of our contemporary customs and even legal provisions reflect it.

5. Chakrabarty (2004: 69). It is important to note in this context that Gandhi too, by Chakrabarty's own admission, insists on a citizen culture that upholds the cleanliness of the public domain. He would have to then put Gandhi too in an 'observer position'. Chakrabarty's overall perspective would recoil from suggesting anything of this kind with regard to Gandhi. It must be noted that Gandhi's concern for the cleanliness of public places remained a continued concern with him throughout his life.

6. Chakrabarty falls back on the work of Mary Douglass for the purpose; see Douglass (1966).

7. See Chakrabarty (2004: 77). While Chakrabarty has employed the distinction between 'the inside' and 'the outside' to underscore opposition to modernity, Partha Chatterjee employs the same to highlight, primarily, the distinctiveness of the nationalist project in India.

8. Ibid.: 77. Chakrabarty produces little evidence to suggest that the measures of the state to enforce sanitation, in particular, has led to mass opposition. In fact, whatever evidence we have in cases like the plague in Surat seems to suggest that there was a broad-based support from the masses to the measures initiated by the administration.

9. The resistance often found in India against such measures as slum clearance, urban beautification, sewage and sanitary measures could well be attributed not as resistance to sanitary and hygienic principles embedded in these measures but as the restriction and undermining of even the feeble resources and opportunities that the affected enjoyed prior to the onset of these measures and the life chances that they held out.

10. Sudipta Kaviraj defines fuzzy identities as those 'where all layers are not exhausted but at the same time they were practically precise'. For further elaboration, see Kaviraj (1997b: 146–8).

11. The prevalence of untouchability all across India is avowed through several exercises under the colonial regime: The diatribes of Swami Vivekananda against untouchability in Kerala; Gandhi's arguments for the eradication of untouchability as an imperative for the consolidation of Indian nationalism; the debates on Census enumeration and the Lothian Committee sojourn all across India to measure the extent of prevalence of untouchability. For an account see Ambedkar (1989: 3–34).

12. Manual scavenging involves physically removing human excreta, often using hand-held metal plates to fill the excreta in buckets and carry it physically to the dumping sites. Sometimes a scavenger may clean hundreds of toilets per day, and, after a few hours of labour, may literally disappear in the dirt he/she has cleaned; all one can hear are the scavengers' grunts and often curses on those whose excreta they have to clean or on their own fate which has driven them to the job. In 1998, there were over 800,000 manual scavengers in India. The Government of India passed The Employment of Manual Scavengers and Construction of Dry Latrines (Prohibition) Act 1993, which expressly prohibited the engagement of any person for manually carrying human excreta. It also prohibited the construction and maintenance of dry latrines. A National Commission for Safai Karmacharis (NCSK) was constituted under the Act to investigate specific grievances and to recommend measures for the social and economic uplift of Safai Karmacharis. The implementation of the provisions of this Act has been tardy although an enormous amount of money has been spent in its name. See Pillai (1999).

13. See Deshpande (2002: 43–54). The mechanisms employed were to tie a broom to one's back whereby one sweeps one's own steps, to tie a small pot on one's neck to spit into, to walk bare-foot, etc.

14. See Parvathamma (1984) for an empirical account of situations involving access to the house (which part of the house, to whom, when, and in relation to what castes), reception in the house (place to sit, use of utensils, kind of food permissible), etc.

15. Gandhi's effort in this direction was caught in a conundrum. While he invited the public to make the public domain clean he argued that it was the duty of the *bhangi* to do so. When the public did not show much enthusiasm to his invitation he increasingly confined the invitation to the satyagrahi. But the satyagrahi was primarily located in a space of choice and more and more in the ashrams. The *bhangi* was thus condemned to public duty with the promise of dignity conferred on his labour. But dignity is an attribute that is garnered in a community and when the community itself did not consider removal of dirt as worth much, Gandhi had little to offer to the *bhangi*. His voice becomes shriller in this regard, reiterating the worth of ancestral

callings and through assertions such as that he would like to stand witness to the dignity of the person of the *bhangi* by being born as one in his next life.

16. There have been several good-intentioned campaigns in India to keep the public domain clean but they have floundered precisely due to the cultural value that maintaining cleanliness is not our responsibility. One of the great success stories in this regard was the cleaning up of Surat in the context of the plague but such public spirit could not be sustained as the social relations and perceptions of the communities were not geared for sustaining such a spirit. For the early enthusiasm in this regard see Shah (1997).

7 Humiliation in a Crematorium*

Peter Ronald deSouza

Perhaps there is an Agatha Christie lesson in the title of this chapter. Just as in her novels the reader is required to suspend his or her hunches on who the real culprit is, and wait for the last chapter to discover the hand that administered the poison; here too do we need to meticulously sift through the evidence, discard first inferences, find significance in the less obvious, and only then arrive at a judgement. While the case being examined here, of a dispute over the cremation of a Dalit in a Goa crematorium, at first take, appears as just another confirming instance of the everyday humiliation of the Dalit by caste society, the details as they emerge demand a more complex explanation. Although the existing social science debates on the multiple transitions taking place in India (deSouza 2000; Thapar 2000) are a valuable resource, in that they help us in preparing a short list of suspects for an identity parade, they still stop short of helping us reach a clear

*The fieldwork for this study was done in 2001. The piecing together of the small details into a coherent and intricate story was only possible because of the keenness, dedication, and social understanding of my students and research assistants Shashank Thakur and Arjun Alanarkar. I wish to record my gratitude to them for their fine fieldwork. I also wish to thank Satish Sonak for giving me access to his newspaper clippings, and to Sushma Pawar, Seema Fernandes, and Reshma Naik for doing the first field study when they were students in my political theory class. Alito Siquiera, as usual, provided both the anthropological appreciation and criticisms that this study has needed to give it both its thick descriptions and its social theory. I alone, however, am responsible for the deficiencies of argument and understanding in this study.

understanding. A full explanation would therefore have to be crafted by using even the minor details. It is clear that we need to read this case of humiliation through multiple lenses. Although it is unique, and therefore not well disposed to sociological generalization, the case still allows us to see the changing personality of Goan society. Through it we can see the residues of a different colonial history as well as the distinct ways by which the processes of modernity and democracy are forging the new rules by which collective life is to be led.

THE 'BURNING' DISPUTE

In the village of Verla-Canca, in the *taluka* of Bardez, 2 kilometres from the famous town of Mapuca, a controversy arose over the cremation of a Dalit on 8 August 2001. While the apocryphal beginnings of the turmoil can be traced to an innocuous remark made by a Dalit in the local taverna (liquor shop) that 'we Dalits have inaugurated the crematorium after it was newly built'—an origin story similar to the assassination of Archduke Franz Ferdinand that was supposed to have led to the first World War—the cremation of the deceased Mahar was seen by the non-Dalits, primarily the majority intermediate caste of Bhandaris, as a case of transgression of caste boundaries. The transgression has many components—place, ritual, power, and status—and these needed to be resisted. The villagers discussed the issue of the cremation after the formal Gram Sabha of 15 August 2001, where both officials and elected members were present, and it was decided that a separate shed for the cremation of the Mahars would be constructed within the crematorium. The Mahars of the village accepted this compromise. After this agreement was reached it is alleged that the President of the Village Crematorium Development Committee (VCDC) along with a Hindu priest performed a *shuddhikaran* (purification) ceremony of the newly built crematorium.[1]

A few days later, on 9 September 2001, another Mahar from the same village died and his cremation in the common shed was obstructed by some of the villagers. The police from the nearby town of Mapuca, under whose jurisdiction the case falls, were brought in to adjudicate the dispute. They persuaded the Mahars to adhere to the originally accepted compromise of a separate cremation shed to be built for them by the panchayat authorities. This agreement, between all groups in the village, brokered by the police, was reached in the presence of the Sarpanch and the Zilla Parishad member. The second Mahar was thus later cremated on a separate platform erected in the burial area that the

Mahars used. This second case added to the dispute because the Mahars felt that since they had now shifted to the practice of cremation they wanted to continue with this new practice. It is interesting to note that in this controversy, of burial or cremation, the wives of the two deceased were not consulted.

At this point the story takes a Marquezian turn. The panchayat elections in the state were to take place in about four months' time, in January 2002. The sitting members were not eager for the dispute to continue since it would affect their electoral prospects. The *panch*, in whose ward the Mahars lived, had won the elections on their support and was a member of the ruling group in the panchayat. Although he was not a Mahar he initially supported the cremation, when the Mahars had informally asked him for permission. They also went to the Zilla Parishad member, a Catholic, to obtain his approval to cremate their dead in the crematorium but he refused to get involved on the grounds that it was an 'internal matter' of the Hindus. This, interestingly, was a position taken by a person who had been Sarpanch for several terms.

Perhaps a small digression is in order here. The position of seeing the issue as an 'internal matter' is also the position of the Catholic community who constitute more than a fourth of the village population. Their voice seems to be absent in the emerging public debate. This is surprising since the dispute is, after all, taking place in an Indian village where anonymity and privacy are not available as strategies behind which one can take refuge as one could in a city. So for the Catholic community to treat the dispute in the village as an internal matter tells us something about the back-to-back character of community relations in a Goan village where the same geographical space is shared but not the same socio-cultural space. There are minimal border crossings between the two communities (Newmann 2001). In addition, the response of the Catholic leadership, including the village priest, to the episode shows that the dispute is seen as a procedural issue and not a substantive one, that is, a matter of 'their' religious procedures for the disposal of the dead, which is an issue of 'their' religion for them to sort out among themselves rather than a secular matter concerning discrimination which, in contrast, is a common concern. The standard response to religious practices, however objectionable these practices may be, in India, is one of non-interference keep off rather than campaign for common attributes of citizenship with cultural rights, in practice, getting pre-eminence over individual rights.

And now, back to the main story. The Mahar campaign for cremation was led by two of their young men, one of whom was a co-opted member of the village panchayat while the other who, because of the campaign, soon won the subsequent panchayat elections to the ward. Since the population of Dalits in Goa is only about 2 per cent of the total population, the state of Goa, to meet the requirements of the 73rd Constitutional Amendment, has followed a policy of co-option of Scheduled Caste (SC) members to give them representation in village governance. The relevant provision of the government order states that 'provided further that the government may, by order published in the official gazette, direct any panchayat to co-opt, in such manner as may be prescribed, a person belonging to the SC, where there is reasonable population of the SC but the reservation may not be made'.[2] As a result, the village panchayat had a co-opted member who provided leadership to the Mahar campaign. It must be noted that the panchayat, of which he was a member, was a party to the agreement on cremation where a separate shed would be used for Mahars to cremate the dead that had been reached between all the parties at the village level.

This dispute over access to cremation, as a form of disposal of the dead, was the result of a deliberate change of practice by the Mahars from burial to cremation. Till 8 August 2001, the Mahars of the village used to bury their dead in the section of the cremation ground where children are also buried. The Chamars of the village had adopted the practice of cremation some decades earlier and it was only now that the Mahars too wanted to adopt the same practice. The practice of burial was apparently followed by the community because, in the less affluent times of the past, the Mahars could not afford the costs of cremation which were higher than the costs of burial. In the intervening decades of development the Chamars had, observers argue, as a jati among the Dalits, benefited more from reservations than had the Mahars in Goa and hence were able to make the shift earlier to the practice of cremation. Subsequently, some decades later, the Mahars too acquired the material capital to want to adopt this common practice of disposal of their dead by the Hindus in the village. By shifting from burial to cremation they now also wanted to acquire the cultural capital and the religious identity that such a practice brings.

The acceptance, by the other castes, of the Mahar's desire to cremate their dead was regarded by the latter as a significant symbolic gain. They did not think that the simultaneous insistence by the Bhandaris, that this cremation be performed in a separate shed, was a decision that needed to be opposed since the struggle was for them about cremation, and not yet for the common place. This had been achieved. For the Bhandaris the acceptance by the Mahars of a separate shed was also a gain since they too were able to establish both the ritual distance, that they thought was their right, and the identity of difference between them and the Mahars. For the police it was mainly a law and order problem and therefore the solution, of having two cremation sheds for the two conflicting groups, was considered as a good compromise. That it may be violative of the Constitution's enabling and protective provisions, that is, Art 15.2, 'Prohibition of restriction of access to public places', or Art 17, 'Abolition of Untouchability', etc., or a contravention of the Scheduled Castes and Scheduled Tribes (Prevention of Atrocities) Act 1989 did not even appear as a possibility. This acceptance of the compromise formula, of 'separate but common', for the disposal of the dead, seemed to be a win-win solution for all concerned as long as the dispute remained within the village alone. (This containment within the village was, however, not to be, as will become clearer as the story unfolds.) Incidentally the *sopo*, where the dead body of the person is kept before performing the last rites, is the same for all communities and is just at the entrance, opposite the place where the body is consigned to the flames.

Returning to the Marquesian village we discover that the Dalits of the village are relatively new residents, having come to this Old Conquest area during the late colonial period about seventy to eighty years ago, from areas in the New Conquests. The New Conquests refer to areas in Goa that were under Portuguese rule for only about 150 years in comparison to the Old Conquest areas which were under Portuguese domination for more than 450 years. These Old Conquests, unlike the New Conquests that came under colonialism during a later phase, suffered the Inquisition (Robinson: 1998), faced the brutalities of the early phase of colonialism (Angle 2003; Mascarenhas 2002), and had to endure and adapt to the Portuguese policies of making Goa a cultural place in the image of Portugal (Cunha n.d.). These dark episodes of history however had a positive underside. It gave the Dalits a chance to escape from the pernicious laws of Manu (Baxi 1995), which operated in the Konkan socio-cultural landscape, since they now became equal subjects of a European king who did not recognize caste distinctions as valid legal distinctions, and also since it gave them a chance, through migration between the two conquest areas, to reinvent themselves.

Although at this juncture there is inadequate scholarly literature on this issue of Dalits reinventing themselves and masquerading as intermediate castes, especially in their new places of habitation, a serious line of argument is developing that some of those claiming to be part of this omnibus caste grouping, the 'Bhandaris', could be Dalits from the new conquests (Siquiera 2003). This would perhaps explain the low number of Dalits in Goa and the high number of Bhandaris as a percentage of the total population. It also gives a new twist to the dispute between the Mahars and the Bhandaris of Verla-Canca village. It is unclear in this case whether the politics of the present requires the invention of the past although it remains a possibility. Many of these Mahars of the village work on the property of the Catholics who do not reside in the village.

The story, as all such village stories go, has another interesting angle. The first Mahar who died had an inter-caste marriage. His wife was a Bhandari from the neighbouring village of Pilerna and in spite of this inter-caste marriage, which constitutes the ultimate transgression or ultimate liberation in India depending on whether one is a Manuvadi or an Ambedkarite (Ambedkar 1979), there were good relations between the wife's natal and married homes. Persons from the natal home used to come to stay at the married home and the husband too used to go there to stay. While the immediate family had good relations, the extended family, or the relatives, were unhappy with the marriage. The case becomes increasingly curious when one discovers that the president of the VCDC is the maternal uncle of the woman and belonged to the family faction opposed to the marriage. He was at the forefront of the campaign against a single shed for cremation. This can be read as a 'teach them a lesson' lesson for transgressing caste boundaries although 'them' here could refer to both the couple and the Mahars. He had gone to the crematorium, after the first cremation, with a Hindu priest to perform a *shuddhikaran* ceremony. He even disingenuously argued that since Dalits were being provided with reservations in several fields there is nothing wrong if a separate shed is to be reserved for them.

These multiple strands of the story are typical of the existential world of the village anywhere, where there is disapproval, punishment, challenge, endorsement, struggle, opposition, remembering, forgetting, inventing of tradition, and crafting of a pragmatic solution. In terms of the debate on 'the changing village' the case constitutes a challenge since one would be unsure not just about where to place it, on the 'oppression–emancipation' continuum, but also about how to interpret the direction of change that is taking place, that is, how to read the fact that such a dispute has taken place. At this point in the tale one could perhaps surmise that the politics of everyday life in the village would have remained of anthropological curiosity alone if it had stayed within the confines of the village. But that was not to be. The social geography of Goa, where village merges with town, and where communication by road and media is very good, leaving few spaces that could claim to belong to the world of the ignored, means that disputed incidents get immediate public attention. For Verla-Canca, which is only 2 kilometres from the town of Mapuca, there was little chance that this incident would be ignored. The politics of the bigger world soon entered the politics of the village and the various parties who had taken stands on the dispute, when it remained confined to the village, now had to position themselves differently making subtle but significant changes to their earlier stands. The larger discourses of equality, and social reform, and democratic politics, and constitutionalism, now entered the public sphere.

Verla-Canca's *Agni-Pariksha*

The local press picked up the story and by the third week of September critical articles began to appear.[3] When this incident of discrimination became a major public issue the initial response of the VCDC was that the crematorium had been built by private donations and thus, by implication, what happened inside was a private matter. When the response by various groups to this claim was that the land was communidade (public) land and that the expenditure for the construction of the sheds and the boundary wall came from public funds, particularly from the Rural Development Agency, the committee changed its stand and accepted that government money was used. The local press also called for prosecution of the VCDC president and the Hindu priests who performed the *shuddhikaran* ceremony of purification. They replied that the ceremony was in fact not a *shuddhikaran* but an inaugural ceremony since the construction of the gate, sheds, and some newer features had only just been completed.

The articles in the press condemned the practice of segregation and called upon the government, especially the panchayat minister, himself a Dalit, to intervene. The government responded by issuing a circular debarring any discrimination in the crematorium built out of public funds. The circular read 'the crematoria in the village panchayat area are built through the public funds of the Rural Development Agency or the grant in Aid of the state government. *Therefore* [italics mine] they should be open for all without any discrimination as regards caste or creed'. The 'therefore' in the circular, when deconstructed, suggests that the government implicitly seems to accept the private–public distinction first made by the VCDC where, in a space produced by public funds, no discrimination will be countenanced, whereas, in a space produced by private funds, it may be acceptable. Political theorists would have a busy time working themselves out of this maze. They would need to take a stand on the issue of when is 'interference by an external agency' permissible and when is it not and whether this domain of 'private' falls within the inviolable area where 'what I do in my home is my business' or whether, the action of building two sheds belongs to the class of 'other regarding actions' and so, irrespective of whether the crematorium is privately or publicly built, the space and the action still constitutes a legitimate area for external interference by the state. It should be seen, in J.S. Mills' terms, as action that causes serious harm to the definite rights of definite individuals.

The political parties responded to this emerging debate in the press merely by issuing press statements. This is a common form of public intervention by those who want to maintain a visible political presence, seen to be responding without materially affecting the case. The Congress president demanded action against the police officials while the Bharatiya Janata Party (BJP) president wanted action against the Sarpanch and the Zilla Parishad member for misusing public funds and promoting feelings of caste discrimination. The local unit of the Shiv Sena called for the arrest of the Hindu priests who had performed the 'purification' ceremony.[4] The BJP Chief Minister, on 2 October 2001, at a function organized by the Dalit Sanghtana, called for the issue to be resolved amicably. Other than issuing press statements the political parties did not mobilize and campaign on this issue. Interestingly, once the incident began to get public attention the police retreated into an administrative shell agreeing to give information only if it came through proper channels. They became very cautious. A different pragmatics took over.

The most interesting response to the incident, however, is from civil society groups particularly the Goan People's Forum (GPF). The GPF was adamant in arriving at a solution that would be of a higher normative order than was the earlier solution. They were critical of the 'similar but separate' compromise fashioned by the police and villagers and sought, in contrast, an acceptance by all parties that this discriminatory practice would be ended together with an acceptance of the equal rights to cremation for all who desire it. The leading members of the GPF were of a progressive persuasion and had in their student days been active leaders of the Progressive Students Union. They had over the years come to occupy important positions in society as lawyers, journalists, politicians, doctors, and business persons. As a group, the GPF was well networked and possessed considerable social capital for its voice to have an impact in the public sphere (Fiorina and Skocpol 1999). Its members wrote articles in the papers. In fact, some the members are important journalists. They held public meetings, visited the village many times to talk to the concerned parties, and even put pressure on the government to take a public position. The circular issued by the panchayat department (referred to earlier), and the statements of the political parties and of the chief minister, can largely be credited to their efforts.

Two of the GPF's activities must get special mention here, as both were very innovative in form and outcome, thereby taking the public discourse to a different, new level. The first is GPF members meeting with Hindu religious leaders in Goa: Haturli Muth Swami, Shree Brahmanand, and Paradeshwar Baba of Borim. They met these leaders in order to condemn the act of discrimination in the Verla-Canca crematorium. The Haturli Muth Swami is a religious leader with a large following among the Bhandaris. His statement that such discrimination is a disgraceful act with no basis in the *dharmashastras* undermined any religious legitimacy that these intermediate caste leaders may have been attempting to give their decision. He lauded the public awareness programme of the GPF, spoke of how great leaders such as Mahatma Gandhi had dedicated their lives to bringing about equality, said it was a shame that discrimination still prevailed in this era of scientific development, and urged the GPF to work towards changing the mindset of society through the practice of humanitarian thought in their day-to-day life. Organizations such as the GPF were necessary, he affirmed, to root out casteist feelings among Goans. Paradeshwar Baba lent spiritual support to the GPF stating he did not enter any place that prohibited any human being on the grounds of caste. Thus by their intervention in the public sphere the GPF was able to put those advocating for separate sheds in the village on the defensive. These statements received wide press publicity.

Parallel with this initiative, of giving the religious aspect of the dispute a humanitarian character, the GPF also sought to give the secular aspect a constitutional character. They invited a prominent retired chief justice of the Bombay High Court to Goa to speak on the issue. At a *Samata Meleva* in Mapuca, organized by the GPF on 3 October 2001, he condemned the act of discrimination. Addressing the public meeting he asked: 'How can you claim to having achieved freedom when a human being is being denied entry, even after death, in a public place on the basis of caste or religion'.[5] He persuaded the village Sarpanch and the VCDC president to publicly state that no such discrimination would take place in the future. The chief justice added that 'it was the primary responsibility of the government to intervene and make the people realize their constitutional rights and privileges'[6] but lamented that the existing system, unfortunately, does not allow that to happen. He opined that the law does not solve the problem but only shows the way and appealed to the youth to unite against the divisive forces since the future belonged to them. His programme of intervention in Goa concluded with the village Sarpanch reading, in the presence of the learned judge and social reformer, the preamble to the Indian Constitution inside the village crematorium. This was done in the presence of the other villagers, and members of the GPF, and was symbolic of the villagers' acceptance that they, henceforth, would shun caste discrimination and follow the principle of equality. This initiative too was able to capture the imagination of the press who covered it in great detail.

FROM THE ASHES

From the foregoing story what can social sciences in India spend some more time talking about? While the more esoteric issues, of the nature of the human estate in terms of envy or retaliation or humiliation (an everyday playing out of the Mahabharata), or the struggle between the humanitarian and the divisive character of religion, or even the paradoxical consequences of the Portuguese colonial rule, would need a dialogue with the humanities, for their fuller understanding it is the political truths here that can be more easily foregrounded. Issues in five domains, in particular, may be worth talking about.

The first issue is on the relative and contrasting roles of state and civil society organizations. The somewhat cryptic suggestion of the chief justice, that the existing system does not allow the government to intervene and cause the people to realize their constitutional rights and privileges, makes one wonder if the dynamics of democratic politics, in a plural segmented society, itself produces such constraints. This dynamics converts the players, particularly the political parties, into political agents who live a political life of only instrumental reason, dominated by an electoral calculus of forging winning social and political coalitions, and, as a result, there is no place for the moral imperative. The relative silence of the political parties and the government, on this issue, points to the prevalence of such a calculus. In contrast, the active and imaginative role of the civil society organizations, particularly the GPF, shows how such civil society activity can both compel government to take action against social behaviour that is reprehensible, as also against the constitution, and also constrain social forces that are regressive. It can compel a reluctant government to act. By being imaginative and engaged in the public sphere the GPF was able to move the public debate towards issues of a humanitarian philosophy and constitutionalism and away from the validity of the traditional practices of a segmented caste society. It is instructive that the members of the GPF acquired their political world view in the decades of the 1970s and 1980s when they were active in progressive student politics. These were years when student politics nationwide was engaging with issues of civil liberties and democratic rights (after the Emergency), with environmentalism, with the Gandhian Socialism of Jayaprakash Narayan, and with a challenge to imperialism, etc. This world view is what the GPF drew on when it rose to challenge the practice of discrimination. The group's networking, or social capital, also gave it an advantage in that it could influence the possible outcomes of its actions. Another group may not have been able to produce these same results and be as effective. It needed a worldwide and ethical frame and a politics to oppose regressive tendencies which were contrary to this frame.

At this juncture, when I am trying to explore the background factors that may be of relevance to our understanding of the incident of discrimination, it is perhaps relevant to also consider the following facts. The government in Goa at that time was a BJP government, the first ever in Goa, which, as is the case in all national political parties, deferred to the strategizing of the BJP government in Delhi. The Congress had been ousted after being in power almost continuously from the time of the formation of the state. It had also been ousted from the centre. In addition, Goa was and is a place, in the cognitive universe and cultural politics of the Sangh parivar, where the residues of its colonial history need to be erased. Goa, which has produced a pluricultural present replete with syncretic religious practices, is a place where the cultural struggle to make it 'truly Indian' is being waged, with one side arguing that 'truly Indian' means a diversity of cultures within the nation and the other arguing against such diversity. The controversy also takes place before the carnage in Gujarat in 2002 where the politics of mobilization, nationally, on the grounds of aggressive majoritarianism and its concomitant symbolic capital, was at this time being intensively adopted and had not yet been discredited. Are these background processes of relevance to explain the happenings in a Goan village? I cannot yet say conclusively. But as Hercule Poirot would have commented, 'there seems to be a prima facie case here'.

The second issue for discussion is the domain of the local. The emergence of the village panchayat as an institutional opportunity space in the village provides for both an assertion of the local arrogance and power of dominant castes (Ambedkar's fear), and also a resistance by the subaltern castes to such assertion (Gandhi's hope). The two stages through which both groups pass is also very interesting. The socially weaker Mahars first accept the less discriminatory of the two options offered: (i) burial and no cremation, or (ii) cremation but in a separate shed. They first choose the latter. Then, on support from the larger society, they insist on a third option that was initially not offered but which now was within reach of (iii) a common shed for cremation. As a result of the intervention of the larger democratic processes they succeed in getting it. The intermediate castes, in contrast, moved from resisting a common shed for cremation to finally accepting it. Again, because of the larger democratic politics, the imaginative intervention by the Press and the GPF against a reluctant state, they had to publicly affirm that they would not practise discrimination again in the village. This democratic lens helps us see the place of the third panchayat tier of government, which constitutes a new institutional opportunity space for struggle against inequity and for giving suppressed groups a voice. And so, even though it is initially a regressive space where dominant groups are able to impose their world view on the village through informal decisions in the Gram Sabha, it later becomes an emancipatory space where subaltern groups can resist such dominance (deSouza 2003).

The third issue of interest concerns the politics of the symbolic. Here the argument moves from a locality specific set of issues to a civilizational level set of issues since the struggle over the symbolic, that is taking place, draws on the cultural resources of the larger Indic world. Three aspects of the incident invite scrutiny in terms of this politics of symbols. The first aspect is the struggle over cremation. The Mahars regard it as an increase in social status when they move from burial to cremation, a move which they see as marking their arrival, more firmly, into Hindu society. Since the practice of cremation is accompanied, should be read as an announcement of belonging by the Mahars to the larger Hindu family. Getting the flaming right is thus important and can be seen in the insistence, by the Mahars when the second person dies, to continue the practice since it had now been started. This was the new tradition. And for this they were prepared to struggle even if it meant accepting two sheds. Presence and equality were more important than the invisibility and difference that had been their lot till then.

The second aspect is the *shuddhikaran* ceremony. The intermediate castes see the use of this ritual as a way to respond to the insolence of the Mahars. The performance of the purification ceremony of the crematorium was a deliberate act of humiliating the Mahars, a putting down of people who had forgotten their place. Through such a ritual the full force of Manu's social order in operation can be seen. It was a reminder to the Mahars that they are members of the polluting castes and even a crematorium can get polluted if they do not stay in their ascribed place. This 'place' refers to both ritual and geographical place where the Manuvadi rules of prohibition operate. The intellectual peculiarity of this idea of pollution stands out when one considers that the *sopo*, where the dead body is kept in the crematorium before cremation, is common whereas the sheds are not. Why does one place get polluted while the other does not? There is something very pernicious about this attempt to humiliate the Mahars at their moment of greatest vulnerability, when a death has occurred and the family is existentially struggling to come to terms with the finality that it represents. For their neighbours and even relatives to humiliate them at such a vulnerable moment shows the great distance we, in India, have to cover to build a world of fraternal feeling. The fact that caste feelings can trump feelings of empathy is a conundrum. For Ambedkar, as long as the caste system persisted such trumping would occur (Rodrigues 2002). It produces a process of continuous 'othering'. This, in turn, produces a sense of emotional as well as ritual distance. Both these aspects, the desire to be granted access to cremation and the purification ritual, seem to suggest that a process of sanskritization is taking place among Hindus in Goan society.

The third aspect is the reading of the preamble of the Indian Constitution in the crematorium. While the previous two aspects should be seen as a political struggle over symbols, within caste society, this third aspect is a political struggle within the domain of democracy. The imaginary of the event is very powerful. To have the local Sarpanch, an elected official under the Constitution, read the preamble to the

Constitution in the crematorium, in the presence of an eminent judge and the other villagers belonging to both groups, is a scripted event of powerful symbolic value. It reminds one of Gandhiji's Dandi March, of Rosa Park's refusal to sit in the back of a bus, of the lone Chinese standing in the path of the advancing tanks at the time of the massacre in Tian-a-Mein Square, of the Afghan refugees who stitched their mouths in protest at the treatment they were receiving from an arrogant and racist Australian regime. The taking of a pledge to uphold constitutional values in the same place where the discrimination had occurred, the crematorium, in symbolic terms, is a great victory for a democratic and just India. By participating in such a ritual the people confirmed the Constitution as the new Holy Book of India and its values as the new guiding principles. While the symbolic goals had been achieved the pragmatic objectives were also met since the event made for good copy, and, in a world dominated by the media, it received good coverage. The event had to be morally acknowledged.

The fourth issue for debate is the domain of caste, that structure of social stratification which gives India both its distinctiveness and it notoriety. While there is, in the public domain, a very important debate on the changing features of the caste system—whether it is dissolving in the face of the triple onslaught from democracy, modernization, and liberalization of the economy (Ambedkar 1979: 36–97), or whether it is actually more fungible than dominant theories suggest, with groups being able to exit and enter the hierarchical and segmented structure (Sheth 2000), and where, as a result of the deepening and expansion of democracy in India, it is becoming more a political than a social category (ibid.), or whether it remains as oppressive as it has always been (Guru 2005)—two fundamental issues need to be noted. The first emerges from the study done in 2004, which showed, using experimental techniques, how deep the caste system is in the social psyche of India. Two groups of students were studied, Dalits and non-Dalits, and through a series of controlled experimental situations it was found that not only did the expectations of the non-Dalits, with respect to their own and the Dalits' performance change, when caste identities were revealed, but the expectations of the Dalits also changed with respect to their own performances. The conclusion of the paper states that it:

provides experimental evidence that a social identity—a product of history, culture, and personal experience of discrimination—creates a pronounced economic disadvantage for a group through its effect on individuals' expectations. In the experiment, participants had a sociocultural category membership activated by the public announcement of their identities and by segregating groups by caste. In controlled settings, in which any possible difference in treatment toward castes was removed, social identity affected behaviour largely because it affected expectations. Thus the findings provide evidence for an additional explanation, *beyond differences in access to various resources,* for the tendency of social inequalities to reproduce themselves over time. (Hoff and Pandey 2004)

This study draws attention to the durability, in terms of personal and social psychology, of the discriminatory rules of the caste order. It goes some way towards explaining why the Bhandari community in Verla-Canca initially insisted on maintaining ritual distance from the Mahars, and, worse, on teaching them a lesson by performing a *shuddhikaran* ceremony. Where it becomes possible to investigate the depth of feelings of prejudice and discrimination, Ambedkar analytically and perhaps even intuitively had already understood this aspect of caste. In a perceptive passage he comments that 'caste is not a physical object like a wall of bricks or a line of barbed wire which prevents the Hindus from co-mingling and which has therefore to be pulled down. *Caste is a notion, it is a state of mind* [Italics are mine]. The destruction of caste does not therefore mean the destruction of a physical barrier. It means a notional change' (Rodrigues 2002). If caste is a state of mind which causes neighbours in a village to fight over the 'right to cremation', then how can this state of mind be changed, how can a more humane state of mind be brought about.

On this too Ambedkar has an answer. While inter-dining goes some way towards dissolving the barriers it is not enough.

I am convinced that the real remedy is inter-marriage. Fusion of blood alone can alone create the feeling of being kith and kin and unless this feeling of kinship, of being kindred, becomes paramount the separatist feeling—the feeling of being aliens—created by caste will not vanish. Among the Hindus, inter-marriage must necessarily be a factor of greater force in social life than it need be in the life of the non-Hindus. Where society is already well-knit by other ties, marriage is an ordinary incident of life. But where society is cut as under, marriage as a binding force becomes a matter of urgent necessity. *The real remedy for breaking caste is inter-marriage. Nothing else will serve as the solvent of caste.* (ibid.) (Emphasis in the original)

The first Mahar who died and was cremated in Verla-Canca, when it all began, had married inter-caste.

The fifth domain for consideration concerns humiliation. I need to explain the title of the chapter. Since most of my story is about discrimination and the responses to it, one could suggest that a more appropriate title would be 'Discrimination in a Crematorium'. I do not agree. I wish here for us to take that additional step in the analysis and meditate over the humiliation that discrimination brings; to think over its sources, its sanctions, its normalization. Social sciences in India needs to reflect over what kind of socialization process makes a group of ordinary people—fathers, brothers, neighbours, friends—humiliate a bereaved family twice, by challenging their use of a crematorium to dispose of their dead and then by performing a *shuddhikaran* ceremony to purify the polluted crematorium. We need to cogitate on not just the process of socialization which makes such responses available but also one which makes them acceptable.

NOTES

1. Sandesh Prabhudesai wrote several articles in the newspaper *Gomantak*, during the month of September, 2001.
2. This provision was inserted by the 1st Amendment Act 1996 to section 7, of sub-section 4, of the Goa Panchayati Act.
3. Sandesh Prabhudesai, 2001, 'Dalits Prohibited in Public Crematorium', Editorial, *Gomantak*, 20 September.
4. Sandesh Prabhudesai, 2006, Editorial, *Gomantak*, 23 September.
5. Sandesh Prabhudesai, *Gomantak*, 4 October 2001.
6. Ibid.

8 Equality *for* What?
Or the Troublesome Relation between Egalitarianism and Respect
Neera Chandhoke

INTRODUCING THE PROBLEM

Let me begin by posing a specific question of egalitarian theories:[1] *equality for what?* To put it bluntly, is there any connection between the redistribution[2] of material resources and (a) extension of respect to the beneficiary on the one hand, and (b) development *of* self-respect in the beneficiary on the other.[3] Admittedly it is not easy to establish a relationship between tangible things such as material resources— income, shelter, education, and health care—and the cultivation of sentiments such as self-respect, self-esteem, and a sense of self-worth. But presumably the deeper logic that underlines and penetrates egalitarian philosophies and policies is targeted towards the inculcation of precisely these sentiments. After all, liberal theorists do seem to suggest that the provision of basic needs happens to be a prerequisite for human flourishing, or for expanding the realm of choices. Marxists argue that redistribution of resources is necessary to neutralize oppressive structures. And that access to resources that meet basic needs allows individuals to realize their humanity in fullness. This is the *maximal* take on redistribution. *Minimally*, the argument holds that if I do not have to beg for my daily food or clothing, if I am not dependent on the charity of others for the satisfaction of my daily wants, and if I can provide for my own social reproduction as well as that of my family, I can be fairly sure that I will not be subjected to humiliation everyday or every hour of the day. Most egalitarians desire that individuals should be protected against the kind of humiliation that will necessarily occur, when they are dependent on others for the satisfaction of their basic requirements to live a decent life.[4] They would not be committed to egalitarianism otherwise.

The link between redistribution (of material resources) and what has come to be known as recognition (development of feelings of self-respect) has however proved more tenuous than originally conceived of by egalitarians. For one, not only is recognition an elusive concept inasmuch as it belongs to the realm of human prejudice, attitude, and notions of group identity, it is a matter that is not so easily commanded by politics. Politics can, to put it differently, negotiate distribution of scarce resources. The matter requires vision, courage, and commitment, but, as history has shown us, it can be done. How does politics negotiate recognition? How does it lay down parameters of what human beings owe each other by virtue of being human? For too many troubling factors cast their dark shadow on this precise issue; aspects that relate to individual and group psychology, all of which does not lend itself easily to political negotiation or intervention.

And yet recognition is vital to human beings, for it determines how they think of themselves, and how they relate to others. There is more. Hegel, making the concept of recognition fundamental to his philosophy, had told us that a good life is dependent on being held in regard by others. Human self-consciousness, he had argued, depends on being recognized by others as someone who possesses worth. If, for Kant, the idea of *Achtung* or respect contains the nucleus of his 'Categorical Imperative', for the Scottish moralists, recognition or disapproval motivates individuals towards the attainment of desirable virtues.

Essentially, therefore, the concept of recognition is theoretically located in the interface between the individual and the community. We achieve recognition of ourselves as people who matter when others show us through their actions and their behaviour that we matter. Conversely, the potential for moral injury arises from inter-subjectivity of human forms of life. Or, that human beings are vulnerable because their practical self-awareness is dependent on the approval or the disapproval of other human beings. Expectedly, the proposition that the constitution of the self is dependent on its being recognized by other selves shifts our focus away from the individualist notion that the self is self-referential to the idea that the self is a relational entity. Selfhood is, in other words, located in the inter-subjective conditions of identity formation.

'Human integrity', suggests Axel Honneth, modifying the Hegelian concept of recognition through employment of the ideas of George Herbert Mead, 'owes its existence, at a deep level, to the patterns of approval and recognition' (Honneth 1995: 131). The only way in which individuals are constituted as persons—as being with certain positive traits and abilities—is by learning to refer to themselves from the perspective of an approving or encouraging other. In this way the prospect of basic self-confidence is inherent in the experience of love, the prospect of self-respect, in the experience of legal recognition, and, finally, the prospect of self-esteem is found in experiences of solidarity. Correspondingly, since the self-image of individuals is based upon experiences of recognition, disrespect carries with it its own form of injury. That is why, suggests Honneth, individuals describe experiences of non-recognition as insult or humiliation. The consequences of disrespect or humiliation are serious: 'psychological death' of those whose bodily integrity has been violated, 'social death' for victims of slavery, and 'scars' for those whose cultures have been denigrated.

Theories of recognition in sum help us to understand that it may not be enough to grant individuals access to material resources through redistribution, it is equally important to recognize them in the sense of validating their self-image. For when an individual is subjected to disrespect in her daily dealings in the public or in the private sphere, or when she is subjected to humiliation, the consequences can be serious—the spectre of demoralized, diminished, and degraded beings on the one hand, and the eruption of struggles for respect or dignity on the other.

Consequently, theorists identify two types of discrete/overlapping conflicts in the world today: struggles over socio-economic resources and struggles over the revaluation of identities. While we can negotiate economic and political marginalization through the distribution of tangible resources, how do we deal with issues of cultural marginalization, which require the revaluation of devalued identities? Will the first negotiation help us to negotiate the second problem? It is doubtful. All this, as we can see, stacks up serious problems when it comes to the politics and policies of egalitarianism. It is to an exploration of some of these problems that this essay is addressed.

I would, however, like to make one point before I continue with the argument. We tend to assume in our daily lives that respect has to do with human properties that we admire, whether these may be talent, skills, exceptional abilities, or indeed loyalty and integrity in friends. And this is true to some extent. We respect Bhimsen Joshi because he has mastered the intricate art of Hindustani classical music. We respect Sachin Tendulkar because he is a skilled cricket player. And we respect

Medha Patkar because she is committed to justice for the powerless, and because she, with great courage, has expanded the political agenda in the country, even as she has led a massive social movement in western India. In normative political theory, however, respect is a generalized concept inasmuch as it has to do with the need to regard each person, no matter how ordinary she or he may be, as being of value. It is premised upon the notion of human worth. The extension of respect, it is important to note, need not be positive; it need not extend to intentional action. We do not have to go up to persons we know or do not know and tell them that we respect or admire them. It is enough if we refrain from actions that humiliate other human beings. Respect for other persons is generally practised through restraint and control over hateful or hurting speech and actions.

THE PROBLEM

Twenty-four years ago, I.P. Desai presented the findings of his research on the practice of untouchability in rural Gujarat. In public arenas that were governed by law, such as schools and post offices, he told us, untouchability was least practised. Only one school in fifty-nine villages had separate seating arrangements for Dalit children, and only 4 per cent of the post offices practised discrimination in their transactions with Dalits. When it came to the private sphere of social transactions, however, matters were different (Desai 1976). In 90 per cent of the villages that he surveyed, Desai found that Dalits were not allowed to enter the houses of caste Hindus. Barbers, shopkeepers, and potters kept their distance from the Dalits who continued to be thought of as polluting. Dalits were prohibited from entering temples frequented by caste Hindus. In 10 per cent of the villages that were surveyed, Dalits were not allowed direct access to common water sources. They were consequently dependent on caste Hindus for access to water (ibid.: 62–3). Other villages had created separate wells from where the Dalits could draw water. Though discrimination could be found in seating arrangements in the public arena of panchayats (ibid.: 258), it was really in the private sphere that untouchability continued to be practised seriously. Desai concluded that Dalits had benefited because 'they do not have to suffer humiliation every day at the hands of the savarna' (ibid.: 114). But though the attitude of caste Hindus had changed at least in public transactions, their beliefs about untouchability had not altered. The world of the Dalits had advanced in the sphere of public transactions that are governed by law; but not in the sphere of private relationships—friendship, intimacy, dining together, visiting each other—which lie outside the ambit of the law.

One would have thought that matters would be different today. After all, the last two-and-a-half decades have witnessed the Dalit movement and Dalit parties moving to the centre stage of Indian politics. The caste question has been foregrounded in public consciousness in and through what is referred to as the Mandalization of politics in the 1990s. The chief minister of the largest state in the country, Uttar Pradesh (UP), is a Dalit, one of the previous presidents of India was a Dalit. Widely respected Dalit intellectuals have aggressively fought out the caste issue in political and intellectual circles.[5] The Dalit movement has raised, and continues to raise vexing issues of caste discrimination publicly. Activists have brought those who violate provisions that are meant to ensure the well-being of the Dalit community to court, as well as to the scheduled caste commission. A Dalit university has been set up in the country. Prominent Indian literary figures writing in English invariably have a Dalit protagonist as the linchpin of their story, for example, Rohinton Mistry, Arundhati Roy, and Sagarika Ghosh.[6] No election can be fought without reference to the caste issue. And Dalit politics have finally generated a politically correct vocabulary in at least the public domain.

Have the Dalits finally come into their own as equal citizens of India? Perhaps yes, and this despite all odds. Most works on protective discrimination (hereafter PD) conclude that the policies have worked rather well given the anarchic nature of the Indian political system, and given entrenched caste discrimination, even though we can count enough flaws in the implementation of PD.[7] A more troubling question follows: have the Dalits finally come into their own as agents who possess equal moral standing in the public as well as in the private sphere? The response to this question is mixed but on the whole pessimistic.

Consider the conclusions of the recent research carried out by Shankar Gaikwad who interviewed about 200 college-going and employed Dalits in Aurangabad. Publishing his findings in 1999, Gaikwad suggests that despite the institutionalization of protective discrimination policies in the public sphere, the attitude of caste Hindus has not changed (Gaikwad 1999). Whereas all of the respondents 'were eager to do away with caste stigmatizing identity', they felt deeply that they continued to be discriminated against (ibid.: 190). And while 80.5 per cent of the Dalits expected that their relationship with caste Hindus would be based on equality, the latter did not respond in terms of inviting Dalits to their homes, dining with them, or entering into other social relationships.

Of the respondents, 66 per cent reported that they continued to feel humiliated and discriminated against. There have been changes in the secular aspects of the Dalit's life concluded Gaikwad, but other aspects of his or her life have not changed (ibid.: 193).

At least four overlapping but nevertheless distinct questions crop up in light of the above observations. First, is it enough to institutionalize protective discrimination, (which I for the purpose of this article identify with reservations in educational institutions and jobs in the government) in the public sphere to reverse historical discrimination? Second, have the policies of PD yielded results other than the material? By material results I mean (a) access to resources such as professional skills through quotas in educational establishments; and (b) access to an income through quotas in government employment. By non-material results I mean the extension of respect to people, in the sense of treating them with dignity just because they, as human beings, possess equal moral standing. To put it differently, have the policies of PD, (which are an avatar of egalitarianism) produced respect for the beneficiaries of these policies. Third, even if people who have been given access to the sphere of education and government jobs through PD are treated with minimal professional courtesy and propriety in the public sphere, are they extended the same respect in the private sphere? Fourth, how important is the private sphere for issues such as respect and dignity?

To put the issue synoptically: does egalitarianism or the redistribution of resources according to need, lead to respect or self-respect? The second question follows the first: are the two pillars of egalitarianism— redistribution and respect—compatible? Does the first lead to the second or vice versa, or do the two exist in some tension? One prefatory point may be in order here. I am personally committed to the policies of PD, and if I have sought to uncover areas of tension in the concept in this essay, it is purely to explore the idea of PD in its fullness. I wish to explore the ambiguities and the complexities of the issue. I want to show that though there is much good in the idea, it can also cause great harm. I wish, in other words, to carry out a reasoned evaluation of the presuppositions and the consequences of fifty odd years of protective discrimination policies, because I care for democratic equality, even though my efforts may verge at times on the politically incorrect.

EQUALITY AND EGALITARIANISM

The concept of egalitarianism was born out of dissatisfaction with the unintended consequences of formal equality or equalitarianism.

The arguments against formal equality, that each person gets an equal share of whatever it is that we are distributing, are well known by now.[8] Essentially, if the members of a constituency are unequal inasmuch as some people possess resources in excess and others do not possess any resource at all, then if we treat them equally in the sense of giving each person equal shares, we will land up by reproducing inequality. The precepts of formal equality were found wanting precisely because they (the precepts) happen to be supremely indifferent to what Fishkin (1983) has called 'background inequalities'. Egalitarians on the other hand hold that if people are unequally situated in a given social order, we need to treat them differently or unequally. The concept of formal equality/equalitarianism is therefore conceptually distinct from that of substantive equality/egalitarianism, inasmuch as the two concepts are built on different and divergent presuppositions: inattention to background inequalities in the case of the first, and attention to such inequalities in the case of the second.

This is not to take away from the realization that formal equality is valuable for two reasons. Firstly, formal equality is valuable because even though people possess different talents and are unequally endowed, all this is morally irrelevant when it comes to the recognition of the rights of citizens. The idea of non-discrimination (which is a second order principle, with equality being a first order principle) among people is of great value simply because it tells us that though people are different in their own special way, they are equal in the eyes of the state and the law. Secondly, formal equality is of value because it generates the idea of procedural fairness. Procedural fairness extends equal respect to the moral claims of each citizen, therefore it can be considered to be both justified and legitimate. It is justified because everyone is given an equal chance of affecting the outcome as in the visible maxim of 'one person one vote'. It is legitimate because it grants equal moral standing to every individual via the same maxim. Therefore, the decisions that are arrived at through procedural equality are considered binding on all. Having said that let us also acknowledge that though procedural equality is an essential principle for any regime of equality, it is inadequate simply because the outcomes of the principle reproduce inequality. Consider the following case, a local government institution is entrusted with the task of distributing 10 acres of land equally among ten people. According to the principle of formal equality, each of these ten people will be allotted 1 acre of land. But out of these ten people four already happen to possess 4 acres of land and six do not possess any land.[9] All that the principle of formal equality will ensure is that four of our constituency of ten will now possess 5 acres of land, and six will now possess 1 acre each of land. Inequality has been reproduced. Witness the dilemma that confronts our egalitarian here. She has begun with the presupposition that everyone has equal moral standing and should be treated equally. But she is also forced to realize that since the principle of formal equality intensifies inequality, it compromises equal moral standing. For when we break up procedural fairness into its components—procedures and outcomes—we realize that adherence to equal procedures needs to lead to equal outcomes. Procedural fairness has simply been found wanting. It needs to be mediated. This I may hasten to add is not a consequentialist argument. A consequentialist argument will suggest that if procedural fairness does not generate equality, it is dispensable. But procedural fairness is not dispensable, it is merely inadequate and it needs to be supplemented. In sum, unless we strongly believe that the task of equality ends with designing fair procedures, we will have to move on to substantive equality or egalitarianism.

Egalitarianism tells us that the principle of procedural fairness needs to be supplemented by a series of measures, which guarantee some modicum of equality before the arena where procedural fairness arbitrates between demands. Or, if we feel committed to equality, we will have to ensure that people enjoy a rough and ready equality in their life conditions. Equality of life conditions is a prerequisite for formal equality. This in turn does not only mean that we distribute material resources equally, it means that we design redistributive policies based on needs and circumstances. To repeat the proposition laid out above, the paradox of equality is that if people are unequal, they will need to be treated unequally. Unless a society provides basic material resources to the deprived sections of the population, goods that the affluent may not require, it cannot seriously claim equality.

Two kinds of distinct arguments have legitimized the move from the practice of formal equality to that of egalitarianism. According to welfare egalitarians, some people in society are endowed with fewer resources—whether talent or income—because of what is termed 'brute luck'. The luckless should be compensated for their deprivation, by the transfer of resources from those who happen to be privileged and affluent. In other words, skills and talents are randomly distributed through a cosmic lottery. Consequently, any society that lays claims to normativity should compensate people for lack of skills and talents. Richard Arneson, for instance, suggests that 'The concern of distributive justice is to compensate individuals for misfortune.... Distributive justice stipulates that the lucky should transfer some or all of their gains due to luck to the unlucky'.[10]

Note that the idea of a cosmic lottery, which is supposed to distribute skills and talents randomly, and, therefore, unequally, does not and cannot acknowledge that society itself is responsible for the fact that some people just do not possess the resources that are needed for leading a good life. They may possess skills and talent but they may not be in a position to translate these skills and talents into enduring assets. The onus of disprivilege is placed not on the functioning of power in society but on intangible and untouchable forces such as the cosmic lottery or fate.

Welfare egalitarians do not consider for instance that though an individual may be talented, her talent may be left unrealized because she just does not possess the resources to develop and fine-tune this talent. Consider the case of two children, both potential M.F. Hussains, whose families possess unequal endowments. The first child has the opportunity to go to an art school, buy the finest equipment to hone her art, be tutored, and in time be feted simply because she has the funds to hire art galleries, wine and dine critics, and get good reviews in newspapers. The second child has nothing—not even the money to buy the implements that will transfer her talents into skills. Is this a case of a cosmic lottery or a case of entrenched social and economic inequality? To hold that inequality is due to the fact that some people are born talented and others are not may actually serve the purpose of legitimizing the status quo. For it just does not address institutionalized structures of discrimination in society.

On the other hand we have the other kind of egalitarian, says Ronald Dworkin, who advocates the equalization of resources and not merely the equalization of welfare. But if people live a hardworking and productive life, it is only just that their share of common resources is far larger than others. Dworkin makes allowance for what he calls 'ambition-sensitive' policies as well as 'endowment-sensitive' policies inasmuch as the latter guarantees that no one is worse off because of un-chosen factors such as lack of talent or disability (Dworkin 1981). Is this adequate as an account of how to redress inequality? Perhaps not. Elisabeth Anderson for instance argues that despite differences between what she calls academic egalitarians, and those who believe that resources should be equalized, 'recent egalitarian writing has come to be dominated by the view that the fundamental aim of equality is to compensate people for undeserved bad luck' (ibid.: 288). But the proper aim of egalitarian justice, suggests Anderson, is 'not to eliminate the impact of brute luck from human affairs but to end oppression' (ibid.). The proper aim of egalitarianism according to her is to allow people to live in a democratic community instead of a hierarchical one.

In a similar vein, in an exchange in the journal *Philosophy and Public Affairs*, Timothy Hinton attacks Jonathan Wolff's argument that egalitarian fairness demands that we distribute resources in order to eliminate the effects of sheer bad luck on people's lives. This, he argues, is open to very strong objections. It is possible, on the other hand, to secure an equal status for all by eliminating 'two basic forms of injustice that attend human interaction, namely economic exploitation and social domination' (Hinton 2002: 80; Wolff 1998). Instead of relying on some kind of cosmic lottery as a basis for egalitarianism, we, argues Hinton, should commit ourselves to the idea of equal moral standing or the idea that 'all human beings, in virtue of their standing, possess a pre-political entitlement to the resources of the world' (Hinton 2002: 81). Radical egalitarianism is therefore concerned with wider issues of ending exploitation, domination, and unjust use of power that inevitably accompanies inequality in a given society.

To put it differently, it is difficult to escape the conclusion that most egalitarians confuse humanitarianism with egalitarianism. Humanitarianism is concerned with the principle that no one should be deprived, and that the poor should be given resources even if these resources have to be transferred from the well-off. It is not concerned with the underlying structures of society, or of the fact that some people in society are rich beyond belief and others are poor beyond belief, and that the gap between one section of society and the other reproduces inequality no matter how many resources we may transfer. Radical egalitarianism on the other hand is a *relational* concept. It is concerned with both endowing the deprived with resources, as well as with the fact that no one should possess resources in excess of her entitlement. It regards every person as—to use the terminology of the corporate sector—an equal shareholder in the material and the symbolic resources of a given society. Humanism is not concerned with the great gap between the rich and the poor. Egalitarian theories in the radical mode concentrate on lessening this gap. For it is only when we have a rough and ready equality in society that the idea of equal moral standing gains some meaning. After all, when some people in society possess resources in excess of what they should possess, and others do not possess anything, not even command over their labour (I have in mind bonded labour or labour in the informal sector), generalized respect for human beings declines into personalized respect. And it is conceivable that personalized respect may be based not only on admiration for skills and talents or exceptional abilities, but admiration for some people just because they possess the kind of material resources which enables them to command how much resources other people have. Humanitarian egalitarianism may not lead to the generalization of respect at all. And it may not question the structuration of society along the axis of power and domination either.

CARING ABOUT GROUP INEQUALITIES

The tension between humanitarianism and egalitarianism becomes even more contentious when we extend the egalitarian argument to inter-group inequalities. But before I go on to discuss this tension, let me point out that the egalitarian argument undergoes two major shifts when it is applied to any society which is marked by inequality between ascriptive groups such as India. For one, we realize that persons are disadvantaged not because they do not possess talent or luck, or because they have suffered exploitation individually, but because they are born into a caste that has been stigmatized in demeaning ways—as the 'inferior' or the 'polluting'. Human beings, in other words, are discriminated against because the group of which they happen to be members has been historically discriminated against. The source of the problem can be located in inequality between groups.

Even die-hard liberals, who are generally suspicious of ascriptive group identity, have been forced to acknowledge that the codification of caste-based disprivileges denies to the member of that caste group equal moral standing. Consequently, an argument that was originally designed to extend to individuals justice through the adoption of egalitarian policies has been adapted to groups for two reasons. One, individuals are subjected to ritualized humiliation because of their membership of a caste group, which has been allotted a lowly status in the social hierarchy. Secondly, by reasons of this membership individuals are denied access to skills, resources, and other material necessities. Material deprivation, in other words, is supervened upon cultural marginalization, exclusion, and deprivation. Individuals are thus doubly disadvantaged by reasons of their membership to a particular caste. Correspondingly, any kind of remedy has to apply to all the members of the group rather than to the individual per se. Thus protective discrimination is designed not for individuals as individuals but to individuals as members of a group.

Secondly, unlike the brute luck argument that legitimizes welfare egalitarianism, in India the case for protective discrimination has been built on a particular reading of history. It is based upon the idea that members of groups have suffered in history because society has allotted to the group a lowly place in the caste hierarchy and excluded the members from the benefits that accrue to other members. The text of history is read as a narrative of collective guilt and collective complicity on the one hand and collective victimization and collective harm on the other. There are no individual exceptions to this story of collective complicity and culpability. No one can claim that they or their ancestors have not participated in practices that exclude members of a society from sharing in the collective benefits that such a society has to offer to its members. No one can claim that they be exempted from the remedial measures that have been adopted for the victims of history. If a particular reading of Indian history[11] has led to the institutionalization of PD, the acceptance of collective culpability led to its legitimization in society and the polity. The general feeling was, and continues to be, that those who have benefited from history should be willing to pay the costs. The issue of compensation for harm done looms large over the conceptual horizon of PD policies. Certainly, the notion of compensation for the harms of history may be a sound basis for building protective discrimination policies and endowing them with legitimacy. Whether it is enough to reverse caste discrimination and whether it is enough to secure respect for the beneficiaries of these policies is more debatable for the following reasons.

For one, the idea that 'we' owe something to 'them' divides society along the axis of 'we-ism' and 'they-ism'. 'We', as the beneficiaries of history, have to pay 'them', as the 'victims' of history. So we design reservations in educational institutions and in government jobs. But does this mean that the resources of a given society are equalized? Does it mean that every person is viewed as an equal stakeholder in society? For it is possible that even if reservations benefit some people, their share of the common resources of a society remain far, far, lower than those possessed by the better off in that society.

Is it enough, we are further compelled to ask, to minimally compensate people for historical wrongs and leave it at that? Should we disclaim any further responsibility for the disprivileged? Should we not be moving towards a shared vision of egalitarian democracy, instead of remaining mired in notions of minimal compensation? Should we not also ensure that all people move towards this vision through persuasion? Correspondingly, if we do not do that, is it possible that the issue of compensation has been caught up in humanitarianism and not egalitarianism? But humanitarianism cannot be substituted for egalitarianism. The philosopher Temkin, for instance, suggests that humanitarians are concerned only with helping the worse off; they are not concerned with equality (Temkin 1993: 8). Therefore, even if the poor have access to quality care, the rich have even greater access to much better care. This is not egalitarianism.

This is more than evident in our own society, when we consider that social justice as a component of egalitarianism, which ideally should include land reform, income generation policies, redressal of inequality, and securing the well being of the disprivileged, has been collapsed into reservations in educational institutions and in government jobs. Reservations, which should have formed one component of social justice, have come to substitute for social justice. The victims of history have been compensated in the most minimal of fashion possible. In the process, the realm of social justice has narrowed down rather than expanded. Whereas issues of land reform have been consigned to the dustbin of history, reservations have expanded to rather absurd proportions.

It is not difficult to figure out why this is so. Reservations in effect have proved a soft option for political elites, who are reluctant to carry out deep-rooted changes in society and would rather opt to enlarge the constituency for reservations in state jobs and in educational institutions. It is, after all, relatively easy to essay reservations in a rapidly shrinking government sector and in an even more rapidly privatizing educational system than change ownership of resources in the country. Moreover, promises of reservations prove especially profitable when it comes to garnering votes. Therefore we witness the somewhat perplexing phenomenon of caste groups, which by no stretch of imagination can be thought of as historically deprived, benefiting from reservations.. Consider how the once proud Jat community, which has historically either owned land or cultivated land, has been granted reservations in Rajasthan and in Delhi.

Even more peculiar is the exchange in the legislative assembly of Rajasthan. A Bharatiya Janata Party (BJP) member, Rajendra Rathore, during the question hour on the 30th of August 2002, criticized the Congress government for not filling in vacancies in the Other Backward

Class (OBC) commission. It would be different if the said member was concerned about the working of government institutions, but that was not his stated aim. His objection was grounded in the fact that since the earlier commission in its tenth report had recommended reservations for the Rajputs and the Brahmins [!], any delay in filling in the vacancies in the commission leads to delay in the implementation of reservations for the said castes.[12] Since when did the Brahmins and the Rajputs, we can ask, become backward castes? The mind, frankly, boggles.

It is difficult to escape the realization that the public discourse of restitution for historical wrongs has inevitably led to competing and spiralling claims of victimhood on the one hand, and demands for compensation on the other. In a world where the victim is the hero, suffering itself has been trivialized because it has been reduced into an index for compensation. Groups now compete over who has been most victimized in history because they aim for reservations as compensation.

All this has had rather serious consequences both for the practice and the legitimacy of reservations themselves. For in the process of being employed as an electoral ploy, they have been de-linked from their normative moorings in visions of social justice and egalitarian democracy, and come to be generally perceived as a convenient tool of amoral electoral politics. Therein the recent discourse of caste reservations rests, on less rather than more firm philosophical (and hence morally justifiable) grounds. Consequently, the arguments that are assembled for caste reservations in the politics of the nation seem to the ordinary citizen less compelling than they should be. This citizen does not view reservations kindly or the beneficiaries of reservations kindly precisely because no policy maker spells out the normative case for these measures in some detail.

Further, even as reservations have been dis-embedded from their moorings in egalitarianism and come to be embedded in cynical electoral considerations, they have transformed caste identity into a self-perpetuating advantage. And recollect is completely contrary to what the leadership of oppressed groups had dreamed of. After all, if Ambedkar had wanted the annihilation of caste, Martin Luther King had in a famous speech dreamed of a situation where 'my four little children will one day live in a nation where they will not be judged by the color of their skin but by the content of their character' (King 1965). It is an indication of our times that Ambedkar's dream that caste identities should become an insignificant category in our public life is today regarded as naively utopian at best and as a limited commitment to caste equality at worst by Dalit parties themselves. People have simply come to acquire a vested interest in caste identities. And it is precisely this which has contributed to a generalized feeling of hostility towards the beneficiaries of these policies in the country today. To put it bluntly, our public discourse over reservations undermines both reservations and the beneficiaries of reservations. Reservations are seen not as a justified component of egalitarianism but as unjustified rewards for things such as support for a particular political party, for instance. Any political or philosophical defence of such policies is rendered wafer thin. Expectedly, any extension of reservation has met with hostility and resentment for the beneficiaries of the policies. Resentment and hostility in turn have been expressed through the perpetuation of demeaning caste stereotypes and stigmatizing imagery. It has in essence reproduced humiliation and disrespect.

There are two uncomfortable facts about reservations that its defenders refuse to recognize. And this refusal to recognize the problem further de-legitimizes reservations. One, given the self-perpetuating nature of reservations because they have become a soft option, it has become extremely difficult to justify them when it comes to questions such as the following: why should a middle-class child who belongs to the lower caste be offered an educational opportunity, which is denied to a poor upper caste student? Secondly, protective discrimination policies perhaps naturally focus on inter-group rather than intra-group inequalities. Demands for social justice are inescapably demands for equality between groups rather than equality within groups. But that groups, even groups that have been historically deprived, can be divided along the axis of inequality is obvious. After all, those who remain at the bottom of a group will be unequal to those who have benefited for two or now three generations from PD policies. A deep problem casts its shadow over PD policies, for we will have to ask the question: why *is inequality between members of a group acceptable when inequality between groups is not acceptable?* Correspondingly, how do we design policies of redistribution that apply to individuals within the group? These are questions that are rarely asked of policies that target entire groups.

The second set of criticism of the way PD has been deployed in India has to with the monopoly of the state over the inscription and the re-inscription of caste identities. Reservations have given the state immense power, even as it (the state) classifies, categorizes, maps, and certifies caste identities, and even as it brings new claimants for PD within the fold of such mapping and certification. Conversely, individuals who are beneficiaries of state action become excessively dependent on what is perceived to be state generosity and largesse. Reservations, consequently, are perceived as emanating from the state and not as part of what is due to human beings because they are equal shareholders in the resources of a given society. Anderson has made an interesting observation in this context. She suggests that 'people lay claim to the resources of egalitarian re-distribution in virtue of their inferiority to others, not in virtue of their equality to others' (Anderson 1999: 306). This not only compromises the tenets of egalitarianism, it reinforces lack of self-respect and self-esteem.

Correspondingly, it is not enough that people belong to a caste that has been unfairly dismissed and insulted in and through history, they need to constantly prove that they have been victims of historically sanctioned inequality and injustice. After all, claimants for PD have not only to show that they lack the opportunities for developing skills that are needed for the workplace, they have to prove it through the tiresome and repetitive production of certificates. And this can be both demeaning as well as humiliating. Consider this: there is considerable conceptual difference between participating in the reconstruction of a society that has been unequally and unfairly organized by asking for an equalization of resources, and demanding compensation because one has been victimized. The first road to egalitarian democracy may reinforce confidence that one is an equal shareholder in the stakes of a society. The second may just reinforce feelings that one approaches the entire system as a complainant.

And this perhaps cannot generate either respect or self-respect. Wolff, for instance, asks us to think how it must feel—how demeaning it must be—to have to admit to oneself and convince others that one lacks the qualifications for getting a job, and that one has to rely on the state and its sanction to acquire employment. 'This removes any last shred of dignity from those already in a very unfortunate position' (Wolff 1998: 114). He employs the point of what he calls 'shameful revelation'[13] to press for unconditional benefits for all without the need of proof that certain people lack talent. The revelation is not less shameful because it results from brute or bad luck. Secondly, it is demeaning because it is iniquitous; the burden of revealing data after all falls only on the disprivileged. The privileged do not need to declare the cause of their privileges (ibid.: 111).

We can arguably reject Wolff's argument of shameful revelation as unimportant for a society such as India. When it comes to reservations, we can stress, matters are different. Reservations have been designed because certain groups have been so oppressed in society that they still bear the scars in the form of lack of opportunity. And yet we cannot deny that demonstration of proof, the pressing need to become a part of a category that certifies lack of opportunity, can subject one to disrespect.

To put it bluntly: does the reinforcement of caste identities reinforce stereotypes about the so-called lower castes or eradicate them? It is a troublesome question simply because while we cannot do without reservations, they may not have achieved what they were meant for—self-respect for the beneficiaries of these policies.

Take another look at the conclusions of the studies on the Dalit question. They, in essence, tell us that whereas a Dalit may be able to access education and jobs through quotas, she may not be able to access the domain of private transactions, that is, friendships, associational life, dining with others, inter-marrying, or indeed membership of exclusive clubs. Do we now proceed to regulate the private world of our individuals? But liberals, for a variety of perhaps good reasons, have been hostile to the idea that the state should regulate all of our social transactions.

At this point someone can raise an expected question: does the world of the private matter? I would suggest that it matters for two reasons. One, it is essential that no one should be barred from a world that allows for emotional support systems, through forming friendships, and through participating in the fullness of social transactions of a given society. The second reason is instrumental. Though PD policies aim to equip the beneficiary with professional skills to negotiate the job market, we all know by now that market exchanges do not always fall entirely in the public domain. For it is precisely the private domain of social transactions that guarantees the acquisition of both social skills, which are indispensable for acquiring and retaining jobs, and influential contacts, which are necessary for the same. Where we spend our time and with whom, who our children go to school with, what neighbourhood we live in, what clubs we belong to, and what sort of persons our children marry, have an inescapable effect on material things like jobs, promotions, and prestigious placements. If Dalits continue to be discriminated against in the private sphere, their chances in the public sphere may amount to little. To sum up the argument, the way that we have gone about remedying the situation of the Dalit community has sidelined visions of an egalitarian society, marginalized the idea that everyone has an equal share in the resources of a society, whether material or non-material, and reinforced the divisions in society between 'us' and 'them'. There is always the danger that all this can have a decidedly negative impact on the self-respect of the members of the group.

CARING FOR GROUP INEQUALITY FOR THE RIGHT REASONS

If we can find little connection between egalitarian measures and the extension of respect should we rethink the way we have tried to negotiate the situation in India? Wolff, for instance, believes that egalitarians should be motivated not only by concern for equality (as fairness), but also by the idea of respect for all (Wolff 1998: 97). Finding the fairest principles of justice, he suggests, does not exhaust the task of the egalitarian political philosopher (ibid.: 102). For, there may be more to a society of equals than a just scheme of distribution of material rewards. There may be goods that depend on the attitude of people towards each other. If the cost of implementing egalitarian principles is high, it may be preferable to think that a system with some exploitation is nevertheless the best of all possible worlds. What is important is that people should not be deprived of their respect. In response to all these vexing problems that seem to be inherent to egalitarianism, Wolff suggests that we adopt unconditional benefits for all, without subjecting the disprivileged to a level of scrutiny not experienced by those better off. If a social minimum were provided unconditionally it would save people from demeaning themselves by publicly announcing that they are disprivileged.

In his response to the argument, Timothy Hinton suggests that inequality results from economic exploitation and social domination, and not only bad luck. Systematized inequality prohibits equality of status because it permits one group to ritually exploit another. And this violates the basic premise that each individual has an equal moral standing. A proper acknowledgement of their equal moral standing, or the fact that all people share equally the world's resources, will ensure that they receive the resources they need, even as the need for shameful revelation is avoided.

Hinton's suggestion, it seems to me, possesses three virtues. One, by concentrating on society as a whole, we dissolve the distinction between 'us' and 'them', which bedevils much of the case for reservations. Secondly, redistributive policies are not targeted towards compensation but towards the creation of a level playing field, where all individuals can participate from a plane of equality and not as victims or as complainants. Thirdly, if our ultimate end is to create a society where the gap between the very rich and the very poor is eliminated through redistribution, this can only be achieved when we relocate reservations within the social whole.

Therefore, one option is to strengthen, as Wolff suggests, the social minimum for all disadvantaged people without trying necessarily to map their disability. The second is to see that PD measures are wrapped up for a particular family, after three generations of that family have availed of them. This will resolve at least two problems coming in the way of respect for Dalits. First, after a family has benefited from these measures for three generations they can percolate to other members of the community who may be more dispossessed—the Dalit, landless woman who is triply oppressed by gender, caste, and class. This will turn attention from inter-group to intra-group inequality and strengthen the case for radical egalitarianism. Second, it will help to dissolve the perception and consequent hostility that a Dalit from a comparatively better off background is given the advantage of PD when a poor member of the upper caste is not given the same benefits. These two measures may conceivably lead us to establish a relation between redistribution and respect.

CONCLUSION

In this article I have suggested that PD policies are today being defended for the wrong reasons. At best they amount to humanitarian caring and at worst they belong to vote gathering devices. Secondly, through the practices of electoral politics, social justice has been reduced to reservations and, in turn, reservations have become a soft option even as they substitute for hard measures such as land reform. Even Dalit leaders, such as the chief minister of Uttar Pradesh, opt for Ambedkar parks rather than hard options such as giving land to the tiller. Thirdly, because the political and philosophical defences for PD have become wafer-thin, they have aroused hostility in the rest of society. This has been revealed in the sphere of private associational life, where PD policies cannot intrude. Therefore, PD in the public arena is completely compatible with continued caste discrimination in the private arena. In their present avatar, some of the arguments that are used for justifying caste preferential policies may actually exacerbate rather than diminish the problems of caste discrimination that bedevils our society. That all this leads to disrespect is more than obvious. The connection between egalitarianism and respect is more elusive that was originally conceived of.

NOTES

1. I employ the concept of egalitarianism because I find it more acceptable than the concept of formal equality as the subsequent discussion will show.

2. The notion of redistribution immediately suggests that resources have been unequally distributed in the first instance for a variety of reasons, and that any good society will seek to equalize the possession of these resources through redistributing them. The idea is thus relational inasmuch as it seeks to establish a connection between the resources that the well-offs possess in a given society, and the resources that do or do not accrue to the poorer sections.

3. I assume that the point that self-respect or self-worth depends on how other people view or treat us is by now fairly well accepted.

4. This recollect was the thrust of a strain of feminist thought in its early phase. Feminists were to suggest that since the kind of humiliation women suffer from in their daily lives stems from their economic dependence on the male component of the family, they should be encouraged to be economically independent. But much to their consternation, women found that economic independence does not always lead to the extension of either respect from others, or even to the establishment of self-esteem and self-respect. The same problem was discerned when it came to the Dalits in India or indeed the Afro-Americans in the US, as well as all those who had been dismissed and marginalized by society, such as the community of gays.

5. I have in mind Kancha Ilaiah's *Why I am not a Hindu*; see Ilaiah (1996). The book can be read as a sharp, emotional, and often bitter polemic against everything that belongs to caste Hindus, from their gods, to their culinary habits, to the position of women, to the marriage rituals. Gopal Guru's critique of caste is perhaps more influential, but his writing is more sober, reflective, and self-critical than Ilaiah.

6. I am by no means denying that earlier novels such as *The Untouchable* written by Mulk Raj Anand had dealt with the disturbing issue of caste discrimination. And regional literatures have systematically carried a critique of caste discrimination, particularly the kind of literature produced by the intellectuals of the Dalit panther movement. But the kind of visibility that has attached itself to contemporary Indian writing in English makes engagement with the caste question both perceptible as well as public.

7. See Joshi (1982). Simon R. Charsley and G.K. Karanth, in the introduction to their 1998 edited work titled *Challenging Untouchability*, suggest that though it is not as if nothing has changed for the Dalits, their current situation remains paradoxical. That protective discrimination policies have fetched mixed results has been pointed out by Marc Galanter (1984).

8. Note that the idea of 'giving' is not related to benevolence or charity but to rights. People have a right to material goods and they can make a claim on the state and on society by virtue of this right. Correspondingly, the state, society, and which ever agent this right is claimed against—the family for instance—is obliged to honour that right. That honouring constitutes 'giving'.

9. We assume that our constituency of six is disprivileged for reasons outside their control, such as historically handed down discrimination or marginalization. We, as a matter of course, do not hold society responsible for those who have frittered away their resources on say drink and gambling. Sarat Chandra's Devdas is not a candidate for justice by this reasoning, but a Dalit, landless woman who is triply disprivileged by reasons of caste, gender, and class is such a candidate.

10. Cited in Anderson (1999: 290). Anderson classifies along with Arneson, Gerald Cohen, and John Roemer as welfare egalitarians. She contrasts this point of view with that of Dworkin and Philippe Van Parajis who are committed to equalizing resources.

11. I take it as a matter of course that this history of caste exploitation, which was narrated by the Bhakti Saints, Jyotiba Phule, or Ambedkar among others, has become a part of collective consciousness through the struggles of the Dalit movement.

12. *The Hindu*, 31 August 2002, p. 5. The tenth report of the OBC commission had included the Brahmins and the Rajputs in the eight categories that should benefit from reservations.

13. Wolff (1998) terms the act of publicly declaring lack of competence as 'shameful revelation'.

Section III
Society, Economy, and Humiliation

9

Political Economy of Humiliation
Tale of a Failed Strike

Suhas Palshikar

...Baluram decided that there was no alternative left but to sell their land and property in Aundh....his mother, who was going to Aundh because of the sale, first had to mortgage a gold ring of one of the neighbours in order to get sufficient money to reach there.

...They tried to economize on practically everything, clothes and food in particular. The days came when they had to eat the flour, which Baluram carefully collected from the floor of a flourmill.

... One day Baluram came home and seeing his eldest son drinking water and preparing to sleep without have had anything to eat that day, he could take no more. It was as if something snapped inside him. Cursing and screaming he rushed out of the house into the street and plunged into a jail bharo campaign which was in progress. He struggled to get arrested but didn't manage. In the end he just stood there and wept. Baluram falls silent when he recollects those moments. (van Wersch 1992: 296–7)

These are not extracts from any powerful fiction and the unfortunate Baluram of this story actually belongs to the much-dreaded organized industrial, proletariat. Again, Baluram's story of misery does not unfold in the oppressive early industrial period. The year is 1982 and the locale Bombay—now Mumbai.

In what follows, I propose to show how humiliation is experienced in a modern, industrial, and democratic set-up by those sections which are sometimes derided as the labour aristocracy, though not in the sense in which Marx and Engels use the term (Marx and Engels 1975: 161). Baluram's story is not his personal tragedy. It was experienced by tens of thousands who were similarly situated. They were all workers in

Mumbai's textile mills. Being the oldest manufacturing industry, workers in the textile industry have had a long history of organization, unionism, confrontations, and victories won from mill owners and the state.[1] More than 2.5 lakh mill workers in Mumbai participated in the textile strike of 1982, which lasted over eighteen months (van Wersch 1992: 78). In fact, the strike has the distinction of never being officially called off. Mumbai's textile workers had at the time (as they have even today) one recognized trade union, the Rashtriya Mill Mazdoor Sangh (RMMS). Most workers believed that RMMS was not militant enough and did not care for the rights of the workers. This dissatisfaction sparked off many sporadic one-day strikes in 1981. Finally, the workers approached Dr Datta Samant who had become famous for his militant unionism among engineering workers in Mumbai. Samant founded the Maharashtra Girni Kamgar Union (MGKU) and organized the workers for a long-drawn battle. The indefinite strike began in January 1982. Since MGKU was not a recognized union and Samant did not follow legal procedures, the strike was declared illegal by the government of Maharashtra. The state government only made half-hearted attempts to resolve the strike. The mill owners refused to both concede workers' demands and to negotiate with Samant's MGKU. As the strike continued without an end in sight, the workers started to desert the MGKU. Owners, too, recruited temporary workers and finally the strike fizzled out in August 1983 when most workers joined duties and most mills resumed production.[2]

HUMILIATION IN DEFEAT

The ill-fated strike resulted in the threat of closure of thirteen mills in Mumbai. The Government of India took over these mills in October 1983. Another effect of the strike was the reduction in the number of workers employed in the mills. The mill owners used the opportunity of the strike to reduce their workforce on the pretexts of modernization, rationalization, or simply disciplinary action. New recruitment, too, came to a halt. Thirdly, some mills sought to avoid payments of dues of retired/discharged workers. This issue has still not been satisfactorily resolved even after almost two decades. Fourthly, the occupational displacement of large numbers of workers put enormous pressure on the employment situation in Mumbai, tearing the city's frail social fabric. Finally, the mill owners have been pushing for the sale of mill land in Mumbai for its commercial (non-industrial) use.

More than three years after the strike had ended, the Government of Maharashtra appointed a committee to enquire into the consequences of the strike. Manohar Kotwal was the chairman of the committee. The Kotwal Committee reported that over 50,000 workers had lost their jobs during the strike (GoM 1987: 12–13). The report calculated that in all 1,06,356 workers were affected by the strike (ibid.: 22). There is an obvious error in this calculation in that it includes as strike-affected those workers who retired (8,929) during the strike period. Yet, it is noteworthy that almost 43,000 workers are reported as having 'resigned' during and after the strike, possibly as a result of modernization. The Kotwal Committee also estimated that over 46,000 workers were not paid their dues (till 1987 at least, when the report was submitted). Not only were workers not paid their dues, but twenty-nine mills also defaulted on depositing the provident fund amounts with the Provident Fund Commissioner (ibid.: 23–4, 48–51). In all, workers' dues amounting to Rs 225 million were not paid.

Apart from dismissals and non-payment of dues, mill managements were alleged to have prepared blacklists of workers who would be either kept out (without formal dismissals) or taken back only after a lot of begging, both with the management and the RMMS leadership (van Wersch 1992: 248–50). In addition, workers were made to sign an undertaking that they had participated in the illegal strike, that they had not joined the strike voluntarily, and that, in the future, they would not join in any agitation (ibid.: 249, 261). As van Wersch has shown, mills resorted to many finer strategies to keep workers on tenterhooks. Sometimes, they were shown as 'surplus' workers, sometimes as 'temporary permanent' workers (on the entry-cards of workers), and so on. Apart from creating suspense about their status, such strategies often meant that workers forfeited their earlier seniority, would be paid less than their co-workers of equal seniority, and could be displaced any time without much difficulty (ibid.).

The entire history of the textile strike of 1982–3 and its aftermath is a long story of continuing humiliation—humiliation of a well-organized and strong sector of industrial labour. It has two parts. One is what happened after the strike—dismissal, demotion, non-payment of dues, etc. The other concerns what was happening to the lives of striking workers and their families during the strike. Baluram's story is related to this other part of the humiliation experienced by the workers. Contrary to the belief about considerable monetary gains made through trade union activity, studies point to the harrowing lives witnessed by striking workers. Perhaps, Baluram's is a typical story. He lost his father during the strike because the doctor at the Employee's State Insurance

Scheme (ESIS) would not treat the patient since by participating in the strike Baluram had lost the right to medical treatment (van Wersch 1992: 296). The study by Bhowmik and More, too, reports how two workers—Kapare and Nandlal—lost their sons due to illness during the strike (Bhowmik and More 2001: 4825–6). The non-availability of ESIS facility and the inability to pay for private medical care were the causes. Since most mill workers do have some rural connection, many workers fell back on farm work during the strike. In most cases, however, this only meant that they were kept engaged, as their family land was anyway being looked after by other family members. At least 20 per cent (of a sample) worked as agricultural labour. While many workers took to power-loom or handloom weaving, others had to work as casual labour, construction workers, etc. (van Wersch 1992: 323). Wives of workers sought employment as domestic servants. Bhowmik reports a case where one worker's son started working in a hotel. He also reports how the wife of the worker worked as a bidi worker. Most workers had to discontinue the education of their children: over one-third from Bhowmik and More's sample had to withdraw their children from school. The duo further reports that thirty-two out of a hundred families had to pawn their jewellery; in thirty-five cases, the wife/daughter worked as domestic servants, and in fifty-four cases, the workers sought to go back to their village but had to return (Bhowmik and More 2001: 4825–6). In fact, the trauma has been of such a magnitude that Bhowmik and More found that most ex-mill workers were reluctant to speak of their past, in particular the stigma or humiliation of being thrown out of the job (ibid.: 4822). In addition to all these, there are the other factors which contribute to humiliation: not being able to provide medical care to near and dear ones, witnessing the end of children's education, or, as Kapare witnesses, sons turning into alcoholics, sons being unemployed, or worse (ibid.: 4825). The experience of one Jairam is as follows: his brother insulted his wife and children, and 'pained and helpless' the brothers thus decided to separate. When the partition became a fact Jairam felt relieved but also very sad 'because of the inevitability of it all' (van Wersch 1992: 270). As one worker saw it, in contrast to her happy memories associated with mill work, 'No one looks after the workers. The mill owner just looks after his own interests: there's only God above for us'. After losing her job, she sold vegetables, and ended up making a living washing utensils (D'Monte 2002: 2). As another ex-mill worker, unable to pay fees for his three children who attended a municipal school, put it: 'I think the beasts are better off than us;

they may be dumb but at least they are fed' (ibid.: 3). Or is it that the beasts are fed because they are dumb, *because* they don't shout slogans and don't join strikes?

ISSUE OF MILL LAND

The foregoing narrative of humiliation is as much or more a narrative of one group as it is a series of tales about individuals. Besides crushing the life chances and self-esteem of thousands of individuals, the strike and its aftermath proved to be catalysts of the process of emaciation of the large section of the workforce. During the 1990s, something happened in Mumbai's textile industry, which apart from being economic fraud was also a social distortion. As an abject appendix to our story of humiliation, this may be subtitled as 'adding insult to injury'. This relates to the controversy about the sale of mill lands in Mumbai. Many textile mills, located in the heart of old Mumbai city, own considerable area of land. Once the strike was over, the mills first resorted to retrenchment and modernization. However, mill owners soon started tapping the possibility of converting their real estate property into extremely lucrative business propositions. Sale, leasing, and non-industrial use of mill lands became attractive alternatives. A large number of complex issues are involved in this. The state government regulates the use of land and mill land has obviously been marked for industrial/manufacturing purposes. Any development activity in the mill lands would also involve the rules regarding floor space index (FSI) allowed by 'competent' authorities. But more importantly, sale/leasing of mill land further involves the question of industrial production continuing in the mills, thus, the future employment of the workers hinges on this. Similarly, many mill lands have *chawls* (tenements) where mill workers have their residences. Sale/lease of the mill lands would thus displace the workers from these residences.

According to the state government's 1973 plan (Mumbai Metropolitan Regional Development Authority or MMRDA Plan), sale/leasing of mill land was not allowed except for industrial purpose. Yet, activity in that direction was kick-started by Rajiv Gandhi in 1987 itself (EPWRF 1997: 2785–7). In 1989, Mumbai Congress chief Murli Deora proposed a scheme for sale of 'surplus' mill land (D'Monte 2002: 121–2). Although this issue was not pursued further, it came to centre stage in the 1990s as real estate prices spiralled sky high in Mumbai. In 1991, the Maharashtra government amended its development control rules. In the case of sick or closed mills, sale of land was allowed under various conditions. This meant that the mill owner could sale/lease one third land for residential or commercial use; and even this had certain loopholes (ibid.: 124). Later, in 1996, the government appointed a study group to draw up an integrated plan for mill land in Mumbai. However, the government chose not to act upon the report of this group and subsequently kept announcing its policy on the issue of mill lands in a piecemeal fashion from time to time. The intricacies and cobwebs of government plans, reports and policies notwithstanding, in at least one famous case of non-industrial development of mill land, the social distortions are evident.

In 1999, owners of Phoenix Mills launched a 'Bowling Company', which has been the main attraction of rich youngsters. This company, with its twenty lanes, has a health club, spa, pool tables, sports bar, etc., with a jazz café, video arcade, and other attractions on the anvil. This development was possible by taking advantage of a fire in the mill premises way back in 1977 and from the ashes of the industrial unit there emerged an entertainment industry catering to the needs of the neo-rich. As much as the social distortion this brings about, the justification given for this development is cause for humiliation. Permission for this venture was sought as an 'addition to the mill of recreation facilities for workers and staff as well as executives of offices located in the premises'. The management told the municipal authorities, '...our mill workers are continuously demanding for the aforesaid facilities'. The company even cited an agitation by workers (which, in fact, was against closure and non-payment) as agitation for these demands (ibid.: 134–5). Many other mills have been engaged in transformation of their lands into commercial propositions. These deals involve hundreds of crores of rupees.

However, more than the astronomical profits on which the city capitalists have set their sights, the sale/leasing of mill lands involves another major factor: As one mill-activist, Datta Iswalkar sees it, this is going to be a clash between two cultures, two classes. He says, 'ultimately, one will have to give way. No prizes for guessing which...' (ibid.: 136). Darryl D'Monte describes the transformation as gentrification of the areas previously/currently occupied by the working class (ibid.: 207–9). In the process, the working class is initially marginalized in its own areas and gradually erased from social consciousness. It may still continue to exist in the dingy corners of the mill area but it will be totally eclipsed by flats and penthouses on the twenty-eighth floor, selling at more than Rs 15 million. D'Monte gives an illustration of the distorted isolation in which the neo-rich surround themselves, ignoring the very existence of lesser mortals: While the residents of the new high-rise buildings in Parel give their address as Worli (east) instead of Parel, builders offer 'would be buyers 'an unrestricted view of the race course and coast' firmly turning their backs on the grimy chimneys of the mills' (ibid.: 209).

DEPRIVATION OF RIGHT TO RESISTANCE

How can we summarize the mill workers' (and ex-mill-workers') experiences of two decades? At the beginning of the 1980s, workers were fed up with their recognized union, the RMMS. Thus, the irony that the entrenched union could neither be made answerable nor could it be removed forms the basis of this whole tale. Once this is realized, we are able to appreciate the adventure in which the workers plunged themselves. They saw no way to confront the mill owners. Already, in the backdrop of emergency and overall industrial stagnation, collective action was becoming less and less feasible. The inter-sectoral disparities, like the one between textile workers and engineering workers, was also becoming visible to the textile workers. Therefore, with great hopes and preparedness for bitter battle, the workers embarked on the strike. Despite the strike being hundred per cent successful, it failed to produce any favourable result. The workers could not even hope for the minimum 'no victimization' guarantee. They were not compensated for the loss of their wages over the eighteen months of strike. Instead, they lost jobs after facing many hardships during the strike. Once the strike fizzled out, workers faced the problem of payment of their dues. Many mills closed down and many others reduced the scale of their operations. With the sale of mill land around the corner, many workers are facing the threat of displacement from their residence. In the course of these developments, workers were variously cheated by the owners. Now they have neither recourse to collective action, nor to the courts. In addition, they have no hopes from the state since state machinery only helps the mill owners, as we shall see later. In the backdrop of this material and political blockade, there has also been a cultural assault in the form of gentrification of the territory occupied by mill workers. This factor is depriving the workers of a sense of belonging. They now exist in Parel but do not belong; they only await their inevitable marginalization. This marginalization means extinction from the collective consciousness of the city. Soon, for typical Mumbaikars, mill workers will have disappeared from their cognitive maps. The mill workers will have dissolved into petty hawkers and vendors, casual labourers, 'unskilled' jobholders, idlers, and worse still, petty criminals or members of this or that mafia. The disappearance of an entire social group, both physically and also from social consciousness, constitutes the highest degree of humiliation, which is a culmination of two decades of humiliating life.

More significantly, there is deprivation of right to livelihood and right to resistance. This deprivation in itself leads to humiliation. In addition, as our narrative of mill workers shows, the deprived group has had some history of organized collective action and a collective consciousness. These assets are threatened in the course of the struggle. Further, the 'deprivation' leads the humiliated to a dead end because the rights to livelihood and resistance are lost through a 'legal' battle: As we noted, the strike was illegal, the workers lost the battle to derecognize the RMMS, and therefore they did not have the right to claim reinstatement at the end of the strike; they had to depend upon the discretion and goodwill of the mill owners. Even non-payment of dues was caught up in technicalities. Similarly, the sale of mill land was also 'properly' based on established legal practices—amendment to rules, applications by owners, scrutiny by 'competent' authority, and so on. Once the mills do close—on the basis of 'sickness' duly certified—and workers lose their jobs, they are left with no alternative skills or training but that is their bad luck! They could still be recruited as watchmen or attendants or peons, and 'rehabilitated' if government rules so 'stipulate'. While mill lands are being developed, workers will be evicted from their *chawl*s if courts so order, and if workers defy court orders they have to be jailed because, after all, it is the rule of the law! In instances of such humiliation, there is displacement from the means of livelihood and a near absence of space for negotiating with this displacement. The law blocks any resistance. This means that collective action by the deprived can be promptly 'handled' as a law and order problem. What makes matters worse is a lack of support from either others who are similarly situated or from society in general. The lack of support from the former is due to the fragmentation of the subalterns, partly caused by the established system of instrumental, parochial, capitalist relations. It is also due to the isolated, issue-based resistance to which we are accustomed since the late 1980s. However, the lack of broader social support is caused by the gentrification of social imagination, the ideological ascendancy of capitalism. The long and short of it is that in the onward march of capitalism, many subaltern sections and no less the proletariat get trampled. The result is a sense of helplessness: as aptly put by one worker, 'there's only God above for us'.

THE STATE AND WORKING CLASSES

Studies of Mumbai's textile strike and the subsequent decline of the textile industry in Mumbai have shown that in the contest between striking workers and the Mill Owners' Association (MOA), there was a third player, acting as a partisan umpire, the Indian state. In fact, the failure of the strike and the humiliation of workers in the aftermath of the strike could not have taken place without the involvement of the state and union governments. The study by van Wersch and the booklet brought out by a civil rights group from Mumbai (Lokshahi Hakka Sanghatna 1996) chronicle the active role of the state in the developments during and after the strike.

The state government made only perfunctory efforts to avoid the strike. Initially, it appointment a 'High Power Committee' but the exit of the then chief minister (Antulay) ended any possibility of reconciliation. More significantly, the mill owners did not want the government to act in any way that would give Samant and the workers a sense of victory. The mill owners even attempted to thwart Rajiv Gandhi's early efforts to find an honourable solution (van Wersch 1992: 87–9). When the strike actually got underway, the state government remained a witness, periodically appealing to the concerned parties to find a solution. At the same time, the state government declared the strike as illegal, thus opening the floodgates for action against the workers. Later on, any initiative regarding the strike rested with the union government (ibid.: 118–29). Perhaps the attitude of the government is best summed up by the ex-Labour Commissioner who handled the strike: 'It was the strategy of the Government to take care of law and order and to take no action. The other point was that *the mill owners were advised to be firm* (ibid.: 199)' (emphasis added). Of course, the police did more than maintain law and order. They protected the mills, allowed/facilitated mill owners to surreptitiously remove goods from mill compounds, persuaded workers to join work, occasionally arrested and beat up the activists of MGKU, even followed the workers in rural areas and warned them about the consequences of the strike. No wonder, van Wersch speaks of 'a common front' of mill owners and the government (ibid.: 191).

This common front continued even after the strike. The government authorities turned a Nelson's eye to the highhanded manner in which the mill owners went about the 'rationalization' of their workforce. The government also did not bother to facilitate payment of arrears to the workers. Even when a committee appointed by the state government recommended 'penal' action against mills for default on depositing provident fund, the government did not take any action. It appears very clearly that the state and union governments shared the views of the mill owners that an 'irresponsible' and aggressive leader like Datta Samant should not be encouraged in any way. In fact, they must have seen this as an opportunity to put an end to Samant's heroic style of leadership. Samant was known for his contempt about legal procedures, formalities, and formal mechanisms. Ironically, the government sought to defeat Samant by itself abandoning the formal mechanisms and colluding with the mill owners. Besides the immediate task of Samant's defeat, however, those acting on behalf of the Indian state seem to have a more serious and long-term agenda: taming the working class.

It may be borne in mind that the chronicle of Mumbai's mill workers is not an isolated matter where the heroics of one maverick leader 'unfortunately' led to such a humiliating experience. In the first place, the textile industry as a whole was facing many challenges during the 1980s. Obsolete technology on the one hand and India's newly born liberalization programme on the other were the two dimensions relevant in the crisis of the textile industry in general (EPWRF 1997; Saksena 2002; and Srinivasulu 1996). Secondly, the strike by the textile workers must also be seen as a part of the overall decline of the industrial workforce. Hailed and criticized for its organized power, the industrial workforce has gradually ceased to be the engine of material activity. In the case of Mumbai, for instance, stagnation and gradual decline of industrial growth stares one in the eye. In particular, the decline in factory employment (D'Monte 2002: 32–8) meant that industrial workers would constitute an increasingly smaller share in the total workforce. Coupled with this loss of employment opportunities and loss of sense of power, the 1980s also witnessed the defeat of collective action by employees. The textile strike, the illegal status of that strike notwithstanding, gives out the message of the futility of industrial action against the alliance of the state and the capitalists. As if to underscore this point, the Government of India brought about in 1981, as a precursor to future policies of liberalization, the Essential Services Maintenance Act (ESMA), banning strikes in industries considered as 'essential'. Thus, in a sense, alongside the humiliating story of textile workers over two decades, there also runs a two-decade old story of anti-labour laws from ESMA, from 1981 to the revision of labour laws in 2001–2. In this way, the 'humiliation' of Mumbai's textile workers spills over and engulfs the issues of the new political economy of the Indian state.

This 'spill over' may be better appreciated if we pause for a moment to re-understand what humiliation implies. Humiliation, as we discuss it here, is not merely frustrations and insults, despicable though they are. We are positing that (i) humiliation refers to a group's helplessness arising out of systemic constraints; (ii) humiliation is loss of dignity or assault on dignity, which involves right to livelihood and right to resistance; and (iii) humiliation involves unfavourable reconstitution of material situation leading to further (additional) deprivation and misery. As such, it becomes relevant to think of humiliation in the context of unequal group relations, and at least for the particular meaning adopted here, the role of the state becomes crucial in shaping actual experiences of humiliation.

THE INDIAN STATE AND CAPITALIST DEVELOPMENT

After independence, the Indian state sought to strike a balance between its avowed goal of democracy and the agenda of capitalist development (popularized as 'development'). This balancing act could be performed by evolving a complex network of legal-bureaucratic policies and procedures. These could be proof of the state's well-intentioned democratic (welfarist) management of public contestations on issues of resource distribution. At the same time, these policies and procedures ensured that while presiding over capitalist development, the state would, nonetheless, retain considerable 'prestige' on account of being autonomous of sectional interests of one class (Palshikar 2004: 147–52; see also Deshpande 2005). As an instance of the state's role in capitalist development, one may look at state policies about 'rehabilitation'. The Indian state devised may detailed policies of 'protecting' and placating the interests of 'persons' affected by the strategies of industrial development. The state usually refused to recognize that affected persons were often from an identifiable segment; they were tribal or the rural poor (since the rural rich anyway took care that they would be beneficiaries but seldom 'affected' by development); or, they were urban slum dwellers or pavement vendors, hawkers, and so on. By refusing to recognize that 'development' frequently affected adversely disadvantaged and subaltern sections, the state sought to deal with them as families or individuals. However, what is pertinent for our purpose here is that state adopted many policies of 'rehabilitation' and claimed to act upon them. This, on the one hand, 'proved' the state's good intentions, while on the other hand it took care that only minimum 'rehabilitation' would actually take place, putting minimum responsibilities on the capitalists.

Activists and concerned scholars have developed a critique of the ideology and content of these policies. The critique developed by Narmada Bachao Andolan (NBA) is a comprehensive one (Sangvai 2000). Many others have also found out that inadequate as the rehabilitation policies are, they are insincerely implemented or only 'formally' implemented resulting in loss of livelihood and dislocation of lifestyles. What is worse, the impressive legal edifice of rehabilitation laws actually means that once an 'affected' person's case has been settled within that framework, there is no further recourse. Except for occasional outbursts of moral indignation, the judiciary cannot go beyond the legalities. On the other hand, the formal–legal process is subverted by corruption, state violence, suppression of collective action, and ideological manipulations. In a wide-ranging survey of displacement and rehabilitation in Maharashtra, Vora has shown both the inadequacy of state action and the insincerity amounting to non-implementation. He looks at two kinds of displacement: displacement due to construction of dams and displacement due to industrial expansion in rural areas. It was estimated that by 1997, there were 1,40,631 families in Maharashtra affected by acquisition of land for various projects (Vora 2002: 381). Vora's account shows how the state vigorously pursues capitalist development and uses government machinery for acquiring land, which is then put at the disposal of the industry, including multinational giants. Thus the 'government is acting on behalf of the businessmen against the interests of the people' (ibid.: 401).

In spite of laws regarding rehabilitation and constitutionally guaranteed civil liberties, collective action against occupational or spatial displacement is often a humiliating experience. As Sanjay Sangavai and Alok Agarwal have noted, the state resorts to 'indiscriminate arrests, spreading terror and fear psychosis...defaming the movements... pitting one section of the people against the organizations...' (Sangvai and Agarwal 1991: 2665). Amita Baviskar has documented, in detail, the war-like treatment of agitations and the bureaucratic insensitivity and police disregard for human rights and human dignity (Baviskar 1995: 202–13). She reports an incident where 'the collector told assembled villagers that the combined might of the state-lathi, bullet and pen-would be used to persuade people to move from their land' (ibid.: 210). Thus, two things emerge: one is the emptiness of legal procedures governing rehabilitation and the other is near impossibility of undertaking resistance. These two sum up the role of the Indian state in the process of capitalist development.

Since the 1980s, many changes in the political economy have taken place. While the state continues to pursue the policy of capitalist development, liberalization and privatization have meant that the ideological emphasis on welfare would decline. Instead, the repressive role of the state has gained prominence along with the strategies of dismantling the working class. The actualization and informalization of labour and various policies of voluntary retirement have been promoted and pursued by the state contributing further to the decline of the organized sector. This has given tremendous flexibility to employers in dealing with the workforce (Deshpande 2004: 380–4). The narrative of Mumbai's textile workers unfolded in this overall context of India's political economy. This narrative vividly brings out the predicament of a liberal-democratic state in a capitalist economy.

THE PREDICAMENT OF THE LIBERAL DEMOCRATIC STATE

A typical liberal-democratic state, invoking the ideology of democracy, seeks to locate itself in a position to arbitrate over material conflicts. However, as capitalism entrenches itself, the focus of the state shifts towards other arenas of social reconstruction with newer themes of empowerment. This shift gives us some clue to how the state gets involved in humiliation relations obtaining in situations other than the material situation, that is, situations arising on the basis of ascriptive markers like race, ethnicity, caste, or gender. What is the likely trajectory of humiliation based on these factors?

Democracy—even only a very formal democracy—cannot be stopped from infusing some amount of democratization. A democratic party, leader, or force has to invoke popular support by positing the ideology of 'power to the people'. The ordinary public thus enters into the arena of power politics. Thus, the moment the bourgeoisie in Europe gave a call for 'liberty and equality' against feudalism, they were admitting the labouring classes into the game of power. Similarly, the moment the nationalists in colonial societies departed from exclusively conspiratorial and secret methods and waged 'people's struggles', they were running the risk of their nations being claimed by the ordinary public. Around the mid-twentieth century, and afterwards, democratization engulfed many ex-colonial societies. Even after the establishment of formal democratic institutions, the process of democratization kept on expanding the meaning of democracy. Many subaltern groups—women, coloured people, ethnic minorities, Dalits, tribals, aboriginals—were at the centre of the process of democratization resulting in mobilization, self-respect, and self-confidence. These groups mounted multi-pronged ideological challenges to their subordination through art, literature, symbols, religious revivals, evolution of alternative lifestyles, through ideological formulations and through political organizations and struggles. These exercises and democratic struggles resulted in the erosion of ideological bases of domination.

Faced with the forces it generated, the capitalist state effected many changes in its authority structure and also in society in general. Certain forms of oppression came to be disallowed. Discrimination on the grounds of race, religion, caste, gender, etc., were/have been prohibited. In the latter half of the twentieth century, the democratic state went a step further and took upon itself the responsibility of caring for certain subaltern sections. States in Europe and North America went further and began to officially respect plurality, giving rise to the language of multiculturalism and minority rights. These developments mean that the state now derecognizes certain forms of domination and discrimination. In conjunction with the awareness achieved by the subaltern sections through prolonged struggles, the state initiative in respect of democratization meant that the physical and legal basis of domination would fast disappear or at least become weak. Policies of the Indian state follow the same pattern. Starting with constitutional injunctions against untouchability and guarantees against discrimination, the Indian state delegitimized the bases of caste/gender discriminations. Of late, the state has even adopted the language of empowerment.

This, though, does not mean that humiliation based on ascriptive markers has been removed or weakened. In the first place, civil society keeps on evolving new and even more sophisticated ways of perpetrating humiliation against subaltern sections like women, Dalits, minorities, etc. These ways often bypass or circumvent the state and its laws. It is possible—though not intended here—to locate the social dynamics through which such social segments are pushed into adverse material situations also. More importantly, in the new political economy of liberalization, all collective action is being denied legitimacy. As such, the targets of social humiliation do not have recourse to political resistance. The isolation of individuals through fragmentation of group identity and the ascendance of non-governmental organizations (NGOs) as a welfare arm of the state means that humiliated groups will be severely constrained in developing organizational assets to resist civil societal humiliation.

Secondly, the trajectory of humiliation arising from material situations may have an important lesson for this other arena of humiliation. True to type, the liberal democratic state apparatus derecognizes certain (humiliating) forms of discrimination. The injunctions enter the statute book; bureaucratic machinery is installed for supervision and protection, etc. And yet, the ground reality does not change. One can find instances of the police not registering complaints by hapless victims of sexual harassment or not conducting a proper enquiry leading to the acquittal of the accused. More than the humiliation arising from social location, the humiliation of being cheated by the state, the humiliation of false promises, the humiliation of systemic constraints, predominates such situations. Thus, it is possible that victims of humiliation will reach a dead end while seeking/relying on state support.

This takes us back to the predicament of the liberal democratic state: it is rich on rhetoric but cannot transcend the political economy. We argue that the existence of humiliation relations at the group level indicates the need for reconstitution of civil society. The Indian state performs a dual role in this context. On the one hand, it has lost its autonomy vis-à-vis the capitalist interests. Therefore, it has lost initiative in reconstituting material situations. The state now follows the lead of capital. This means that it has neither the power nor the willingness to handle issues of material deprivation and resulting humiliation. On the other hand, we argue that the state can claim to be the formal liquidator of some forms of humiliation based on ascriptive situations. But given the fact that the state is often favourably disposed towards dominant interests, it is doubtful if the state will/can pursue actively any agenda of social reconstruction. Contemporary liberalism, and particularly radical constructions of liberalism (and those who distance themselves from neo-liberal approach), have been aware of this predicament of the discourse of liberal democracy. This awareness reflects in the attempts to expand and radicalize the scope of rights. Liberals are also painfully aware that the dignity of person remains rather as a precept than practice in liberal democratic states. This unease gives rise to formulations such as exclusion, marginalization and humiliation; formulations which will hopefully focus on the shortcomings of liberal practice. The contention of this article is that in formulating the concept of humiliation and in comprehending social relations in the framework of humiliation, a critical enquiry into the political economy of state is very necessary. It is hoped that this article draws attention to the point that liberal

constructions of humiliation, which bypass or obfuscate the issue of
deprivation and exploitations, would miss the predicament in which
liberal-democratic states find themselves.

NOTES

1. On trade union activity among textile workers, see Chandavarkar
   (1994). See also Thakker (1962).
2. For details of the strike, see van Wersch (1992: 66–233).

10 Against Untouchability
The Discourses of Gandhi and Ambedkar
Thomas Pantham[†]

INTRODUCTION

Untouchability is abolished and its practice in any form forbidden by Article 17 of the Constitution of India.[1] That emancipatory constitutional provision is implemented through the Scheduled Castes and Scheduled Tribes (Prevention of Atrocities) Act, 1989, which is the amended version of the earlier Acts on the subject.[2] These constitutional and legislative measures, by which the centuries-old practices of untouchability have become cognizable as punishable offences, owe much to the anti-untouchability movements that were mobilized and led, in their truly emancipatory though largely different, ways, by *Mahatma* Mohandas Karamchand Gandhi (1869–1948) and Bhimrao Ramji Ambedkar (1891–1956). Despite basic differences between, and serious conflicts over, their respective political, social, and religious philosophies and practical-political strategies, both shared a genuine and deep commitment to the eradication of untouchability. As noted by Eleanor Zelliot, a pioneer scholar of the Dalit movement, Article 17 of the Constitution 'stands as a triumph—for Congress, for Gandhi, for Ambedkar, and for India—however imperfectly the idea of complete equality and justice has been realized' (Zelliot 1986, 1988: 194).

†The author retains the copyright of this paper. It is partly based on research carried out by him when he held a Mahatma Gandhi National Fellowship of the Indian Council of Social Science Research.

There can be no denying that our constitutional and legislative measures have served to delegitimize the centuries-old ideology of, or belief in, untouchability and to drastically reduce the extent of its practice. Yet, untouchability has not disappeared fully from our society; some of its customary practices continue to be present even today. Writing in 1994, Mendelsohn and Vicziany noted that in terms of their poverty, the discriminations and occasional violence to which they are subjected, and their own self-perceptions, the Scheduled Castes (SCs) 'remain deeply subordinated' (Mendelsohn and Vicziany 1996: 64). A similar finding has been reported more recently by another team of eminent social scientists, who studied the incidence and extent of untouchability in 560 villages across eleven states in 2001–2. They write:

...many Dalits are still confined to those occupations that were traditionally assigned to ati-shudras.... Limited occupational mobility has meant that, in almost all parts of rural India, Dalits continue to dispose of animal carcasses, collect human filth and clean toilets and streets....

...untouchability is practised in one form or another in almost eighty percent of the villages. It was most extensive in the private and religious spheres, and least present in the public and political spheres. Though the most blatant and grotesque practices have significantly declined, they have not yet been relegated to the yellowing pages of history. Every other day, untouchability-related instances make news stories in the media. (Shah *et al.* 2006: 145–6)

Obviously, the persistence of untouchability today is a pointer to the limitations of our theory and practice of untouchability-eradication. Some of those limitations lie in a debilitating divergence that has developed between the trajectories taken by the Gandhian and Ambedkarian approaches to untouchability-eradication.[3] Among their partisan inheritors, there is, as pointed out by Suhas Palshikar, 'a standardized positioning of the two [Gandhi and Ambedkar] as each other's enemies'. As a result, our movements for social transformation have become 'weak and localized' and ideologically 'fragmented or stagnant'. This is indeed an enfeebling condition of our, as yet incomplete, movement for the eradication of untouchability. We need to get out of this situation and, as suggested by Palshikar, attempt to move forward by 'building bridges between the two rich discourses of our times [that is, Gandhi's and Ambedkar's emancipatory discourses]' (Palshikar 1996). Such a bridge-building calls for interpretive understanding, by us, of the making of our complex political heritage from the mutually conditioned and, arguably, complementary or compatible emancipatory interventions of Gandhi, Ambedkar, and other thinker-leaders of our Freedom Movement.

Accordingly, I shall, in what follows, try to review some selected instances of the political and intellectual interactions or exchanges between Gandhi and Ambedkar during their pursuit, either co-operatively (as was rarely the case) or (as was more often the case) in opposition to each other, of what in fact were their interlocked and arguably complementary/compatible discursive approaches to the eradication of untouchability. Ever since their first meeting in Mumbai on the eve of their journeys to London for the second Round Table Conference in 1931, they responded to each other's criticisms of their respective approaches to social transformation with regard to caste and untouchability. There was a running political debate between them. They learned and unlearned a good deal from each other. This has not been given sufficient appreciation or attention by social and political theorists.[4] I feel that in Gandhi's and Ambedkar's sustained discursive responsiveness to each other's criticisms or objections, we may find grounds of complementarity or compatibility between their emancipatory approaches. In fact, while they did express their opposition to each other's views and actions on some occasions, they also expressed, on some other occasions, their open or tacit acknowledgement of the value or justifiability of each other's line of thought and action on the issue of untouchability-eradication.

GANDHI AGAINST UNTOUCHABILITY

Gandhi, born in a Vaishnava family at Porbandar in Gujarat, started his anti-untouchability activities when he was about twelve years of age and continued to do so till his death at the hands of his 'conservative assassin'.[5] At the age of twelve, Gandhi had tussles with his mother over the issue of his touching Uka, an 'untouchable' cleaner of the family's latrines. Although he obeyed his mother by performing the ablutions demanded of him, he told her that she was wrong in considering physical contact with Uka as sinful. In 1898, Gandhi nearly pushed his wife out of their house in Durban, South Africa, for her refusal to clean the chamber pots used by their Christian guest, whose parents had been untouchables. In 1915, Gandhi had to weather a big storm of protest and opposition from his wife, some fellow inmates of his ashram at Ahmedabad, and from some of its caste Hindu benefactors over the issue of his admitting an untouchable family into the ashram.

Initially, Gandhi's anti-untouchability work was informed or guided, in the main, by his reformist social-religious morality. He regarded untouchability as an historically institutionalized sin or *adharma* on the part of the caste Hindus, who, he maintained, should bear a primary responsibility for ending it. He found no warrant for untouchability in the true teachings of Hinduism. In a speech to a Suppressed Classes Conference held at Ahmedabad in 1921, he said: 'How can the Ramayana... in which...an "untouchable" took Rama across the Ganga in his boat... countenance the idea of any human beings being untouchables?' (CW 19: 331).[6] Three years earlier, in his presidential address to the Gujarat Political Conference held in the same city, he had said: 'It is no good quoting verses from Manusmriti and other scriptures in defence of this orthodoxy [untouchability]. A number of verses in these scriptures are apocryphal, a number of them are quite meaningless' (CW 14: 77).

In August 1917, when the British colonial government, in anticipation of its 1919 Constitutional Act for the Government of India, announced that they intended to set up self-government bodies, the untouchables, who constituted about one-seventh of the population, became a politically important group. They began to make demands for their representation, in proportion to their numerical strength, in the promised self-government bodies. It was in that year (1917) that the Congress passed, for the first time in its history, a resolution calling upon the people to remove 'disabilities imposed by custom upon the Depressed Classes, the disabilities being of a most vexatious and oppressive character'. Yet, besides passing that resolution, the Congress as an organization did little for the eradication of untouchability until Gandhi's rise to its leadership.

In 1920, in the wake of the oppressive Rowlatt Acts of the colonial government and the Jallianwala massacre, the first all-India Non-cooperation Movement (against the British colonial government) was launched by the Congress under Gandhi's leadership. The fight against untouchability, along with the promotion of Hindu–Muslim unity and the settlement of the disputes between the Brahmins and the non-Brahmins, were made integral parts of that Movement. The 1920 resolution passed by the Congress for the launch of that Movement read, in part, as follows:

Inasmuch as the movement of non-cooperation [against the colonial government] can only succeed by complete co-operation amongst the people themselves, this Congress calls upon public associations to advance Hindu-Muslim unity and the Hindu delegates of this Congress call upon the leading Hindus to settle all disputes between Brahmins and non-Brahmins, wherever they may be existing, and to make a special effort to rid Hinduism of the reproach of untouchability, and respectfully urges the religious heads to help the growing desire to reform Hinduism in the matter of its treatment of the suppressed classes.[7]

Gandhi's anti-untouchability programme was strongly resented and stubbornly opposed by the orthodox Hindus. For instance, in 1920, when the Gujarat Vidyapith, the national university founded by him at Ahmedabad, decided not to recognize schools which did not admit untouchables, the Hindu orthodoxy opposed the decision and threatened to withdraw from the Gandhi-led Freedom Movement. In reply, Gandhi wrote the following in *Navajivan* (5 December 1920):

The advice I receive from one and all is that if I do not exclude the Antyajas from the national schools, the movement for swaraj will end in smoke. If I have even a little of the Vaishnava in me, God will also vouchsafe me the strength to reject the swaraj which may be won by abandoning the Antyajas. (CW 19: 73)

Some critics alleged that Gandhi's anti-untouchability work was only of instrumental value to him for mobilizing the untouchables into his mass-based Freedom Movement, which, it was further alleged, was meant to transfer power from the colonial rulers into the hands of the caste Hindus. Even C.F. Andrews, Gandhi's friend, seemed to think that he was subordinating anti-untouchability work to the programme of non-cooperation against the colonial government. Regarding this issue, Gandhi wrote to Andrews in January 1921:

You are doing an injustice to me in even allowing yourself to think that for a single moment I may be subordinating the question [of untouchability] to any others.... It [untouchability] is a bigger problem than that of gaining Indian independence but I can tackle it better if I gain the latter on the way. It is not impossible that India may free herself from English domination before India has become free of the curse of untouchability.... Do you know that today [the orthodox] who are opposing me in Gujarat are actually supporting the Government and the latter are playing them against me? (CW 19: 288–90)

Actually, Gandhi's anti-untouchability work preceded and, in the value that he attached to it, was not less important than any other work or programme of the national mass movement for political independence. He believed that the caste Hindus, who denied freedom to the untouchables, were themselves morally deficient and were thereby devoid of any moral right to undertake or support any satyagraha movement for freedom from oppression and exploitation by the external colonizers. He stated: 'We have become "pariahs of the Empire" because we have created "pariahs" in our midst. The slave owner is always more hurt than the slave. We shall be unfit to gain Swaraj so long as we would keep in bondage a fifth of the population of Hindustan' (CW 19: 20). He also said:

If it is necessary for us to buy peace with the Mussalmans as a condition of Swaraj, it is equally necessary for us to give peace to the Panchama [untouchables] before we can with any show of justice or self-respect talk of Swaraj.... Hence for me the movement of Swaraj is a movement of self-purification. (CW 24: 227)

And,

When I ask you to purify your hearts of untouchability, I ask of you nothing less than this—that you should believe in the fundamental unity and equality of man. I invite you all to forget that there are any distinctions of high and low among the children of one and the same God. (CW 57: 147)

In February 1922, the Congress Working Committee (CWC), in its meeting held at Bardoli, resolved to provide to the Depressed Classes the ordinary facilities which were available to the other citizens. Taking note of the strong prejudices of the caste Hindus against the untouchables in many places, the CWC decided to set up and maintain, with Congress funds, separate schools and separate wells for the untouchables in such places. In the following year, the CWC made a further move to tackle the persistence of caste Hindu prejudices against the untouchables. A resolution passed by the CWC in that year noted that the question of untouchability was of particular concern to the Hindu community and, accordingly, it (CWC) called upon the Hindu Mahasabha to join in the programme for the eradication of untouchability.

In 1925, Gandhi played a leading role in a satyagraha campaign of the untouchables at Vaikkam in Kerala.[8] That satyagraha was launched by the local untouchable community, with the active support of reformers from other communities, to secure for the untouchables the right to pass through the roads surrounding the Siva temple. The satyagrahis included Periyar E.V. Ramaswamy Naicker from Tamil Nadu and were once addressed by Sree Narayana Guru. Gandhi visited Vaikkam and had a long discussion with the trustees and priests of the temple at the residence of Indanthuruthil Nambudiri on 10 March 1925.

Gandhi began the debate with the question: 'Is it fair to exclude a whole section of Hindus, because of their supposed lower birth, from public roads which can be used by non-Hindus, by criminals and bad characters, and even by dogs and cattle?' Nambudiri replied that the untouchables were reaping the reward of their karma and that God is using the orthodox Hindus 'as His instruments in order to impose on them the punishment that their karma has earned for them'. He beseeched Gandhi 'to prevent the avarnas from depriving us of our age-old privileges'. To Gandhi's pleas (to Nambudiri) 'to talk with some reason at least', he replied: 'Reason is out of place in matters religious'. He referred to Sankaracharya's books in support of the prohibition against the untouchables. Gandhi's suggestions for a referendum or arbitration by reputed pundits were not accepted by Nambudiri. Gandhi asked: '...if the Maharaja [of Travancore] were to issue a smriti throwing open the roads like the Sankaracharya's smriti that you claim there is in support of the prohibition, what will you do?' Nambudiri replied that the state has the authority to issue such a smriti and that he would have to obey it (CW 26: 261–3).

From Vaikkam Gandhi went to Thiruvananthapuram, where he met the Maharani, the Prince who was soon to ascend the throne, and the Diwan, whom he apprised of the situation at Vaikkam. Gandhi also met Sree Narayana Guru at his *Math*. Before long, the Maharaja of Travancore ordered that the roads on three sides of the Vaikkam temple be opened to all.

The Vaikkam satyagraha and Gandhi's leadership of it were deeply resented and resisted by the orthodox Hindus, but Ambedkar, as we shall see ahead, regarded it, while it was going on, as an emancipatory move by Gandhi.

Ambedkar against Untouchability

Ambedkar was born in an untouchable Mahar family at Mhow in Madhya Pradesh, where his father was a Subedar Major in the British Indian army. The family hailed from Ambavade village in Ratnagiri district in Maharashtra. Ambedkar's father taught him the epics of Hinduism, the songs of Thukaram, and the egalitarian teachings of Kabir. After graduating from Elphinstone College, Mumbai, Ambedkar received financial support from the Maharajas of Baroda and Kolhapur to study abroad. He secured the PhD and DSc degrees in Economics from Columbia University and the University of London, respectively. He also qualified as a lawyer and was called to the Bar from Grey's Inn, London. In spite of all these achievements, he experienced, even when he held high office, some of the humiliating discriminations meted out to the untouchables by the caste Hindus.[9]

Ambedkar was a profound scholar of India's social, economic, and political problems. On the caste system, he wrote books which show the Shudras to be of Kshatriya lineage and the untouchables as descendents of the defeated, 'broken' tribes of ancient India, who had suffered oppression partly because of their allegiance to Buddhism, and partly because of their beef-eating.

While Gandhi believed that the historical Hinduism of his time could be reformed to purge it of untouchability and of the rigid, high-or-low rankings of the caste system, Ambedkar, through his historical analysis and experiences, arrived at the conclusion that untouchability is inseparable from the caste system and Hinduism. In his view, the untouchables and the Shudras constituted the sustaining bases of the 'graded inequality' of the caste system, whose legitimation was provided by the dogma of human inequality that is central to Brahmanic Hinduism.

Broadly speaking, there were two distinct phases in the strategy and tactics which Ambedkar actually followed for the emancipation of the untouchables from their oppressive and humiliating situation. In the first phase (roughly till the end of 1934), he sought to gain, for the Depressed Classes, equality within Hinduism by trying to reform it through non-violent direct actions by the untouchables themselves, rather than, as Gandhi insisted, by expiatory or penitential actions by the caste Hindus.[10] In the second phase (from 1935 onwards), Ambedkar, while continuing to demand emancipatory and welfare measures by the government, redefined the primary objective of the movement of the Depressed Classes to be the gaining of social equality, which called for 'liberation from Hinduism and not reform of Hinduism'.

Ambedkar himself explained the difference between these two phases in the following words:

I thought for long that we could rid the Hindu society of its evils and get the Depressed Classes incorporated into it on terms of equality. That motive inspired the Mahad Chaudar [Water] Tank Satyagraha and the Nasik Temple Entry Satyagraha. With that object in mind we burned the Manu Smriti and performed mass thread ceremonies. Experience has taught me better. I stand today absolutely convinced that for the depressed classes there can be no equality among the Hindus because on inequality rest the foundations of Hinduism. We no longer want to be part of the Hindu society.[11]

Commenting on the aforementioned Vaikkam satyagraha while it was going on, Ambedkar said that it was, for the untouchables, 'the most important event in the country today'. In his address to a 1925 conference of the depressed classes at Belgaum, he expressed his appreciation of Gandhi's anti-untouchability work in the following words:

Before Mahatma Gandhi, no politician in this country maintained that it is necessary to remove social injustice here in order to do away with tension and conflict, and that every Indian should consider it his sacred duty to do so.... However, if we look closely, one finds there is a slight disharmony...for he does not insist on the removal of untouchability as much as he insists on the propagation of Khaddar or the Hindu-Muslim unity. If he had he would have made the removal of untouchability a precondition of voting in the party. Well, be that as it may, when one is spurned by everyone, even the sympathy shown by Mahatma Gandhi is of no little importance.[12]

The Mahad Satyagraha, which Ambedkar refers to in the foregoing quotation, was conducted to establish the right of the untouchables to the drinking water of the Chowdar water tank at Mahad—a right which, though recognized in a resolution passed by the Mahad municipality in 1924, had remained unexercised by the untouchables because of the hostility of the caste Hindus. In organizing this satyagraha, Ambedkar seems to have been influenced, to some extent, by Gandhi. In his presidential address of 19 March 1927 to the Mahad conference of the depressed classes, Ambedkar, broadly in consonance with Gandhi's conception of some of the qualities which a satyagrahi should cultivate in himself or herself, said:

No lasting progress can be achieved unless we put ourselves through a three-fold process of purification. We must improve the general tone of our demeanor, re-tone our pronunciations and revitalize our thoughts. I, therefore, ask you now to take a vow from this moment to renounce eating carrion.... Make an unflinching resolve not to eat the throw-out crumbs. We will attain self-elevation only if we learn self-help, regain our self-respect, and gain self-knowledge. (Keer 1991: 71)

One of the resolutions passed at the Mahad conference called upon the caste Hindus to bury their dead animals themselves and to help the untouchables to secure their civic rights. On the second day of the conference, Ambedkar and his followers marched to the water tank and drank from it. Before long, they were attacked by the orthodox Hindus. The latter also performed a ceremony of purification of the water 'desecrated' by the touch of the untouchables. Some months later, the attackers were arrested and given short-term rigorous imprisonment. On 4 August 1927, the Mahad municipality revoked its earlier decision, taken in 1924, which had granted the untouchables access to the tank.

In preparation for another round of the struggle, Ambedkar organized a series of public meetings in Mumbai and publicized the issue in the press. Meanwhile, the orthodox Hindus of Mahad filed a civil suit claiming the tank to be their private property and obtained, on 14 December 1927, a temporary injunction preventing the untouchables access to the tank. Undeterred, Ambedkar and his followers organized a conference at Mahad on 25 December 1927 for launching a satyagraha. At the inaugural session (in a pavilion featuring Gandhi's photo), which was attended, among others, by several prominent Hindu social reformers as well as by the District Collector and the District Superintendent of Police, Ambedkar gave his historic presidential address, in which he said:

The Hindu community is set in the steel-frame of Caste system in which one caste is lower than another in social gradation involving particular privileges, rights, inhibitions, and disabilities with regard to each caste. This system has created vested interests which depend upon maintaining the inequalities resulting from the system...

...The Caste system must be abolished if the Hindu society is to be reconstructed on the basis of equality, it goes without saying...

...If we achieve success in our movement to unite all the Hindus in a single caste we shall have rendered the greatest service to the Indian nation in general and to the Hindu community in particular. (GoM 1982: 14–16)

Many of the speakers, who followed Ambedkar, denounced the *Manusmriti*. Thereafter, following a resolution passed by the conference, the *Manusmriti* was ceremoniously burned in the presence of the District Collector, Mr Hood, and the District Superintendent of Police. On the following day, however, heeding Hood's advice, Ambedkar postponed the satyagraha till the decision on the pending civil suit. That decision, taken by the local court, and upheld in appeals to the higher courts, was in favour of the depressed classes.

In March 1930, Ambedkar played a leading role in launching a satyagraha campaign against the exclusion of the untouchables from the Kalaram temple at Nasik. However, after launching the campaign, he did not continue to be personally active in it because he felt that the limited objective of the temple-entry movement, namely, to conscientize and energize the depressed classes, had already been achieved and that henceforth they should 'concentrate their energy and resources on politics and education'. Ambedkar believed that social equality is a bigger goal than getting access to the temples and that for the former Hinduism needed to be purged of the doctrine of *chaturvarna*.

THE POONA PACT

In 1928, in his speech before a Pune session of the Simon Commission (which had no Indian members on it and was therefore boycotted by the Congress), Ambedkar summarized the relative advantages, to the

Depressed Classes, of 'separate electorates' on the one hand and 'joint electorates accompanied by adult suffrage' on the other. He said:

At any rate, this must be said with certainty that a minority gets a larger advantage under joint electorates than it does under a system of separate electorates. With separate electorates the minority gets its own quota of representation and no more. The rest of the house owes no allegiance to it and is therefore not influenced by the desire to meet the wishes of the minority. The minority is thus thrown on its own resources and as no system of representation can convert a minority into a majority, it is bound to be overwhelmed. On the other hand, under a system of joint electorates and reserved seats the minority not only gets its quota of representation but something more. For, every member of the majority who has partly succeeded on the strength of the votes of the minority if not a member of the minority will certainly be a member for the minority.[13]

Ambedkar's view of the merits of a joint or common electorate was shared by Gandhi, although it must be remembered that the former was firm in his view that no joint electorate should be forced upon the depressed classes unless and until it (the joint electorate) was accompanied by adult suffrage. While Ambedkar clearly and firmly preferred a separate electorate for the untouchable minority as long as adult suffrage was not granted, Gandhi, as we shall below, maintained that untouchability was a social-religious evil or 'bar-sinister', which he and many other Hindu social reformers and freedom fighters believed had to be eliminated, and that making it (untouchability) a basis for separate electorates would be a deleterious move.

In November 1930, in a major effort to consult Indian leaders on what was eventually to become the 1935 Constitutional Act for the government of colonial India, the British Government convened the first of three London Round Table Conferences. It was boycotted by the Congress. Ambedkar participated in it and in his opening speech stated that it is 'the viewpoint of the depressed classes' that the colonial government has 'not dared to touch' the social evils from which the depressed classes have suffered and that it must be replaced by 'a Government of the people, by the people and for the people'. 'It is only in a Swaraj constitution', he went on to say, 'that we stand any chance of getting the political power in our own hands, without which we cannot bring salvation to our people'. In a historic memorandum submitted to the Conference, Ambedkar and Rao Bahadur Srinivasan stated that the depressed classes must be given adequate special representation *either* through separate electorates (in the absence of adult suffrage) *or* through 'joint electorates accompanied by adult suffrage'.

In a Supplementary Memorandum submitted to the second Round Table Conference, Ambedkar and Srinivasan reiterated their demand for separate electorates of the depressed classes and provided details of the proportional special representation to be made for them in the Central and Provincial Legislatures. They also added that the nomenclature of depressed classes was 'degrading and contemptuous' and that it should be changed to some other name, such as, 'Non-Caste Hindus', 'Protestant Hindus', or 'Non-Conformist Hindus'.

At that second Round Table Conference, with Gandhi in attendance as the sole representative of the Congress, Ambedkar, like the leaders of the other minority communities, demanded separate electorates and reserved seats for the Depressed Classes. This demand was strongly opposed by Gandhi. In his speech, he stated that the Congress represented all the interests and classes of India and that its demand for *purna swaraj* or complete independence was the only legitimate solution to India's basic problems. Recognizing Ambedkar's participation, Gandhi clarified that 'Congress will share the honour, with Dr Ambedkar, of representing the interests of the Untouchables'. Gandhi spoke:

I can understand the claims advanced by other minorities but the claims advanced on behalf of the untouchables, that to me is the 'unkindest cut of all'. *It means the perpetual bar-sinister.* I would not sell the vital interests of the untouchables even for the sake of winning the freedom of India. I claim myself in my own person to represent the vast mass of untouchables.... And I would work from one end of India to the other to tell the untouchables that *separate electorates and separate reservation is not the way to remove this bar-sinister, which is the shame, not of them, but of orthodox Hinduism.*

Let this Committee and let the whole world know that today there is a body of Hindu reformers who are pledged to remove this blot of untouchability. We do not want on our register and on our census untouchables classified as a separate class. Sikhs may remain as such in perpetuity, so may Mohammedans, so may Europeans. Will untouchables remain untouchables in perpetuity? I would far rather that Hinduism died than that Untouchability lived.... It hurts me to have to say this, but I would be untrue to the cause of the untouchables, which is as dear to me as life itself, if I did not say it. I will not bargain away their rights for the kingdom of the whole world. I am speaking with a due sense of responsibility, and I say that it is not a proper claim which is registered by Dr Ambedkar when he seeks to speak for the whole of the untouchables of India. It will create a division in Hindusim which I cannot possibly look forward to with any satisfaction whatsoever. *I do not mind untouchables, if they so desire, being converted to Islam or Christianity. I should tolerate that, but I cannot possibly tolerate what is in store for Hinduism if there are two divisions set forth in the villages.* Those who speak of the political rights of untouchables do not know their India, do not know how Indian society is today constructed, and therefore I want to say with all the emphasis that I can command that, if I was the only person to resist this thing, I would resist it with my life. (CWCD 54: 158–9. Emphasis added.)

While concluding the conference, the British prime minister said that the matter of communal representation in legislatures was of 'supreme importance' and that given the deep disagreement between Gandhi and Ambedkar, he would himself take a decision on it. Subsequently, on 17 August 1932, he announced the 'Communal Award', which gave a separate electorate and reserved seats to the Depressed Classes. He clarified that the Award could be revised only if the caste Hindus and the Depressed Classes were to come up with an agreed alternative.

Meanwhile, since his return from the Round Table Conference, Gandhi had been imprisoned at Yeravada near Pune to prevent him from resuming the civil disobedience movement. From his prison, he wrote to the Secretary of State for India that if the government were to decide to grant separate electorates to the Depressed Classes, he would, as he had pledged in the London conference, undertake a fast unto death. After the Communal Award was announced, he wrote again to confirm that he will go on a 'perpetual fast' till death or till the 'British Government, of its own motion or under pressure of public opinion, revise their decision and withdraw their scheme of communal electorates for the Depressed Classes'. On 9 September 1932, replying to a letter from the British prime minister, Gandhi summarized his reasons for opposing the separate electorate for the untouchables in the following words:

...In the establishment of separate electorate at all for the Depressed Classes I sense the injection of poison that is calculated to destroy Hinduism and do no good whatsoever to the Depressed Classes....

I should not be against even over-representation of the Depressed Classes. What I am against is their statutory separation even in a limited form, from the Hindu fold, *so long as they choose to belong to it*. Do you realize that if your decision stands and the constitution comes into being, you arrest the marvelous growth of the work of Hindu reformers, who have dedicated themselves to the uplift of their suppressed brethren in every walk of life?

I have therefore been compelled reluctantly to adhere to the decision conveyed to you. (CWCD 57: 8–9. Emphasis added.)

Reacting to Gandhi's resolve to adhere to his decision to resist the 'Communal Award' with his life, Ambedkar said that it was strange and 'beyond my comprehension' that Gandhi, who claimed to be a well-wisher of the Depressed Classes, was staking his very life in order to deprive them of the little political power they were getting through that Communal Award. On the eve of Gandhi's fast, Ambedkar stated:

I hope that the Mahatma will desist from carrying out the extreme step contemplated by him. We mean no harm to the Hindu society when we demand separate electorates. If we choose separate electorates, we do so in order to avoid the total dependence on the sweet will of the Caste Hindus in matters affecting our destiny....

... [T]he Mahatma is...fostering the spirit of hatred between the Hindu community and the Depressed Classes by resorting to this method and thereby widening the existing gulf between the two. (Ambedkar 1990b: 316–17)

Ambedkar had the support of most of the leaders of the Depressed Classes. A significant opposition was that of M.C. Rajah, the leader of the Depressed Classes of the Madras Province and Member of the Central Legislature, who had (before the announcement of the Communal Award) entered into a Pact with B.S. Moonje of the Hindu Mahasabha in support of joint electorates. He felt that the Depressed Classes, who were already 'socially untouchable', would become, under the Communal Award's scheme of separate electorates, 'politically untouchable' as well.

As Gandhi prepared to begin his 'epic fast' on 20 September 1932, in the Yeravada Jail at Pune, leaders of the caste Hindus and the Depressed Classes intensified their consultations for finding an agreed alternative to the scheme of separate electorates for the untouchables so as to save Gandhi's life.

By that time it had become clear to all concerned that Gandhi's objection was only to the creation of separate electorates for the untouchables, and not to the reservation of electoral seats for them. It was also clear to them that Gandhi was in favour of the widest possible franchise for, and representation by, them.

Ambedkar found himself placed 'in a greater and graver dilemma' than any other negotiator. On the same day of the start of Gandhi's fast in jail at Pune, Ambedkar, in a meeting with caste Hindu leaders and other leaders (for example, M.C. Rajah) of the Depressed Classes at Mumbai, agreed to have the scheme of separate electorates replaced by a scheme combining primary election, by the Depressed Classes, of a panel of Depressed Classes candidates and a secondary election by the common or joint electorate. When this development was conveyed to Gandhi, he desired a dialogue with Ambedkar. They met in the jail on 22–23 September 1932. The mutual respect and concern shown in their conversation was as remarkable and, arguably, as consequential as was their hard bargaining on the terms of their agreement. Ambedkar began by saying: 'Mahatmaji, you must come to our rescue'. Gandhi, at one point during their discussion, said to Ambedkar:

You have a perfect right to demand cent per cent security by statutory safeguards, but from my fiery bed I beg of you not to insist upon that right. I am here today to ask for a reprieve for my Caste Hindu brethren. Thank God, their conscience has been roused.... I entreat you...not to deprive Hinduism of a last chance to make a voluntary expiation for its sinful past. Give me the chance of working among the Caste Hindus. (Pyarelal 1932: 70–1)

With the consent of Gandhi and Ambedkar, the scheme of primary and secondary elections was formally drafted into the 'Poona Pact' and signed by the leaders of the caste Hindus and the Depressed Classes on 24 September 1932. It was cabled to the British government, who was soon to convey its approval. Meanwhile, on 25 September, a public meeting of the leaders of the caste Hindus and Depressed Classes, chaired by Pandit Madan Mohan Malaviya at Mumbai, ratified the Poona Pact and passed an accompanying resolution on a trans-election programme of actions for the removal of untouchability. That resolution, which had the pre-endorsement of Gandhi (from his prison at Yeravada) and which was passed by the Mumbai conference in the presence of Ambedkar, Rajah, etc., read, in part, as follows:

This Conference resolves that henceforth, amongst Hindus, no one shall be regarded as an untouchable by reason of his birth and those who have been so regarded hitherto will have the same rights as the other Hindus in regard to the use of public wells, public roads and other public institutions. *This right shall have statutory recognition at the first opportunity and shall be one of the earliest acts of the Swaraj Parliament, if it shall not have received such recognition before that time.* (CWCD 57: 118. Emphasis added.)

Gandhi regarded this resolution to contain the vital, necessary condition of the formal Poona Pact (1932) in settlement of the conflict over the colonial government's 'communal award' of a separate electorate for the untouchables. It was only on the promisory strength of that resolution of the leaders of the caste Hindus and the Depressed Classes, and after the approval of the Poona Pact by the British government, that Gandhi broke his fast, in the presence of, among others, Rabindranath Tagore, on 26 September 1932.

Immediately after breaking the fast, Gandhi, in a press statement, thanked Ambedkar and the other leaders of the untouchables and promised that he would hold himself hostage for the fulfilment, by the caste Hindus, of their untouchability-abolition resolution. He also said that if the caste Hindus failed to relentlessly pursue their resolution for abolishing untouchability, he would resume his fast. A part of his press statement is quoted below:

The settlement arrived at is, so far as I can see, a generous gesture on all sides. It is a meeting of hearts, and *my Hindu gratitude is due to Dr Ambedkar, Rao Bahadur Srinivasan and their party on the one hand and Rao Bahadur M.C. Rajah on the other.* They could have taken up an uncompromising and defiant attitude by way of punishment to the so-called caste Hindus for the sins of generations. If they had done so, I at least could not have resented their attitude and my death would have been but a trifling price exacted for the tortures that the outcastes of Hinduism have been going through for unknown generations. But they chose a nobler path and have thus shown that they have followed the precept of forgiveness enjoined by all religions. Let me hope that the caste Hindus will prove themselves worthy of this forgiveness and carry out to the letter and spirit every clause of the settlement with all its implications. (CWCD 57: 123–5. Emphasis added.)

Ambedkar's gratitude to Gandhi was expressed by him in his speech in the Mumbai Conference, which ratified the Poona Pact. After giving to Gandhi 'a large part of the credit' for the amicable settlement of their dispute, he added: 'I must confess that I was surprised, immensely surprised, when I met him that there was so much in common between him and me' (Pyarelal 1932: 188). Ambedkar, however, went on to say that he still remained 'unconvinced that for minority representation separate electorates are an evil'. He also said that joint electorates or any other electoral arrangement 'cannot be a solution of the larger social problem'. He hoped that ways and means would be devised 'whereby it would be possible for the Depressed Classes not only to be part and parcel of the Hindu community but also to occupy an honourable position, a position of equality of status in the community' (ibid.: 190).

HARIJAN SEVAK SANGH

After the Poona Pact, Gandhi pursued a concerted programme of action to persuade the caste Hindus to remove untouchability. That programme included the founding of the Harijan Sevak Sangh (which was originally named All-India Anti-Untouchability League), publication of a new weekly journal, *Harijan*, three fasts for the cause of the Harijans and a nine-month 'Harijan Tour' through the length and breadth of the country from November 1933 to August 1934. In all this, Gandhi faced stiff opposition from the orthodox Hindus and virulent criticism from Ambedkar. The latter blamed Gandhi for his failure to recognize that untouchability and inequality of status are inherent in the caste system or the *varnashramadharma*, and that the former cannot be abolished without the annihilation of the latter. The orthodox Hindus opposed Gandhi's anti-untouchability movement, which they perceived to be undermining the Hindu community and its *varnadharma*. They organized protest demonstrations against him during his Harijan Tour. Some of those demonstrations turned violent, with even an incidence of bomb throwing, in July 1934, at what was mistakenly taken to be the car in which Gandhi was travelling in Pune.

The opposition of the orthodox/*sanatanist* Hindus did not deter Gandhi from his commitment to purge Hinduism of the evil of untouchability, but it did make him extremely cautious about his reformist strategy towards caste and varna. According to him, the participation of the caste Hindus was necessary both for the effectiveness of the non-violent mass political movement for freedom from colonial rule and for the success of the movement against untouchability.

After Vaikkam, Gandhi had been feeling that he, even in his fight against untouchability, had to be seen as a protector of the caste Hindus as well. Until about 1935, he did not share Ambedkar's sense of urgency to extend the anti-untouchability programme into a wider public-political programme that would include campaigns against the caste-based discriminations on inter-dining, intermarriages, etc. As noted by Bhikhu Parekh, Gandhi was 'involved in several battles, that against untouchability being only one of them, and political exigencies inevitably dictated their order of importance' (Parekh 1999: 270). Similarly, Rajmohan Gandhi writes: 'He [Gandhi] would have united pro-orthodox ranks in opposition if he had commenced with an attack on caste. He chose to zero in on an evil [untouchability] none could defend' (Gandhi 1995: 241).

Both the caste Hindus and the Depressed Classes were part of the Gandhi-led, non-violent, mass-movement of all the peoples of India for freedom from colonial rule. His emancipatory genius lay in the fact that he perceived that the unity of this mass movement, consistent with 'the universally accepted first principles of morality', had to be created and maintained if it was to withstand and overcome the ideological defence and the divide-and-rule mechanisms of imperialist rule. His life-risking political fasts, which was incomprehensible not only to his opponents but also to many of his close colleagues, were part of his satyagrahic mass movement for *swaraj*. His message to the caste Hindus was that untouchability is a sin or adharma and that as long as they denied freedom to the 'untouchables', they lacked both the moral integrity and the political capacity for a non-violent political struggle for freedom from imperialist oppression. His message to the Depressed Classes was that they should, besides following the rules of cleanliness and self-empowerment, join or support the social reformers in sensitizing the caste Hindus to the fact that untouchability is primarily a sin or crime on their part and that they should remove it for purifying their religion and thereby making the Hindu society conform to the principles of truth and justice.

Gandhi did not view his anti-untouchability programme as a subordinate component of the Swaraj movement. After his release from the Yeravada jail in May 1933, he, in fact, temporarily suspended the Mass Civil Disobedience Movement in order to concentrate on anti-untouchability work.

Regarding the varnadharma of the caste system, however, Gandhi had, till the mid-1930s, a conservative attitude.[14] The Hindu epics had given him a romantic picture of varnashramadharma in ancient India. He imagined it, in an uncritical manner, to have been a harmonious division of occupations or duties, which he believed had been free from untouchability or the high/low status-discriminations of the present-day caste system. He wrote:

My varnashrama enables me to dine with anybody who will give me clean food, be he Hindu, Muslim, Christian, Parsi, whatever he is. My varnashrama accommodates a Pariah girl under my own roof as my own daughter. My varnashrama accommodates many Panchama families with whom I dine with the greatest pleasure—to dine with whom is a privilege. (CW 34: 511–12)

In September 1927, he admitted that 'varnashrama as it is at present understood and practised is a monstrous parody of the original' and that it should be demolished (CW 35: 2). From 1935 onwards, Gandhi's approach to the reform of caste and varna took a radically liberal-egalitarian direction. This change had partly to do with Ambedkar's vehement criticisms. Those criticisms and Gandhi's responses to some of them were occasioned by, and pertained to, the working of the Harijan Sevak Sangh and its weekly journal, Harijan.

The Harijan Sevak Sangh was the new name chosen by Gandhi (in November 1932) for the All-India Anti-Untouchability League that was established on 26 October 1932, with G.D. Birla as President and Amritlal Thakkar as General Secretary.[15] The Central Board of the League included Ambedkar and two other leaders of the Depressed Classes. The objective of the League was to carry out propaganda against untouchability and to take steps to get public wells, roads, schools, temples, etc., declared open to the Depressed Classes.

On 3 November 1932, Birla and Thakkar issued a press statement indicating that the work of the League would be confined to a constructive programme for 'the uplift of Depressed Classes educationally, economically and socially, which itself will go a great way to remove untouchability'. They noted that 'reasonable persons among the Sanatanists', who are 'not much against the removal of untouchability as such', are against inter-caste dinners and marriages. Hence, they stated: 'Social reforms like the abolition of the caste system and inter-caste dining are kept outside the scope of the League' (CWCD 62: 291).

Concurring with the Birla-Thakkar statement, Gandhi wrote:

Correspondents have asked whether inter-dining and inter-marriage are part of the movement against untouchability. In my opinion they are not. They touch the caste men equally with the outcastes. It is, therefore, not obligatory on an anti-untouchability worker to devote himself or herself to inter-dining and intermarriage reform. Personally, I am of opinion that this reform is coming sooner than we expect. Restriction on inter-caste dining and inter-caste marriage is no part of Hindu religion.... Wherever...people voluntarily take part in functions where 'touchables' and 'untouchables', Hindus and non-Hindus are invited to join dinner parties, I welcome them as a healthy sign. But I should never dream of making this reform, however desirable in itself it may be, part of an all-India reform which has been long overdue. (CWCD 57: 328–9)

Since my youth upward I have consistently dined with all so long as the rules of cleanliness have been observed. But that has nothing to do with the present movement. Inter-dining and the rest is a question for each individual to determine for himself. The movement organized by the Servants of Untouchables Society stands for simple removal of untouchability in every shape and form, in so far as it is special to the so-called untouchables. They would have the same public rights and facilities as are enjoyed by every other Hindu, that is to say, they should have access to all public institutions, such as wells, schools, roads, temples, etc. (CWCD 62: 138)

Ambedkar had agreed to join the League/Sangh on its Central Board. During his sea voyage to London for the third Round Table Conference, he wrote, on 14 November 1932, to Thakkar, giving his suggestions as to what the Sangh should do. He wrote that instead of attempting to help 'a few [untouchable] individuals at random' to become personally virtuous through temperance, gymnasium, co-operation, libraries, schools, etc., the League/Sangh should try to secure civic rights and social justice for the untouchables, for example, their right of access to the village wells, village schools, public conveyance, etc. He also suggested that the

Sangh should have an army of workers to lead the Depressed Classes in direct action for securing civic rights and to facilitate their admission to the houses of the caste Hindus as guests or servants. He concluded his letter by stating that these measures of social justice, rather than the electoral mechanism of joint or separate electorate, would bring about love and unity between the touchables and untouchables.

Ambedkar however did not receive any response from the Sangh, from which he and the two other leaders of the Depressed Classes soon dissociated themselves. The consequent absence of any leader of the Depressed Classes in the Central Board of the Sangh was justified by Gandhi in the following words:

The welfare work for the Untouchables is a penance which the Hindus have to do for the sin of untouchability. The money that has been collected has been contributed by the Hindus. From both points of view the Hindus alone must run the Sangh. Neither ethics nor right would justify Untouchables in claiming a seat on the Board of the Sangh. (Ambedkar 1990b: 142)

Ambedkar understandably disapproved this decision taken by Gandhi. Their relationship soured considerably over this issue.

On Caste and Hinduism

In preparation for launching his weekly newspaper, *Harijan*, Gandhi requested Ambedkar for a message for its inaugural issue that was to come out on 11 February 1933. Instead of any message, which he felt would not be received with respect by the caste Hindus, Ambedkar gave, for publication, the following statement of his views on 'the momentous issue of Hindu social organization': 'The outcaste [untouchable] is a bye-product of the caste system. There will be outcastes as long as there are castes. Nothing can emancipate the outcaste except the destruction of the caste system. Nothing can help to save Hindus and ensure their survival in the coming struggle except purging of the Hindu faith of this odious and vicious dogma' (CWCD 59: 227).

In Gandhi's rejoinder, which he published in the same inaugural issue, he wrote that Ambedkar has every reason to feel bitter about what the caste Hindus have been doing to him as a member of the Depressed Classes. This, Gandhi added, is a shame to the caste Hindus and not to Ambedkar, whom Gandhi assured that 'there are today thousands of caste Hindus who would listen to his message with the same respect and consideration that they would give to that of any other leader'. However, expressing his disagreement with Ambedkar's views on the caste system, Gandhi went on to write:

I do not believe the caste system, even as distinguished from varnashrama, to be an 'odious and vicious dogma'. It has its limitations and its defects, but there is nothing sinful about it, as there is about untouchability..... Untouchability is the product...not of the caste system, but of the distinction of high and low that has crept into Hinduism and is corroding it. The attack on untouchability is thus an attack upon this 'high-and-low'ness. The moment untouchability goes, the caste system itself will be purified, that is to say, according to my dream, it will resolve itself into the true varnadharma....
...[S]uch being my faith, I have always respectfully differed from those distinguished countrymen, Dr Ambedkar among them, who have held that untouchability will not go without the destruction of varnashramadharma.... At the present moment, it is the 'untouchable', the outcaste, with whom all Hindu reformers, whether they believe in varnashrama or not, have agreed to deal. The opposition to untouchability is common to both. Therefore, the present joint fight is restricted to the removal of untouchability, and I would invite Dr Ambedkar and those who think with him to throw themselves, heart and soul, into the campaign against the monster of untouchability. It is highly likely that at the end of it we shall all find that there is nothing to fight against in varnashrama. If however, varnashrama even then looks an ugly thing, the whole of Hindu society will fight it. (CWCD 59: 228–9)

In response to an open letter from Sir Govindrao Madgaonkar, a former judge of the Bombay High Court, Gandhi wrote in *Harijan*, dated 16 November 1935:

Varnashrama of the Shastras is today non-existent in practice. The present caste system is the very antithesis of varnashrama. The sooner public opinion abolishes it the better.
    In varnashrama there was and should be no prohibition of intermarriage or inter-dining.... Though there is in varnashrama no prohibition against intermarriage and inter-dining, there can be no compulsion. It must be left to the unfettered choice of the individual as to where he or she will marry or dine. (CWCD 68: 151–2)

The above distinction which Gandhi made between the caste system and varnadharma and his qualified upholding of the latter were restated and re-emphasized by him in his critique of Ambedkar's monograph, entitled 'The Annihilation of Caste' (1936).[16] In that monograph, Ambedkar argued that the Hindu society has been ruined by caste and *chaturvarnya*, both of which, besides denying knowledge to the masses, are opposed to the principles of liberty, equality, and fraternity. Hence, he went on argue that the divine authority of the Hindu *shastras*, which uphold caste and chaturvarnya, should be rejected, as was done by the Buddha and Guru Nanak. Ambedkar stated that the doctrine of chaturvarnya, as upheld, somewhat differently, by the Arya Samajists and by Gandhi, was unacceptable to him.

In a two-part review-article on Ambedkar's monograph,[17] Gandhi wrote that the *savarna* Hindus 'have to correct their belief and their conduct' in the light of Ambedkar's criticism. Both the reformers and the orthodox Hindus, Gandhi admitted, would gain by reading Ambedkar. Gandhi also admitted that the caste system 'is harmful to spiritual and national growth'. He however went on to state that the *varnadharma* 'teaches that we have each one of us to earn our bread by following the ancestral calling' and that it has 'neither untouchability nor any high or low status-ranking' and that therefore it is 'conducive to the welfare of humanity'. Gandhi also criticized Ambedkar for judging Hinduism by its worst specimens rather than by the best it has produced, for example, Chaitanya, Jnyandeo, Tukaram, Tiruvallur, Ramkrishna Paramahansa, and Vivekananda.

In his response to Gandhi's criticism, Ambedkar appreciated Gandhi's admission that caste is harmful to spiritual and national growth. Yet his continued belief in varna troubled Ambedkar as it is 'fundamentally opposed to democracy' and, as the Buddhists have shown long ago, cannot be rationally defended. He added that Gandhi was 'preaching caste under the name of varna' in order to sustain the support of the orthodox and unorthodox Hindus for the movement for Swaraj. According to Ambedkar, there is, under Hinduism and its caste/varna system, a 'fundamentally wrong relationship' between high-caste men and low-caste men. Without attempting to bring about any structural change of that wrong relationship, Gandhi, Ambedkar stated, was trying to present the Hindu society as a tolerable and good religious community. He went on to write that by focusing on improving the 'personal character' of the caste Hindus, Gandhi was 'wasting his energy and hugging an illusion'. The social system of the Hindus, namely, the caste/varna system, said Ambedkar, is what has to be changed. In other words, according to him, the Hindu society had to be transformed into a casteless society.[18]

Some of these criticisms were restated and elaborated by Ambedkar in two publications: 'Mr Gandhi and the Emancipation of the Untouchables' (1942/1943)[19]; and *What Congress and Gandhi Have Done to the Untouchables* (1945).[20] In the former, Ambedkar wrote that Gandhi's Quit India programme was not a 'war for freedom', equality, justice, or democracy, but was in fact a 'war for power' for the Hindu middle class and capitalists. Gandhi, like every other Hindu, was for

Ambedkar, 'a social Tory and political Radical' (Ambedkar 1990b: 430). He went on to add that Gandhi's 'liberalism is only a very thin veneer which sits very lightly on him as dust does on one's boots'. Ambedkar wrote that the Hindu majority and the Untouchable minority constitute two 'permanent communities', which are 'separated by a fundamental and deadly antagonism' (Ambedkar 1990b: 416). Hence, according to Ambedkar, the untouchables were justified in demanding constitutional safeguards of their political rights, including, among other things, a separate electorate and separate settlements.

In the second of the two aforementioned publications, Ambedkar criticized Gandhi and the Congress for maintaining separate wells and separate schools for the untouchables. That policy revealed to Ambedkar that 'the Congress was not out for the abolition of untouchability', but was only trying 'to undertake amelioration of the condition of the Untouchables'. He also wrote that the Congress 'washed its hands off the problem of Untouchables' by calling upon the Hindu Mahasabha to join in the programme for the eradication of untouchability. Viewing the 1932 Poona Pact as a 'mean deal', he went on to point out that the Congress was using the electoral arrangement of that Pact to manoeuvre the election of docile or subservient candidates from the SCs. Even the temple-entry movement, he said, was being used for the sake of the political power of the Congress. 'Under Gandhism', he added, 'the Untouchables are to be eternal scavengers' and, at best, 'classed as Shudras instead of being classed as Ati-Shudras'. 'Barring this illusory campaign against Untouchability', wrote Ambedkar, 'Gandhism is simply another form of Sanatanism which is the ancient name for militant orthodox Hinduism' (Rodrigues 2002: 170).

A reply to some of these criticisms was given by Gandhi's colleague, C. Rajagopalachari, in his *Ambedkar Refuted* (Rajagopalachari 1946). He tried to show that the condition of the SCs has improved considerably as a direct result of the untouchability-abolition movement undertaken by Gandhi and the Congress and that it compared favourably with the conditions of similar sections of society in USA, South Africa, etc.

Gandhi himself continued to appreciate the fact that Ambedkar's bitterness towards the caste Hindus, including himself, was based on his humiliating experiences of caste-based oppression. Recognizing the validity of some of his criticisms, Gandhi pursued a more radical approach to caste-reform. As if in reaction to Ambedkar's criticism that Gandhism stands for the iron-law of hereditary professions in respect of the SCs, Gandhi stated in December 1947 that a *bhangi* 'should not be forced to clean lavatories today' and that if he can become a barrister, he should not be prevented from doing so. Since a decade earlier, Gandhi, as we saw above, had been advocating the voluntary removal of the caste-prohibitions on intermarriages and inter-dining. He in fact exemplified the practice of inter-dining in his home and ashrams. In the last few years of his life, it was his practice to attend or bless only those weddings, of which one of the parties was a Harijan.

Gandhi seems to have come to believe that by eradicating untouchability, he was in fact undermining the caste system. Regarding this, Nehru spoke to the Hungarian journalist Tibor Mende in January 1956, as follows:

I spoke to Gandhi repeatedly: why don't you hit out at the caste system directly? He said that he did not believe in the caste system except in some idealized form of occupations and all that; but that the present system was thoroughly bad and must go. 'I am undermining it completely,' he said, 'by my tackling untouchability.'.... 'If untouchability goes,' he said, 'the caste system goes'. (Mende 1958: 24–7)

When they met at the Yeravada prison on 4 February 1933 to discuss the issue of two pending temple-entry bills, on which Gandhi sought Ambedkar's support, the latter replied that the immediate concern of the Depressed Classes was not temple entry, but securing political power. He added:

The object of this effort [temple-entry legislation] could be that you want the depressed classes to be retained in the Hindu religion, in which case I am inclined to believe that it is not sufficient in the present awakened state of the depressed classes.... If I call myself a Hindu I am obliged to accept that by birth I belong to a low caste. Hence I think I must ask the Hindus to show me some sacred authority which would rule out this feeling of lowliness. If it cannot be, I should say goodbye to Hinduism. (CW 53: 499)

Ambedkar's intention to leave Hinduism and to convert to another religion was reiterated by him at a conference of the Depressed Classes at Yeola in Maharashtra on 13 October 1935. There, he declared: 'Unfortunately for me, I was born a Hindu Untouchable.... I solemnly assure you that I will not die a Hindu'.[21] Less than two months before his death on 6 December 1956, he actually converted to Buddhism, which he said was a religion of equality and compassion.

It is beyond the limited scope of the present paper to analyse the implications of Ambedkar's conversion to Buddhism. Here, I can only very briefly indicate the nature of Gandhi's reaction to Ambedkar's 1933 and 1935 announcements of his intention to leave Hinduism.

In reaction to Ambedkar's threat (of February 1933) to leave Hinduism, Gandhi said to him: 'If you repudiate us and go away I would think that we only deserved it' (CW 53: 499). Gandhi added that the *savarna* Hindus should, in atonement for their sin, give equal status to the Harijans not only in schools, railways, etc., but also before God and that therefore they should, as a matter of their duty, 'throw open the temple doors for the Harijans whether or not they wish to come in'. Gandhi admitted that 'the secession of stalwarts like Dr Ambedkar can but weaken the defences of Harijans' (CWCD 68: 93–4). He advised the *savarna* Hindus as follows:

If...any Harijan wants to give up Hinduism, he should be entirely free to do so.... The course before savarnas is...on the one hand not to interfere with Harijans wishing to leave the Hindu fold...and, on the other hand, to insist on full justice being done to Harijans in every walk of life.... The greatest hardship felt by thousands of Harijans is want of pure water for drinking and domestic use, denial of access to public schools and other institutions, constant pinpricks in villages and, last but not least, denial of access to temples of worship.... If they as a mass give up Hinduism, they will do so because of these common disabilities which brand them as lepers of Hindu society. (CWCD 68: 315–16)

Two Complementary Moves against Untouchability

In 1946, Ambedkar was elected to the Constituent Assembly (CA) from Bengal. After Bengal was partitioned in the following year, he lost his seat in the CA and was re-elected into it on nomination by the Mumbai Legislative Congress Party. In August 1947, he became chairman of the Constitution Drafting Committee of the CA. Gandhi publicly expressed his appreciation of Ambedkar's role in the Constituent Assembly and is reported to have effectively advised Jawaharlal Nehru and Sardar Vallabhbhai Patel to invite Ambedkar into independent India's first cabinet of ministers.[22]

In a very valuable jurisprudential reading of Ambedkar's pioneering contribution to the emancipation of the Dalits, Upendra Baxi singles him out as 'the first, and so far the only major, Indian thinker' to have interrogated 'the organized millennial lawlessness structured through the "sacred" law of an ancient civilization' (Baxi 1995: 143). Baxi points out that Ambedkar, departing from 'the liberal paradigm of rights and justice', pioneered an emancipatory conception of the rights of the untouchables in two interrelated ways. Firstly, he identified their basic human needs and transformed them into human rights. Secondly, in his theory, those rights 'emerge as legal entitlements casting corresponding obligations on the members of civil society', with the state being recognized as having the power and the duty 'to eradicate obdurate discriminatory practices in civil society'. With reference to Articles 17 and 23 of the Constitution, Baxi writes insightfully: 'The constitutional articulation is remarkable in that it, in a chapter on fundamental rights, creates specific offences and that the rights themselves are limitations on the *power* of civil society rather than that of the state' (ibid.: 144).

Turning to Gandhi, without denying his 'unquestioned commitment to the cause of "eradication" of untouchability or his moral integrity', Baxi, following E.M.S. Namboodripad, seems to think that Gandhi's 'constructive work' for Harijans was more 'an aspect of political tactics' to serve the class interests of the bourgeoisie than 'an aspect of conscientious struggle to fundamentally change the social structure of Hinduism' (Baxi 1995: 137). According to Baxi, the untouchables, as a result of Gandhi's political tactics, may be 'the immediate and perhaps long-term losers'. Hence, in Baxi's view, the identity of Ambedkar as an iconoclast or rebel (who, for instance, set aflame the Manusmriti in 1927 and converted to Buddhism shortly before his death) is preferable to the identity of the Ambedkar, 'whose spirit was domesticated, for all practical purposes, by the Mahatma and whose national presence was marginalized by his political heir' (ibid.: 130).

While I find much to admire and accept in Baxi's stimulating analysis of Ambedkar's emancipatory thought and work, I feel that his reading of its relation to Gandhi's untouchability-eradication programme is somewhat problematic. His reading seems to me to be deficient in that it does not recognize the collective authorship of the Indian constitutional innovation of the conventional liberal theory of rights and justice. In the collective authorship, which I am alluding to, Ambedkar, as I learn from Baxi's path-breaking jurisprudential analysis, played a truly pioneering emancipatory role. Not a less pioneering emancipatory role, I feel, was also played by Gandhi, who, as I have tried to show in the foregoing pages, was in constant discursive or dialogic interaction with Ambedkar.[23] It was a discursively interactive process, which seems to me to be reflective and, perhaps, generative of a certain complementariness or, at least, compatibility between their different approaches to the rights and the duties of the untouchables and the touchables.

Regarding the Indian Constitution's innovation of the conventional liberal notions of rights and justice, I feel that we need to recognize the collective authorship of what may be called the pre-drafting of some of those innovations before the CA was formed. Instances of such pre-drafting may be seen in: (i) the 1931 Karachi Resolution of the Congress on the Fundamental Rights of the citizens, which was drafted by Nehru in consultation with Gandhi, who, in fact, was the mover of that Resolution in the Congress session; (ii) the two Memoranda on the Claims of the Depressed Classes, submitted by Ambedkar and Srinivasan to the Round Table Conferences; (iii) Gandhi's statements on untouchability-eradication during and after the second Round Table Conference; and (iv) the 1932 Poona Pact and its related Gandhi-endorsed untouchability-abolition resolution of the Mumbai conference of the leaders of the *savarna* Hindus and Depressed Classes, including, among others, Ambedkar himself.

In fact, when Article 17 of the Constitution (which abolishes untouchability) was passed by the CA on 29 November 1948, its members invoked the memory of Mahatma Gandhi, who had died at the hands of his assassin ten months earlier, with the chanting of '*Mahatma Gandhi Ki Jai!*' In that chanting, Baxi sees a slighting of the emancipatory role of Ambedkar (Baxi 1995: 129). Somewhat differently from that reading, I am inclined to think that the memory invoked by the CA was of a Mahatma, who had publicly expressed, immediately after the 1932 Poona Pact was signed, his 'Hindu gratitude' to Ambedkar, Srinivasan, and Rajah for generously and forgivingly sharing the collective authorship of a pre-constitutional formulation of what may be called a joint or common approach of the untouchables and the touchables to removing the millennial social-religious evil of untouchability. 'The agreement between the Mahatma and Ambedkar [in the Poona Pact]', as noted by Ravinder Kumar, 'saved a society from turning into itself and committing collective suicide'. In this connection, it may be noted that Ambedkar's eventual conversion to Buddhism was a legitimate and respectable reaction by him to the actual limitations of the working of the joint approach that was begun with the Poona Pact.[24]

On the eve of the day of his assassination, Gandhi wrote a draft resolution for the consideration of the Congress. In it, which has come to be known as his 'Last Will', he called for the disbanding of the Congress and the formation of a new organization to be called the Lok Sevak Sangh, to which the Harijan Sevak Sangh was to be affiliated. He stipulated that every Hindu member of the Lok Sevak Sangh had to abjure 'untouchability in any shape or form in his own person or in his own family'. In writing that draft resolution for the Congress, Gandhi, I presume, had in his mind, among other considerations, some of Ambedkar's long-standing criticisms of himself (Gandhi) and the Congress. Gandhi seems to me to have been appreciative of the fact that Ambedkar's emancipatory approach, which emphasized the human rights of the Dalits,[25] was, in a broad sense, compatible with, if not complementary to, his own approach, which emphasized the primary or co-primary responsibility or human duty of the caste Hindus to remove the denials or impairments which they have been causing to the human rights of the so-called untouchables.

As we saw above, although 'Gandhism' was denounced by Ambedkar in the later phase of his public-political career, he had earlier expressed his appreciation of the value of Gandhi's distinctive emphasis on the duty of the caste Hindus to remove untouchability. For instance, when they met to negotiate the terms of the 1932 Poona Pact, Ambedkar said to Gandhi (then on the third day of his fast): 'We do realize that you are of immense help to us [depressed classes]'. A few years earlier, Ambedkar, as we saw above, had acknowledged at a conference of the Depressed Classes that Gandhi's approach, which emphasized the 'sacred duty' of 'every Indian' to remove social injustice, was 'of no little importance'.

Hence, we may conclude that Gandhi and Ambedkar made, sometimes together and sometimes separately, truly pioneering contributions to a mass political movement for an as yet incomplete multifaceted programme for human freedom from untouchability, imperialism, etc.[26] Recognizing the compatibility, if not a mutual supplementarity, between their emancipatory legacies in the religious and political spheres may perhaps be needed today for a co-operative revitalization of our unfinished moral-political movement against untouchability.

NOTES

1. Relatedly, Article 15 of the Constitution prohibits the state from discriminating against any citizen only on grounds of caste, religion, race, sex, place of birth, or any of them. Similarly, traffic in human beings and *begar* and similar other forms of forced labour are prohibited by Article 23.
2. In this essay, 'scheduled castes', 'depressed classes', 'untouchables', '*avarnas*', 'Harijans', 'Dalits', '*antyajas*', and '*Panchama*' are used interchangeably.
3. Valerian Rodrigues (1994: 137) writes: 'Our political and intellectual arena is still stamped with these legacies [from Gandhi and Ambedkar]'. See also Rodrigues (2002).
4. Pertinently, taking note of an 'organized neglect', by the academia, of Ambedkar's thought and work, Upendra Baxi wrote in 1995: '... our understanding of leading historic figures like Gandhi or Nehru

is bound to remain incomplete, both in the sense of biography and history, in the absence of the grasp of their relations with Ambedkar' (pp. 123–4).

5. In this context, see Nandy (1980: 71).

6. I shall be using CW and CWCD to refer to the printed version and the CD Rom version, respectively, of *Gandhi's Collected Works*. The two versions—both brought out by the Publications Division of the Government of India—do not tally in all respects, especially as regards the volume numbering and pagination.

7. As quoted in Zelliot (1988: 184–5).

8. For a valuable contextual analysis of Gandhi's role in this satyagraha, see Parekh (1999).

9. Ambedkar served as Professor and Principal of the Government Law College, Bombay, Member of the Bombay Legislative Council, Labour Member of the Viceroy's Executive Council, Law Minister in Nehru's cabinet, and Chairman of the Constitution Drafting Committee of the Constituent Assembly. He founded and led the Independent Labour Party and the Scheduled Caste Federation (SCF), and conceived the Republican Party of India, which was organized after his death.

10. In his first political activity for the Dalits, Ambedkar, in his testimony before the Southborough Committee (1919), called for lowering the taxable rating level for the franchise of the Depressed Classes and for either reserved electoral seats or a separate electorate. In the following year, he launched a journal, *Mook Nayak* (Leader of the Dumb).

11. From Ambedkar's speech in April 1942; see GoM (1982: 250).

12. As quoted in Jaffrelot (2004: 63).

13. Quoted in Jaffrelot (2004: 55).

14. It should however be noted that from as early as 1897, if not earlier, Gandhi had begun following, both in his home and in his ashrams, the anti-caste practice of inter-dining. Even his crossing the seawaters to go to London for studies was in violation of a customary rule of his caste!

15. By then Gandhi had begun to call the untouchables 'Harijans' (people of God).

16. This was originally written as an address to the 1936 annual conference of the Jat Pat Todak Mandal of Lahore, a social-reform organization set up by the Arya Samaj. But the senior leaders of the Mandal objected to Ambedkar's attack, in his advance lecture-text, on the *chaturvarnya* and they succeeded in cancelling the conference. Ambedkar then published his lecture-text separately. It is included in Ambedkar (1979: 22–96), vol. 1. Selected parts of it appear in Rodrigues (2002: 263–305).

17. *Harijan*, 11 and 18 July 1936; CWCD 69: 205–7, and 226–7.

18. Ambedkar's 'Reply to the Mahatma' is included in Ambedkar (1979), vol. 1. Selected parts from it appear in Rodrigues (2002: 306–19).

19. This was written as a Paper for a Conference of the Institute of Pacific Relations, held in Quebec, Canada, in December 1942. It was published in the Proceedings of that Conference, republished as a monograph by Thackar & Co., Bombay, in 1943, and is included in Ambedkar (1990b).
20. Ambedkar (1990b: 274–97). It is included as an Appendix in Ahir (1995: 79–106).
21. Quoted in Jaffrelot (2004: 120).
22. See Gandhi (1995: 260–1) and Jaffrelot (2004: 100). Ambedkar was Law Minister in Nehru's cabinet till September 1951, when he resigned partly because his proposals for reforming the Hindu Code Bill were not effectively backed by Nehru.
23. On the distinctive discursive merits of Gandhi's satyagraha, see Pantham (1987).
24. Kumar (1987). For valuable analyses of Ambedkar's conversion, see Valerian Rodrigues, 'Making a Tradition Critical: Ambedkar's Reading of Buddhism', in Peter Robb (ed.), *Dalit Movements and Meanings of Labour in India* (New Delhi: Oxford University Press, 1993, 299–338) and Gauri Viswanathan, *Outside the Fold: Conversion, Modernity, and Belief* (New Delhi: Oxford Unversity Press, 1998).
25. See Busi (1997); Guru (2001); Jaffrelot (2004); Omvedt (1994); Verma (1999).
26. On the present writer's attempts to understand the extent to which Gandhi was ideologically linked or de-linked with some of his other political colleagues or rivals, see Pantham (1995a, 1995b, 2006).

11 Rejection of Rejection
Foregrounding Self-respect
Gopal Guru

The history of the development of any human civilization shows that human beings have been engaged in a twofold struggle to survive, and survive meaningfully. The first kind of struggle is aimed at the preservation of the self, both from nature and the barbaric nature of man. Food, shelter, and clothing become natural needs for this preservation of the self, which is natural to all animals with organic properties. However, human beings seek discontinuity from nature or animals on grounds that the former possess reflective qualities. Human beings invest these qualities to not only survive but also to survive meaningfully. To put it differently, man seeks discontinuity from the natural-like existence by adding to his life cultural, aesthetic, and rational dimensions. The first level of elevation thus signifies discontinuity. At still higher levels of elevation, human beings seek differentiation from other humans. This differentiation by some is sought by adding ethical and moral dimensions to their life. Thus human life becomes meaningful through double elevation, first from nature and second from one culture to another. The second level thus involves cultural hierarchies.

Elevation, needless to say, is uniquely human simply because human beings do not subtract their moral worth from animals. They might demand loyalty from the animal, particularly from cats and dogs. On the contrary, they seek recognition from other human beings as they have a capacity of moral grading. Recognition as a vital cultural need becomes available only in the society of humans. It is the human society that provides the background condition within which a desire to look either culturally superior or different from other beings emerges. However, the realization of desire for recognition is not without social cost, which someone in the society has to bear for someone else's elevation within society. In this regard it is important to raise related questions. What is this social cost? And which notion of elevation or recognition involves this cost?

Desire for recognition or elevation logically assumes corresponding reduction, rejection, cancellation, and annihilation of certain human beings. It has to be kept in mind that there is a difference between reduction and rejection. Reduction happens at different levels. A person is reduced to a natural level through his/her comparison with animal, plants, and stones.[1] This kind of reduction has a cultural orientation as it is achieved through assigning hierarchical meanings to some. In another sense, it could also be fundamentally structural as well. For example, the reduction of a human being to a commodity or thing is basically structural (Bernstein 1984: 18). For reducing a person to a thing, the physical existence of that person becomes a precondition. It cannot be an imagined reduction. Rejection especially achieved by assigning a repulsive meaning to the human body assumes a much more pernicious dimension. Unlike reduction it does not require the existence of a person as the precondition for its definition. The very idea of untouchables in India creates among the upper caste a deep sense of repulsion. In its extremity it cancels out or erases the human being from the memory. We shall discuss these levels of rejection in greater detail in the following pages. At the moment it is necessary to answer a set of questions raised above.

It is possible to argue that it is the surplus recognition that provides the defining condition for the idea of reduction. To put it differently, minimal recognition eliminates the possibility of such reduction. Minimal recognition could be defined not in terms of the material attributes that one has externally acquired but moral worth that is internally enjoyed by every human being without distinction. Everyone is guaranteed a worthy personality in isolation, separated from one's activities and relationships in which we seek to express our empirical self (Seidler 1986: 191). To put it differently, minimal recognition could be defined in terms of the principle of one-man-one-value or the normative understanding that every human being is inherently worthy of respect. Obviously, the desire for surplus recognition is the ground for battle.

Social Context of Recognition

The battle that the bourgeoisie successfully fought against the feudal forces during the French Revolution of 1789 was basically for gaining surplus recognition. Ironically, this desire for surplus is contingent upon the promise of minimal recognition. The trilogy of equality, liberty, and fraternity in the context of the French Revolution embodied this promise. In the Indian context, it was documented in the Constitution. The desire for surplus recognition presupposes a permanent gap between the elite and the subaltern cultural aspirations for recognition. This desire for surplus recognition forces the modern social elite to produce a new form of reduction, rejection, and exclusion sustained by modern conditions. Modernity has an inherent tendency to exclude more in favour of few. In fact, reduction is endemic to structures that underlie and renew the desire for surplus. However, it plays out differently in societies with the differential cultural context. Thus, it might take different routes—class, gender, race, and caste to name a few.

As mentioned in the introduction to this volume, in nineteenth-century England, the rich white people excluded the poor whites from the public sphere (Smith 1966: 371). In the context of British material life, it is also interesting to note that structures involving economic transaction were divided on moral hierarchy. Thus, in the 1840s, trade in London came to be organized under different moral codes: honourable trade and dishonourable trade (Thomson 1963: 277). In the West, particularly in France and the US, the category of race provided decisive parameters in terms of assigning differential but derogatory meaning to some social groups like the Jews and the blacks. In the US, the socially superior white males keep reducing the blacks to the level of animals. Thus the blacks are virtually reduced to zebra or water buffalo.[2] It has been argued that the French white people seem to have adopted two different but negative attitudes towards the blacks and the Jews. The blacks were thus considered a social evil while the Jews were considered a menace. The latter were considered a menace because Jews, according to Fanon, created a sense of fear among the French who thought that the former might take over everything in France (Fanon 1967: 157). Differently put, for the French a Jew could be a source of nuisance, while the 'black' surely is perceived as a *source of nausea* (with my emphasis).

As far as reduction of human beings from cultural to natural is concerned, it could be argued that both societies—the West and the East—share common ground. Like the West, in India too, the upper caste establish continuity between the natural (animal) and the cultural life experience. In the Indian context, the ideology of purity-pollution helps the socially dominant elite to reduce some human beings to the level of an animal.[3] Secondly, like the blacks, the untouchables in India are treated as a source of nausea.[4] Finally, as in the West, the reduction or rejection is achieved through enclosure in ghettos; in India, too, the untouchables are folded into the Indian ghettos which are known by different names—*Chamar tola* in the north, *Cheri* and *hulgeri* in the south, and *wadas* in the west of India. Yet these two situations differ from each other in the following fundamental ways. First, as noted earlier, in the West the cultural rejection of blacks involves the virtual identification of human beings with animals. Ironically, in such a treatment, certain symmetry of worth is granted between the animal and the human being. In India, however, the politics of rejection involves asymmetry that turns the worth in favour of the animal rather than the human being. Thus, the upper castes treat cows as more important than the Dalits.[5] That is to say, the four-legged animal is privileged over the human being. The relative worth of a person is pushed much below the ritual worth of an animal, which otherwise forms the part of the natural order.

Secondly, as the social history of the US shows, during slavery, a black person was treated as a commodity, to be sold and bought by the white masters. Ironically, a black carried some price, which brought him or her some luck to the extent that he or she remained visible/touchable for the master. He/she was lucky to be touched by the master. In India, however, the rejection of the untouchable continues to be complete, suggesting a concentrated expression of repulsion. It not only makes the untouchable invisible but even unimaginable.[6] The ideology of purity-pollution cancels out a vast section of people from the social interaction, both in terms of time and space. The caste system and the ideology of purity-pollution produces a kind of total rejection which seeks to push a person or an entire social group in question beyond the civilizational framework, rendering the latter completely un-seeable, unapproachable, and untouchable.

The reduction to a 'walking' carrion is completely mind numbing as it seeks to reduce a person to an obnoxious level where he/she even the scented body are treated as 'walking carrion'.[7] The cultural construction of the human body into 'mobile dirt' is treated by the upper castes as a source that creates a deep sense of nausea within the latter. This repulsive sense gets communicated to the 'object' of the nausea through deploying a sign language. For example, the upper caste women still cover their noses whenever in close proximity to an untouchable in the public sphere.[8] It is this negative image of the human body, associated with a deep sense of nausea and disgust, that must have prompted the *Sawakar* moneylenders to use these *walking carrion* (my emphasis) for timely recovery of loans.[9]

Finally, in the West, the struggle of the modern social elite (bourgeois) was not so much to prove what one was in the past but to prove continuously what one is in the present. For the blacks, however, the struggle is to reject what one was in the past and to retain at least what one is (the citizen, intellectual, a poet with a generic identity) in the present. The dalits in India and perhaps blacks in the US would ultimately want to become a Bodhisattva as understood in Buddhist philosophical tradition. Arguably, the struggle of the Jews is almost over. In India, however, the struggle of the 'bourgeoisie' or caste elite is focused more on what one was in the past.[10] Therefore, for the upper castes, the struggle is for the affirmation of the old, a belief which is deeply Brahmanical in nature and hence inherently hierarchical, and which faces a cultural challenge from the lower strata. To put it differently, the conservative social elite in India treats the arrival of modernity (including colonial modernity) as co-terminus with 'kaliyug' (Sarkar 1993). For the affirmation of modernity logically requires the rejection or reduction of some social groups and women. Their struggle thus is to retain or reproduce the hierarchical past in the cultural present. The hierarchical past was based on the total rejection of a large chunk of social groups. For the Dalits and women the struggle is similar to that of the blacks. The top of the twice born have created in Dalits a social leper or walking carrion which is sociologically dangerous and hence needs to be physically quarantined. The ideology of purity-pollution helped the top of the twice born to transmute the human body as an aesthetic idea into a 'filthy reality'. Untouchables are forced to eat human excreta.[11] This atrocious act seeks to reduce the Dalits to the level of dogs, pigs, and cows that are considered wretched as these animals (not the pampered pets) also eat human excreta. The body of the Dalits is treated as if it is trapped into a septic tank even if it is vibrant think tank. This is obnoxiously special to the Indian form of reduction.

The construction of the untouchable as a 'sociological danger' is different from the idea of biological danger (Sarkar 1996: 290) as perceived particularly by the Hindutva forces in India. The difference lies in the differential attitudes that the Hindutva forces have adopted towards these two social groups—the Minorities and the Dalits. In case of the untouchables, as mentioned earlier, it is the deep sense of repulsion that makes even the scented body a source of nausea. This negative attribution is so complete that the Dalits even today have to announce their arrival in the public sphere that is infected by the ideology of purity-pollution.[12] The nineteenth-century construction of untouchables as sociological danger consequently led to the exclusion, ex-communication, and segregation of the former. They became part of what is called 'quarantined India'.[13] They continue to remain quarantined in small but repulsive enclaves, both in the villages and also the metros, and also remain a source of anxiety for the upper castes particularly in the urban cities.

The Hindutva forces, on the other hand, perceive some sections the biological danger, as a source of rage and not so much of repulsion. Why do they become the source of rage? The answer to this question lies with the perception of the Hindutva forces. These forces, as scholars on modern Indian history rightly argue, perceive that a particular religious minority would achieve demographic preponderance over the Hindus. This fear of being outnumbered by the minorities appears to be biologically dangerous to Hindutva imagination. This perceived threat of demographic preponderance has led Hindus to develop an unmitigated rage against the Muslims.

The Hindutva reduction of the Dalits and the minorities oscillates, to paraphrase Connolly, between conversion, exclusion, and conquest (Connolly 1988). Since the untouchable constitute the source of ritual pollution they need to be excluded at least from the more intimate, sociologically familiar spheres and intellectual imagination. The untouchables in India face comprehensive exclusion to the extent that their construction as 'ritual dirt' permeates mainstream life in India. The minorities, as the history of social relationships between the minorities and Hindus show, according to the Hindu attitude constitute primarily a biological danger, which cannot be completely annihilated, and hence need to be conquered and kept under subjugation and servility. Thus, the political project of rejection involves the creation of two different images of the Dalits and the minorities. Thus, the minorities are converted into the 'significant other 'and are forced to remain on probation as far as nationalism is concerned. The untouchables on the other hand are treated as the 'insignificant other', whose servile attitudes feeds into the social dominance of the upper caste Hindus. The rejection of the untouchables to sociological danger through the process of exclusion and ex-communication produces and perpetuates a servile attitude among the former. Servility could be defined in terms of a person who is too ready to obey the master and too quick to run down his own peers. This is done with the hope to seek accommodation on the margins of the totality of social dominance and finally fight the stigma of being treated as sociological danger. Let me explain this using an illustration.

I cite the case of a Dalit teacher from one of the regional universities in the state of Maharashtra.[14] This, I believe, is a paradigmatic case of humiliation through reduction.

In the context of the elections of the teachers association, a head of department (HoD) from the university I cite, 'summons' his Dalit colleague to his house at 6 a.m. Understandably, the 'Dalit' teacher responds to these summons quite promptly. Since the Dalit teacher fears being late, he forgets to put on his footwear and a proper dress. Even though the Dalit teacher wastes no time in reaching the HoD's place, this promptness does not help him avoid the repulsive gaze that the HoD casts on him. Here, the Dalit's response to the command of the high caste head suggests the complex nature of reduction of a person. At one level, the ordeal of the response seeks to attach a dark aesthetic to Dalit reduction; the HoD enjoys the state in which the Dalit appears as comical. On the other hand, the Dalit response also acquires the genre of tragedy for the following reasons. First, the disciplining of the Dalit body forces the Dalit to gain physical power (for speeding to the head's house) and this only adds to the political power of the HoD, who defends his own power by striking fear within the Dalit. Secondly, the faster the Dalit runs to the HoD, the more self-respect he loses. This is analogous to the economic law of diminishing returns. The fear of death, thus, separates the moral force from self-respect and eventually turns it in favour of self-abasement. Finally, the Dalit teacher also offers himself as the means to the end of the HoD who wants the former to vote for a candidate of his choice. Thirdly, the Dalit teacher is reduced to an automobile machine. Like a machine the Dalit teacher also generates horsepower only to be subordinated to the power of fear produced by the HoD. It is in this sense that self-respect establishes its own moral scale. The more one delays the response the more one creates the possibility of retaining one's self-respect. Dragging foot is the subaltern method of restoring self-respect.

IDEOLOGY AND SELF-RESPECT

Paradoxically, in the discourse on reduction or humiliation it is necessary for the tormentor to retain the sense of self-respect within the victims (Millar 2000: 54). In other words, for seeking moral disintegration, it is necessary to create within the victim a sense of moral worth. The tormentor requires a sensitive human being in order to communicate the sense of reduction. A victim needs to develop an insight into his/her reduction. Those who fail to gain this insight do not provide the defining condition of rejection. Taking cue from Richard Rorty it could be argued that the ironist self cannot develop an insight into humiliation.[15] Thus, gaining insight into humiliation is neither integral nor natural to the self. Feigning ignorance of reduction, on the other hand, eliminates the moral conditions that are necessary for developing an insight into reduction and its transcendence. For example, many political leaders who are otherwise politically competent choose to act dumb in front of party bosses. This could be interpreted as a deliberate act of self-deception where the person does not spell out to the bosses his/her ability to excel. They deliberately accept the reduced position in the institutional settings primarily because they want to hold on to power at some level.[16] This is analogous to what Charles Taylor calls reduced mode of being (Taylor 1989: 213). This reduction of being however is permanent. In fact, the dialectics of reduction suggests that the victim cannot be permanently folded into their reduced being. They make moves, both intellectual and political, to overcome this reduction. The reduced, fixed bodies become fluid and start flowing across time and space.[17] It is this fluid nature of bodies that forces the tormentor to destroy the possibility of this moral insight. The tormentor has a stake in eliminating this possibility as insight can lead to subversion and assertion against domination. As mentioned above, striking fear into the victim is a coercive way to reduce a person to servility. In addition, the tormentor also uses ideology as a potent source to destroy this insight.

The dominant often use ideology to destroy the possibility of this insight that one might develop in order to detect his/her reduction and later on resist it. Ideology often operates by either taking on symbolic or some times fake forms of elevation. For example, raising Indian women to the level of goddess constitutes a spiritual elevation of the former. This elevation into the spiritual time often leads Hindu women to gloss over their trauma, exploitation, and subjugation in lived/real time. The tactical elevation of women—that 'behind every successful man there is a woman'—also suggests an ideological construction that often naturalizes the survival status of women. Thus, raising woman to mother India tends to wrap their servility within a nationalist frame, while elevating them symbolically to the status of Annapurana (Goddess of bounty) and Laxmi (Goddess of wealth) is a smart move to achieve women's acquiesce to patriarchical domination over bounty and wealth.

Patriarchical ideology acquires a specific form when it seeks to justify what could be termed as the multilayered reduction of women belonging particularly from the lower caste. In order to further elucidate this point let us look at the Devadasi system that is still prevalent in certain parts of India (Kamble 1986). In this system a woman gets married to either a god or a goddess. Women who are married to gods or goddesses treat this marriage as a rare opportunity that is available only to them. In their self-perception becoming the wife of God King is the highest form of elevation (Marglin 1987). Hence they do not find anything objectionable in becoming 'dasis' of the God King. However, in actual practice, they are reduced to a level where they become objects of free sexual exploitation by the temple priests or the village upper caste lords. However, as social activism among the Devadasis informs us, these women are not pathologically incapable of smashing the ideological frame that ties them into servility. On many occasions they have displayed the moral stamina needed to develop an insight into their humiliation, and have walked out from this system.[18] Many of them have started a 'normal' life by tying the nuptial knot. Marriage in this context becomes a radical alternative to fight reduction. But in another context, there is a danger that marriage might reproduce new forms of reduction. Marriage with a person in lived time and not in spiritual time certainly demonstrates Devadasis' ability to communicate to the tormentor that the former refuse to participate in her own reduction by the latter. Thus, developing an insight into humiliation is an epistemological act while communicating it to the tormentor is political.

Ideological mediation can also produce a complex form of humiliation involving layers of reduction. That is to say, a person seeks to humiliate others without realizing that his attempts to humiliate others also involve his own humiliation at the same time. This complex process takes place through an internalization of the ideology of humiliation. This internalization of ideology becomes one of the subtle ways to define reduction. Let us explain it further by decoding an act of confession or lamentation as offered by some of the members of the minority community. For example, look at the following lamentation made by one of the minority persons, who, in the context of the communal riots, is reported to have said, 'hamko acchuto se pitwayya'. Here, the upper caste forces got the minority person thrashed by the 'acchut' (untouchable).[19]

This lamentation thus adopts a very complicated route to communicate reduction. First, it suggests a certain kind of hierarchy for the tormentor/ humiliator. The higher the position of the tormentor the lesser is the feeling of humiliation within the victim. To put it differently, the complainant would not lament the loss of dignity if he/she were to be beaten up by the upper caste and not the untouchables. The lamentation is much deeper, not because the untouchables were weak opponents (as it happens in the game of cricket where the strongest team is beaten by a very weak team as a matter of chance) but because they were already humiliated. The ritually negative power to humiliate, however, is different from the negative power of the eunuch, who is used as a poison weapon to humiliate the strong candidate in the elections. In the latter case, it is the masculine that acts as the governing context while in the first it is framework of purity-pollution that has bearing on the intensity of the feeing of humiliation. Secondly, this lamentation also suggests order of value in which an untouchable acquires negative worth that is used for disturbing the stable conception of the minority self. The tone of the complaint in the aforementioned lamentation also suggests that the minority person enjoys this stability until he/she is shaken out of their moral complacency. Thus the untouchable as a poison weapon plays a crucial role in producing a sense of humiliation within the minorities. Finally, reduction (of the minority person to the level of the untouchable) on its way to its confirmation is both comic and tragic. Comic for those who are alleged to have deployed the untouchables for the job which produces 'dark pleasure' for the former. It is also comic in another sense; the Hindu upper caste is doubly pleased with the minority person's confirmation of the ideology of purity-pollution. This is clear from the lament that they were beaten by the untouchables. It is tragic in the sense that those who are alleged to have been involved in the plot themselves are the recipients of humiliation—the untouchables. This lamentation is also tragic in that on the one hand it merits sympathy, but on the other it also undercuts the significance of this sympathy. This is because the lamenting person (in the present case the minority person) continues to be the repository of the ideology of purity-pollution which seeks to push the untouchable to the lowest level where he/she is used as the common denominator for measuring the relative height of the ritual purity of a person. Ironically, the attempt to impute more obnoxious meaning to those 'guilty' untouchables tends to neutralize the more punitive power of the latter. That is to say, the moral strength of the complaint would have been much more effective had it been framed outside the parameters of purity-pollution ideology. In India, the ideology of purity-pollution cutting across other religions provide the overall governing principle which gets internalized by the members of these religions. This internalization of an ideology on the part of the minority person however eliminates the possibility of developing an insight into reduction. This internalization also suggests a different kind of servility in which a minority person depends on the ideology of purity-pollution for his own self-definition. The question that needs to be raised here is: what are those conditions that enable the victim of reduction to fight the fear of death, servility, and ideological illusion? What are those normative grounds on which the struggle for rejection of rejection is carried out by the subaltern masses?

The struggle for rejection of rejection becomes a possibility only within certain objective conditions. In a Hegelian sense the work process which goes hand in hand with the struggle for recognition leads to the emancipation and education of the subject. Abstract work produced by the division of labour of subjective individuals requires objective recognition by means of exchange and contracts. And this recognition transforms their fortuitous possession into property, and themselves into a person, that is, legal subject (Kortian 1984: 201). In addition to the division of labour, the rotation principle, which is considered the hallmark of modernity, can also help achieve de-linking of a person from traditional occupations that are co-terminus with the cultural moral reduction of some people (Walzer 1983: 134). The rotation principle, if taken seriously, can put the old status arrangement upside down. This has happened both in the US and in India. Thanks to modernity that has made this rotation possible. However, this principle is not without problems for it can reproduce new forms of reduction of rejection.

The socially dominant elite, the upper castes in India, and whites (female no exception) find it difficult to accept the arrival of the ex-communicated, branded, and marginalized. The arrival signifies elevation of women, blacks, tribes, and Dalits at various levels of opportunity structures where some of these groups have been elevated from the corporeal to the abstract identity. Thus, some of them have become citizens, poets, artists, and so on and so forth. This is all due to the arrival of modernity, which has made this elevation possible for the subaltern groups in India. Modernity to some extent has achieved the standardization of cultural and social hierarchies. However, this elevation does not enjoy the recognition of the twice-born, even if it is just symbolic. In fact, the twice-born keep devising and deploying newer ways to reduce the Dalit from whatever social height the latter could manage to achieve for themselves. For example, the blacks and the Dalits still appear in public life with prefixes like Dalit president, Dalit intellectual, or black president or black intellectual. This use of such attributions with a prefix is humiliating. It involves an attempt to socially bracket a modern status or position with the caste background of a person. This bracketing forms the part of an exception and not the rule. This is so because bracketing all the modern positions with social background is not specific to India. The upper castes in India and the whites in the US form part of the rule. They can exist without the negative prefix. That is to say, no one is called a Brahmin president or a white president (in the White House). The reduction of the body and not its elevation as the idea of an abstract self constitutes humiliation. This chaining to the physical body, which obviously is not a celebrated body, which exists in the genre of tragedy or comedy, tends to introduce fragmentation in the truth. This bracketing with the sociological (Dalit and black) by implication separates the partial truth (Dalit or black president) from the universal truth (the white male president or the Brahmin president). Thus the Dalits and the blacks are permanently reduced to the sphere of partiality that the upper castes deploy while assigning recognition. This partiality is evident in the sceptical attitude adopted by the socially dominant in order to retain their panoptical position. For example, look at the following attribution to a Dalit intellectual: 'you are more than' your own people but 'less than us'. The rejection of Dalits and blacks lies in the notion of double exception. They are exceptions in as much as they are more than those who belong to the social constituency of the former, and they are less than in relation to the upper caste in India and the whites in the US. This scepticism, which results from the inability to offer what is due to a black and a Dalit, essentially questions the upper caste/white claims about the robustness of rationality. If rationality, as Connolly (1988) has argued, as it develops historically is an achievement through which the self comes closer to truth and spirit then it could be argued that the whites and the upper castes are still to arrive at this rationality as they refuse to come closer to truth (that the Dalits and the blacks have arrived). This weak sense of rationality looks pathological because it suggests that the Dalits in India and the blacks in the US never grow in the eyes of the upper castes in India and the whites in the US respectively. It is within this view, one could argue, that the upper caste's act of rejection is a defence mechanism that is adopted with the intention to compensate for the social loss resulting from the modernist arrival of Dalits and women in India and the Blacks in the US. To put it differently, it is the fear of the arrival of 'Kaliyug', which suggests the assertion of Dalits and women in India and the Blacks in the US. It is the fear of being evened out or, in worst cases, being surpassed by those who were historically inferior. This is not to suggest that the rejection of rejection is total, both in India and in the West. As mentioned in the earlier section, the Dalits and the blacks, for example, chose to remain on the probation of the upper castes and the whites respectively. This is because they lacked the moral courage to take risks and challenge their hegemonic rejection by the socially dominant. Thus, at the subjective level, developing courage provides the necessary moral conditions to produce the counter rejection.

DIALECTICS OF REJECTION

Taking a cue from Hegel and Hannah Arendt moral courage could be defined in terms of the ability to liberate oneself from the fear of death or the preservation of self that puts a premium on individual interest (Bernstein 1984: 35). Moral courage presumes the ability to achieve the shift, from worrying for the individual to making the worries of the world one's own. For in emancipatory politics it is not so much personal life but the whole world that is at stake. Arguably there are several social and political revolutionaries across the world who have showed this moral courage of moving from the personal to the universal. The moral passage from the personal to the universal is particularly unique as far as B.R. Ambedkar is concerned. Thus, he along with his people sought to walk out from the given image of 'walking carrion' and went on to become the walking storm. It would not be an exaggeration to attribute this identity to Ambedkar, for he acquired storm-like qualities, both political and epistemological, to explode into the structures (caste, class, colonialism, and patriarchy) of rejection. Ambedkar, with his intellectual power and moral ability to lead from the front, imposed dialogue on the recalcitrant tradition in India. His argumentative force and authenticity of purpose did produce moral/ethical and political crises for those who sought other's reduction. Thus, moral courage to take risk and avoid soft paternalism offers the first subjective condition in the struggle for counter rejection.

Secondly, the untouchables like the black used the principle of fairness to substantiate their move to reject the rejection. They argued that seeking the reduction of human beings and treating them as wretched animals on the basis of their skin colour and nature of occupation (as in the case of India) is absolutely unfair. It is unfair on the grounds of ontological equality. From the point of view of this notion of equality every organic body—animal and human—is constitutive of common organic properties both positive and negative. Animals and humans come into being and survive on the basis of life-giving properties like air, water, earth, fire, and space. These are present in everybody in equal degree and quantity. Equal distribution of these natural properties, therefore, should form the basis on which all the organic bodies deserve equal recognition irrespective of caste, colour, size, and gender. All the organic bodies are also equally condemnable because they consist of negative properties. As pathological investigation would reveal, every organic body—human or animal—consists of organic refuse. Discharging human refuse is natural to any organic body and to that extent such bodies share ontologically equal status—that all the organic bodies contain refuse. Bodies in general are undifferentiated because they contain underneath their skin all kinds of refuse or filth. Such bodies containing filth are not treated as repulsive as long as the filth remains hidden within them. Bodies become objects of ridicule depending on their capacity to emit the filth in a controlled way and in an appropriate context. Thus urinating in trousers or ferreting in public can lead to embarrassment and loss of self-esteem. Four-legged animals do not suffer from this embarrassment. Similarly, the disposal of dirt by human beings seeks to reduce the latter to the level of dirt. In India, a large number of people who are still forced to dispose dirt through manual scavenging have been treated like dirt. In fact, these sanitary workers who call themselves as 'walmiki' have been treated as mobile dirt. This is so because they have been denied a generic identity. To conclude, in the dialectic of the rejection of reduction, those who have been rejected by pre-modern society and social protocols seek to reject this reduction by adopting modern egalitarian protocols. However, treating people culturally equal remains a theoretical promise as those who have taken the lead in rejecting the feudal norms of social status have ended up reproducing new forms of reduction. Thus, the struggle for the rejection of rejection acquires an endemic character as far as the subalterns are concerned.

THE STRUGGLE FOR GENERIC IDENTITY

The struggle to retain a generic identity has been the core concern of the Dalit and also the black imagination. The Dalit and the Shudra tradition first led by Jotirao Phule[20] and later by B.R. Ambedkar signifies this struggle for generic identity. Dalit politics led by Ambedkar succeeded in achieving their elevation through the Indian constitution. Thus, at least formally, they have become the right-bearing citizens of the country. The political passage of Dalits from walking carcasses to citizens is no mean feat that was made possible through the struggle for recognition that was launched by Ambedkar in 1920 from Mangao, a village in the Kolhapur princely state led by the socially most radical raja, Raja Chatrapati Shahu Maharaj. As a result one finds social hierarchy has no place in the Indian constitution, for it has abolished all the feudal titles that existed during the feudal period. As I have argued elsewhere this elevation to 'citizen' has not been redeemed in terms of one-person-one-value.[21] What is promised in the political realm is summarily denied in the social. Dalits, for all practical purposes, are treated as walking carcasses despite the fact there exist pernicious acts to regulate this passage from walking carcass to citizen. Ironically, the Indian state has been responsible for reducing them from being active citizens to dole receivers. They are known as target groups or the card holders/certificate holders. Their failure to enjoy elevation in material life has been compensated in the literary, metaphorical life.

Thus, Dalit literary figures have deployed certain powerful modes of transvaluation in order to produce counter rejection through resignification of what was previously stigmatized (Taylor 1989). One leading Dalit writer, known for his serious philosophical bent of mind, used these principles as a potent source of assertion. Bagul asks the upper castes a question: 'you call us untouchable! Sun is also untouchable' (Bagul 1978). He further argues that the untouchables are like death, which human beings try hard to avoid and normally do not embrace it. But the efforts, however laudable they may be, remain at the level of the war of semantics. The subjective affirmation of one stigmatized identity has no meaning as it is denied by the objective condemnation of the dominant adversary. To put it differently, these attempts at positive self-definition have limitations in that they are not sustained at the objective level both in the US and in India. This is borne out the by the wall of separation that the upper castes from one of the villages in Tamil Nadu in south India have raised between them and the untouchables. The continuous rejection of Dalits could lead a reaction along the lines what Babuaro Bagul has said: 'the self-respect of Dalit has to be achieved either leaving the nation or completely transforming it on decent line'. Thus the idea of not just the developed society but also a decent society, and the struggle to redeem this society, should warrant the need for a paradigm of thinking.

NOTES

1. In the Indian context, the Manu Dharma Shastra text has compared the untouchables and women to four-legged animals. Dalits are seen

in the form of cactus and stone. In fact, they were forced to adopt names signifying stone. Stone symbolically means a person who is dumb/stupid.

2. The upper castes in India and the whites in the US reduced, respectively, the untouchables and blacks to the level of animals by using metaphoric language. For example, in the US, the whites use the metaphor of water buffalo for the black woman while the upper castes in India use the term 'dead animal' for the untouchable.

3. In India, for the upper castes, the cows are more valuable than the untouchables, as was publicly defended by the *Mahanta* (religious priest) from a Hindutva Right wing outfit in the context of the Jhazzar killings of Dalits in Haryana, in 2002. The *Mahanta* went on record saying that the cow is more valuable than the life of a Dalit. This statement was made in the context of the Jhazzar killing in which five Dalits were killed by caste Hindus on the false pretext that the latter were responsible for killing a cow.

4. In the southern part of India, the upper castes cover their noses whenever they happen to cross the path of an untouchable. This has been also documented in a study by Khare (1984).

5. See the example given in note 3 above.

6. See Kamble (2006). This has also been observed by Naipaul (1990: 166).

7. Moor (1978: 69). In this work, Moor uses the metaphor of 'walking corpse'. As Veena Das has observed, there are different meanings for corpse in ritual Hinduism. For example, Das observes that there are two kinds of corpses—pure and impure; see Das (1977: 124). I have chosen to borrow the metaphor of 'walking carrion' as used by Naipaul (1988: 37).

8. The upper caste women in India still cover their noses with the ends of their sarees so as to give the untouchable women a feeling that they are the mobile dirt.

9. Untouchables were used for efficient recovery of loans in many parts of the country during the nineteenth century in India. The subaltern history shows this very clearly.

10. The upper castes do not feel the loss of prestige even if they lose the electoral battle to a lower caste person. They are often found claiming that traditional social status is still higher than the political status.

11. The untouchables are forced to eat human excreta in various parts of the country. This had happened in a village in Chikodi taluka of Belgaum district of Karnataka state in 1989.

12. Dalits are considered a sociological danger by the upper castes that deploy the ideology of purity-pollution to construct this danger. This is not the perceived but rather the experienced danger.

13. B.R. Ambedkar termed the untouchables as people who belong to 'Bahiskrut Bharat'.
14. This is my own observation in one of the regional universities in Maharashtra.
15. Richard Rorty quoted in Gender (1999: 94).
16. This has been the story about one of the prominent Dalit leaders of the early 1970s. I thank Professor V.K. Natraj for sharing this information with me.
17. Upendra Baxi, in this volume.
18. There are a few rehabilitation centres for Devadasis, supported by the government of Maharashtra. One of the active centres is located at Gadhinglaj, District Kolhapur, Maharashtra, headed by Vithhal Bane, a Marathi professor. Acchut Mane, a Marathi professor at Nipani, has also been active in these projects.
19. Ashis Nandy in this volume.
20. Jotirao Phule was the nineteenth-century thinker from Maharashtra. His ideas involve self-respect for the Shudra and ati-Shudra caste.
21. There are about twenty-three volumes on the writings and speeches of Ambedkar. The education department of the Government of Maharashtra publishes these volumes.

Bibliography

Ahir, D.C. 1995. *Gandhi and Ambedkar: A Comparative Study*, Third Revised and Enlarged Edition, New Delhi: Blumoon Books.

Alam, Javeed. 1999. *India: Living with Modernity*, New Delhi: Oxford University Press.

Ambedkar, B.R. 1957. *The Buddha and His Dhamma*, Bombay: Siddartha Publication.

_____. 1979. *Writings and Speeches*, vol. 1, Department of Education, Bombay: Government of Maharashtra.

_____. 1987. *Writings and Speeches*, vol. 3, Department of Education, Bombay: Government of Maharashtra.

_____. 1989. *Babasaheb Ambedkar Writings and Speeches*, vol. 5, Department of Education, Bombay: Government of Maharashtra.

_____. 1990a. *Ambedkar: Writings and Speeches*, vol. 3, Bombay: Government of Maharashtra.

_____. 1990b. *Source Material on Dr Babasaheb Ambedkar, Writings and Speeches*, vol. 9, Bombay: Government of Maharashtra.

_____. 1993. *Writngs and Speeches*, vol. 12, Department of Education, Bombay: Government of Maharashtra.

Anderson, Elisabeth S. 1999. 'What is the Point of Equality?' *Ethics*, vol. 109, no. 2, pp. 287–337.

Angle, Prabhakar, 2003. *Goa, Concepts and Misconcepts*, Panaji: Gova Hindu Association.

Arendt, Hannah, 2000. 'The Origins of Totalitarianism', in Peter Baehr (ed.), *The Portable Hannah Arendt*, Harmondsworth: Penguin Books.

Asad, Talal. 1987. 'On Torture, or Cruel, Inhuman, and Degrading Treatment', in Arthur Kleinman, Veena Das, and Margaret Lock (eds), *Social Suffering*, Berkeley: University of California Press.

_____. 1998. 'On Torture, or Cruel, Inhuman, and Degrading Treatment', in

Arthur Kleinman, Veena Das, and Margaret Lock (eds), *Social Suffering*, Oxford: Oxford University Press.

Austin, J.L. 1976. *How to Do Things with Words*, London: Oxford University Press.

Bagul, Baburao, 1978. *Dalit Sahitya Ajche Kranti Vidnanayn* (Marathi), Nagpur: Buddhist Publication.

Baher, Peter (ed.). 2000. *The Portable Hannah Arendt*, Harmondsworth: Penguin Books.

Ball, Terence. 1995. *Reappraising Political Theory*, Oxford: Clarendon Press.

Baviskar, Amita. 1995. *In the Belly of the River*, New Delhi: Oxford University Press.

Baxi, Upendra. 1982. *The Crisis of Indian Legal System*, New Delhi: Vikas.

————. 1984. 'Legislative Reservations for Social Justice', in R.B. Goldman and J. Wilson (eds), *From Independence to Statehood: Managing Ethnic Conflicts in Five African and Asian States*, London: Pinter, pp. 210–24.

————. 1987. 'What is Wrong with Sycophancy?' in Bhikhu Parekh and Thomas Pantham (eds), *Political Discourse*, New Delhi: Sage Publications.

————. 1995. 'Emancipation as Justice: Babasaheb Ambedkar's Legacy and Vision', in Upendra Baxi and Bhikhu Parekh (eds), *Crisis and Change in Contemporary India*, New Delhi: Sage Publications, pp. 122–49.

————. 2002. 'The Second Gujarat Catastrope', *Economic and Political Weekly*, vol. 37, 24 August.

————. 2009. *The Future of Human Rights*, 3rd edition, New Delhi: Oxford University Press.

Baxi, Upendra and Bhikhu Parekh (eds). 1995b. *Crisis and Change in Contemporary India*, New Delhi: Sage Publications.

Bernstein, J.M. 1984. 'From Self-consciousness to Community', in Z.A. Pelnczynski (ed.), *State and Civil Society: Studies in Hegel's Political Philosophy*, Cambridge: Cambridge University Press.

Bhargava, Rajeev and Helmut Reifeld (eds). 2005. *Civil Society, Public Sphere and Citizenship: Dialogues and Perceptions*, New Delhi: Sage Publications.

Bhattacharya, Neeladri. 2005. 'Notes Towards a Conception of the Colonial Public', in Rajeev Bhargava and Helmut Reifeld (eds), *Civil Society, Public Sphere and Citizenship*, New Delhi: Sage Publications, pp. 130–56.

Bhowmik, Sharait and Nitin More. 2001. 'Coping with Urban Poverty: Ex-Textile Mill Workers in Central Mumbai', *Economic and Political Weekly*, vol. 36, no. 52, 29 December.

Bohra K. and Janak Pande. 1984. 'Ingratiation Toward Strangers, Friends, and Bosses', *The Journal of Social Psychology*, vol. 122, pp. 217–22.

Bourdieu, Pierre. 2000. *Pascalian Meditations*, Oxford: Polity Press.

Branaman, Ann (ed.). 2002. *Self and Society*, Massachusetts: Blackwell.

Butler, Judith, Ernesto Laclau and Salvoj Žižek. 2000. *Contingency, Hegemony, Universality: Contemporary Debates on the Left*, London: Verso.

Busi, S.N. 1997. *Mahatma Gandhi and Babasaheb Ambedkar*, Hyderabad: Saroja Publications.

Catriona, Mckinnon. 2002. *Liberalism and the Defense of Political Constructivism*, London: Palgrave Macmillan.

Cesairé, Aimé. 1972. *Discourse on Colonialism*, trans. Joan Pinkham, New York and London: Monthly Review Press.

Chakrabarty, Arindam. 2005. 'The Moral Psychology of Revenge', *Journal of Human Values*, vol. 11, no. 1, pp. 31–6.

Chakrabarty, Dipesh. 1996. 'Remembered Village: Representation of Hindu-Bengali Memories in the Aftermath of Partition', *Economic and Political Weekly*, vol. 31, no. 32, 10 August, pp. 2143–61.

———. 2002. *Habitations of Modernity*, New Delhi: Permanent Black.

Chandavarkar, Rajnarayan. 1994. *The Origins of Industrial Capitalism in India: Business Strategies and the Working Classes in Bombay, 1900–1940*, New Delhi: Foundation Books.

Charlesworth, Hilary, Christine Chinkin and Shelly Wright. 1991. 'Feminist Approaches to International Law', *American Journal of International Law*, vol. 85.

Charsley, Simon R., and G.K. Karanth (eds). 1998. *Challenging Untouchability*, New Delhi: Sage Publications.

Coetzee, J.M. 2000. *Disgrace*, London: Vintage.

Connolly, William, 1988. *Political Theory and Modernity*, Oxford: Basil Blackwell.

Cunha, T.B. (n.d). *Denationalism of Goas*, Panaji: Government Press.

Daniel, Valentine. 2000. 'The Arrogation of Being by the Blind-Spot of Religion', Paper presented at the Conference on the Twentieth Century: Dreams and Realities, Graduate School of Social Science, Hitotsubashi, University, Tokyo, 2 December.

Das, Veena. 1977. *Structure and Cognition*, New Delhi: Oxford University Press.

DeMause, Lloyd. 1982. *Foundations of Psychohistory*, New York: Creative Roots Publication.

Dent, Nicholas. 2004. *Rousseau*, London: Routledge.

Derrida, Jacques. 2002. *On Cosmopolitanism and Forgiveness*, London and New York: Routledge.

Desai, I.P. 1976. *Untouchability in Rural Gujarat*, Bombay: Popular Prakashan.

Desai, Prakash. 1995. 'Personality Politics: A Psychoanalytic Perspective', in Upendra Baxi and Bhikhu Parekh (eds), *Crisis and Change in Contemporary India*, New Delhi: Sage Publications.

Desai, Meghnad. 2001. *Marx's Revenge: The Resurgence of Capitalism and the Death of Statist Capitalism*, London: Verso.

Deshpande, G.P. (ed.). 2002. *Selected Writings of Jotirao Phule*, New Delhi: Left Word Books.

Deshpande, Rajeshwari. 2004. 'Social Movements in Crisis?' in Rajendra Vora and Suhas Palshikar (eds). *Indian Democracy: Meanings and Practices*, New Delhi: Sage Publications, pp. 379–409.

_____. 2005. *State and Democracy in India*, Pune, Department of Politics and Public Administration, University of Pune, Occasional Paper III: 4.

deSouza, Peter R. (ed.). 2000. *Contemporary India: Transitions*, New Delhi: Sage Publications.

_____. 2003. 'The Struggle for Local Government: Indian Democracy's New Phase', *Publius*, Fall, vol. 33, no. 4, pp. 99–118.

Devi, Maheshweta. 1997. *Breast Stories*, trans. Gayatri Spivak Chakravorty, Kolkata: Seagull Books.

Dhagamwar, Vasudha. 2002. 'Personal Law and Criminal Law Interaction', Paper presented at an International Conference, New Delhi, under the auspices of Lawyer's Collective.

Digeser, Peter. 1998. 'Forgiveness and Politics: Dirty Hands and Imperfect Procedures', *Political Theory*, vol. 26, no. 5, October, pp. 700–24.

D'Monte, Darryl. 2002. *Ripping the Fabric: The Decline of Mumbai and its Mills*, New Delhi: Oxford University Press.

Douglas, Mary. 1966. *Purity and Danger: An Analysis of Concepts of Pollution and Taboo*, Harmondsworth: Penguin Books.

Dworkin, Ronald. 1981. 'What is Equality? Part 2: Equality of Resources', *Philosophy and Public Affairs*, vol. 10, no. 4, pp. 283–345.

_____. 1984. *Taking Rights Seriously*, London: Duckworth.

Ellul, Jacques. 1985. *The Humiliation of the Word*, trans. Joyce Main Hanks, Eerdmans Publishing.

EPW Research Foundation (EPWRF). 1997. 'Mumbai's Textile Mills and the Land Question', *Economic and Political Weekly*, vol. 32, no. 43, 25 October, pp. 2785–7.

Fanon, Frantz. 1967. *The Wretched of the Earth*, Harmondsworth: Penguin Books.

_____. 1967. *Black Skin White Masks*, New York: Grove Press.

Faubion, James D. 2000. *The Essential Works of Michel Foucault*, vol. 3, New York: New Press (Paul Rainbow Series).

Fraser, Nancy. 2000. 'Rethinking Recognition: Overcoming Displacement and Reification in Cultural Politics', *New Left Review*, 3 May/June.

Fraser, Nancy and Axel Honneth. 2003. *Recognition and Redistribution*, London: Verso.

Fishkin, James. 1983. *Justice, Equal Opportunity, and the Family*, New Haven: Yale University Press.

Fiorina, Morris P. and Theda Skocpol. 1999. *Civic Engagement in American Democracy*, Washington D.C.: Brookings Institution.

Foucault, Michel. 1979. *Discipline and Punish: The Birth of the Prison*, New York: Random House.

Gaikwad, Shankar L. 1999. *Protective Discrimination Policy and Social Change: An Analytical Study of State Action on Scheduled Castes in Aurangabad City*, Jaipur: Rawat Publications.

Galanter, Marc. 1984. *Competing Equalities: Law and Backward Classes in India*, New Delhi: Oxford University Press.

Galsman, Maurice. 1996. *Unnecessary Suffering: Managing Market Utopia*, London: Verso.

Gandhi, M.K. 1963. 'Hind Swaraj', in *Collected Works of Mahatma Gandhi*, New Delhi: Publications Division, Ministry of Information and Broadcasting, Government of India, vol. 4, pp. 81–208.

———. 1967. *Collected Works of Mahatma Gandhi*, New Delhi: Publications Division, Ministry of Information and Broadcasting, Government of India, vol. 25.

Gandhi, Rajmohan. 1995. *The Good Boatman: A Portrait of Gandhi*, New Delhi: Penguin Books.

Gary, Romain.1978. *The Dance of Genghis Cohn*, Harmondsworth: Penguin Books.

Gender, Eric. 1999. *The Last Conceptual Revolution: A Critique of Richard Rorty's Political Philosophy*, Albany: State University Press.

Goodin, Robert. 1987. 'Exploiting a Situaton and Exploiting a Person', in Andrew Reeve (ed.), *Modern Theories of Exploitation*, London: Sage Publications.

Government of Maharashtra (GoM). 1982. *Source Material on Dr Ambedkar and the Movement of Untouchables*, vol. 1. Bombay: Government of Maharashtra.

———. 1987. *The Bombay Textile Strike Affected and Un-employed Workers and their Legal Dues Assessment Committee Report* (Kotwal Committee), Bombay: Government of Maharashtra.

Grover, Verinder (ed.). 1992. *Political Thinkers of Modern India*, vol. 16, New Delhi: Deep and Deep Publications.

Guha, Ranajit. 1983. *Elementary Aspects of Peasant Insurgency*, New Delhi: Oxford University Press.

———. 1997. *Dominance without Hegemony: History and Power in Colonial India*, Cambridge: Cambridge University Press.

Guru, Gopal. 2001. 'Ambedkar's Idea of Social Justice', in Ghanshyam Shah (ed.), *Dalits and the State*, New Delhi: Concept, pp. 40–50.

———. 2005. (ed.) *Atrophy of Dalit Politics, Intervention*, Mumbai: Vikas Adhyayan Kendra.

Habermas, J. 1991. *The Structural Transformation of the Public Sphere: An Inquiry into a Category of Bourgeois Society*, Massachusetts: The MIT Press.

Hagginbotham, Evelyn Brooks. 1992. 'African American Women's History and the Meta-language of Race', *Signs*, vol. 17, no. 2.

Haldar, Baby. 2006. *A Life Less Ordinary*, English Translation by Urvashi Butalia, New Delhi: Zubaan/Penguin.

Hamber, Brandon and Richard Wilson. 2002. 'Symbolic Closer through Memory, Reparation and Revenge in Post-Conflict Societies', *Journal of Human Rights*, vol. 1, no. 1, March, pp. 35–53.

Harvey, David. 1996. *Justice, Nature and Geography of Difference*, Oxford: Blackwell.

Heller, Agnes. 1985. *The Power of Shame: A Rational Perspective*, London: Routledge and Kegan Paul.

———. 1987. *Beyond Justice*, New York: Basil Blackwell.

Herman, Ellen, 1995. *The Romance of American Psychology: Political Culture in the Age of Experts*, Berkeley: University of California.

Hinton, Timothy. 2002. 'Must Egalitarians Choose Between Fairness and Respect?' *Philosophy and Public Affairs*, vol. 30, no. 1, pp. 72–87.

Hoff, Karla and Priyanka Pandey. 2004. 'Belief Systems and Durable Inequalities: An Experimental Investigation of Indian Caste', Policy Research Working Paper Series 3351, The World Bank.

Honneth, Axel. 1995. *The Struggle for Recognition: The Moral Grammar of Social Conflict*, trans. Joel Anderson, Cambridge: Polity Press.

Ilaiah, Kancha. 1996. *Why I am not a Hindu. A Sudra Critique of Hindutva Philosophy, Culture, and Political Economy*, Calcutta: Samya Publication.

Jaffrelot, Christophe. 2004. *Dr Ambedkar and Untouchability*, New Delhi: Permanent Black.

Joshi, Barbara. 1982. *Democracy in Search of Equality*, Delhi: Hindustan Publishers.

Kahan, Dan. 1996. 'What do Alternate Sanction Mean?', vol. 63, *University of Chicago Law Review*, 591.

Kamble, Baby. 2006. *The Prison That We Broke*, trans. Maya Pandit, Delhi: Orient Longman.

Kamble, Uttam. 1986. *Debdasi te Nagna Puja* (Marathi), Mumbai: Lok Wangmay Graha.

Kaviraj, Sudipta, 1995. 'Religion, Politics and Modernity', in Upendra Baxi and Bhikhu Parekh (eds), *Crisis and Change in Contemporary India*, New Delhi: Sage Publications.

———. 1997a. 'Filth and the Public Sphere: Concepts and Practices about Space in Calcutta', Fall, *Public Culture*, vol. 10, no. 1, pp. 83–113.

———. 1997b. 'On the Construction of Colonial Power', in Sudipta Kaviraj (ed.), *Politics in India*, New Delhi: Oxford University Press, pp. 141–58.

———. 2001. 'The Culture of Representative Democracy', in Niraja Gopal Jayal (ed.), *Democracy in India*, New Delhi: Oxford University Press.

Keer, Dhananjay. 1991. *Dr Ambedkar: Life and Mission*, Bombay: Popular Prakashan.

Khare, R.S. 1984. *The Untouchable as Himself: Ideology and Pragmatism among the Lucknow Chamars*, Cambridge: Cambridge University Press.

Khattak, Saba. 2001. 'Case Study of a Woman Twice Displaced', Paper presented at workshop of the project, Delhi: Centre for the Study of Developing Societies.

King, Martin Luther, Jr. 1965. 'I Have a Dream' speech cited in F. Broderick and A. Meier's *Negro Protest Thought in the Twentieth Century*, Indianapolis: Bobbs Merril.

Kortian, Garbis. 1984. 'Subjectivity in Civil Society', in Z.A. Pelczynski (ed.), *The State and Civil Society: Studies in Hegel's Political Philosophy*, Cambridge: Cambridge University Press.

Kosambi, D.D. 2002. *Combined Methods in Indology and Other Writings*, edited by Brajadulal Chattopadhyay, New Delhi: Oxford University Press.

Kumar, Ravinder. 1987. 'Gandhi, Ambedkar and the Poona Pact, 1932', in Jim Masselos (ed.), *Struggling and Ruling: The Indian National Congress 1885–1985*, New Delhi: Sterling, pp. 87–101.

Linder, Evelin Gerda. 2001a. 'The Psychology of Humiliation; Summary of Results and What Research on Humiliation Added to Pre-Exiting Knowledge' (on file with the author and quoted with Dr Linder's kind permission. See also http://www.uio.no/-evelinl).

———. 2001. 'Humiliation: Trauma that has been Overlooked: An Analysis Based on Fieldwork in Germany, Rawanda/Burundi and Somalia, 7m *Traumatology*, 51.

———. 2001. 'Humiliation and Human Condition: Mapping a Minefield', *Human Rights Review*, vol. 2, no. 46.

Lokshahi Hakka Sanghatna (LHS). 1996. *Murder of the Mills: An Enquiry into Bombay's Cotton Textile Industry and its Workers*, Mumbai: LHS.

Lukes, Steven, 1997. 'Humiliation and the Politics of Identity', *Social Research*, spring, vol. 64, no. 1.

Margalit, Avishai. 1996. *The Decent Society*, trans. Naomi Goldblum, Massachusetts: Harvard University Press.

Marglin, Frédérique. 1987. *Wives of the God-King: The Rituals of the Devadasis of Puri*, New Delhi: Oxford University Press.

Margalit, Edna-Ullmann, 1997. *The Emergence of Social Norms*, Oxford: Oxford University Press.

Margalit, Edna-Ullmann and Cass R. Sunstein. 2002. 'Inequality and Indignation', John M. Olin Law and Economic Working Papers, 141, 2nd series; University of Chicago website (last visited 28 August).

Markel, Dan. 2001. 'Are Shaming Punishments Beautifully Retributive: Retributivism and the Implications for the Alternative Sentencing Debate', vol. 54, *Van. L. Rev.*, 2157.

Mascarenhas, Delio. 2002. *Conversion and Citizenry: Goa Under Portugal*, Delhi: Concept Publication.

Massaro, Toni M. 1880. 'Shame, Culture and American Criminal Law', *Michigan Law Review*, vol. 89.

———. 1997. 'The Meanings of Shame', 3 *Psychology, Public Policy, and Law*, pp. 645, 648.

Marx, Karl. 1975. *Early Writings*, trans. Rodney Livingstone and George Benton, London: Penguin Books.

Marx, Karl and F. Engels. 1975. *Collected Works*, vol. 21, Moscow: Progress Publishers.

Mendelsohn, Oliver and Marika Vicziany. 1996. 'The Untouchables', in O.

Mendelsohn and U. Baxi (eds), *The Rights of Subordinated Peoples*, New Delhi: Oxford University Press, pp. 64–116.

———. 1998. *The Untouchables: Subordination, Poverty and the State in Modern India*, Cambridge: Cambridge University Press.

Mende, Tibor. 1958. *Conversations with Nehru*, Bombay: Wilco.

Millar, David. 1999. *Principles of Social Justice*, Massachusetts: Harvard University Press.

Millar, William D. 2000. *Humiliation*, New Jersey: Princeton University Press.

Miller, W.I. 1993. *Humiliation and Other Essays on Honor, Social Discomfort and Violence*, Ithaca: Cornell University Press.

Mills, Nocolaus. 1997. *The Triumph of Meanness: America's War Against its Better Self*, Boston: Houghton Mifflin.

Millet, Kate. 1994. *The Politics of Cruelty: An Essay on the Literature of Political Imprisonment*, New Delhi: Penguin Books.

Misra, B.B. (ed.). 1963. *Select Documents of Mahatma Gandhi's Movement in Champaran, 1917–18*, Patna: Superintendent Secretariat Press.

Mohapatra, Bishnu. 1998. 'Understanding Indignities', *Seminar*, 461.

Moor, Barrington. 1978. *Injustice: Social Basis of Obedience and Revolt*, New Delhi: Macmillan.

Moore, Michael. 1997. *Downsize This! Random Threats from an Unarmed American*, Harper Paperbacks.

Mukhopadhyay, Anindita. 2006. *Behind the Mask: The Cultural Definition of the Legal Subject in Colonial Bengal (1715–1911)*, New Delhi: Oxford University Press.

Nagaraj, D.R. 1994, 'From Political Rage to Cultural Affirmation: Notes on the Kannada Dalit Poet-Activist Siddalingaiah', *India International Quarterly*, Winter, vol. 21, no. 4, pp. 15–26.

Naipaul, V.S. 1964. *An Area of Darkness*, London: Picador.

———. 1988. *India: A Wounded Civilization*, New Delhi: Picador.

———. 1990. *India: A Million Mutinies Now*, London: Minerva Press.

Nandy, Ashis. 1980. *At the Edge of Psychology*, New Delhi: Oxford University Press.

———. 1983. *The Intimate Enemy: Loss and the Recovery of the Self Under Colonialism*, New Delhi: Oxford University Press.

———. 1994. *The Illegitimacy of Nationalism: Rabindranath Tagore and the Politics of Self*, New Delhi: Oxford University Press.

———. 2002a. 'Telling the Story of Communal Conflicts in South Asia: Interim Report on a Search for Defining Myths', *Ethnic and Racial Studies*, January, vol. 25, no. 1, pp. 1–19.

———. 2002b 'Time Travel to a Possible Self: Searching for the Alternative Cosmopolitanism of Cochin', in *Time Warps: The Insistent Politics of Silent and Evasive Pasts*, New Delhi: Permanent Black, pp. 157–209.

Newmann, Robert. 2001. *Goddesses and Dreams: Essays on Goan Culture and Society*, Goa: Other India Press.

Nussbaum, Martha C. 2004. *Hiding from Humanity: Disgust, Shame and the Law*, New Jersey: Princeton University Press.

Ogborn, Miles. 1998. *Spaces of Modernity*, New York: The Guilford Press.

Ollman, Bertell. 1976. *Alienation: Marx's Conception of Man in Capitalist Society*, Cambridge: Cambridge University Press.

Omvedt, Gail. 1994. *Dalits and the Democratic Revolution*. New Delhi: Sage Publications.

Orwell, George. 1975. *Down and Out in Paris and London*, London: Penguin Books.

Pande, Janak. 1980. 'Ingratiation as Expected and Manipulative Behaviour in Indian Society', *Social Change*, vol. 10, nos 3 & 4, September–October.

_____. 1981a. 'Ingratiation Tactics in India,' *The Journal of Social Psychology*, vol. 113, pp. 147–8.

_____. 1981b. 'Effects of Machiavellianism and Degree of Organizational Formalization on Ingratiation', *Psychologia*, vol. 24, pp. 41–6.

_____. 1981c. 'Social Influence Processes', in his *Perspectives on Experimental Social Psychology*, New Delhi: Concept, pp. 55–93.

_____. 1986. 'Cross-cultural Perspectives on Ingratiation', in B. Maher and W. Maher (eds), *Progress in Experimental Personality Research*, New York: Academic Press, pp. 205–29.

Pande, Janak and R. Rastogi. 1979. 'Machiavellianism and Ingratiation', *The Journal of Social Psychology*, vol. 108, pp. 221–5.

Palshikar, Suhas. 1996. 'Gandhi-Ambedkar Interface...When Shall the Twain Meet?', *Economic and Political Weekly*, 3 August, pp. 2070–72.

_____. 2004. 'Whose Democracy Are We Talking About?: Hegemony and Democracy in India', in Rajendra Vora and Suhas Palshikar (eds), *Indian Democracy: Meaning and Practices*, New Delhi: Sage Publications.

Pantham, Thomas. 1987. 'Habermas's Practical Discourse and Gandhi's Satyagraha', in Bhikhu Parekh and Thomas Pantham (eds), *Political Discourse: Explorations in Indian and Western Political Thought*, New Delhi: Sage Publications, pp. 292–310.

_____. 1995a. *Political Theories and Social Reconstruction: A Critical Survey of the Literature on India*, New Delhi: Sage Publications.

_____. 1995b. 'Gandhi, Nehru and Modernity', in Upendra Baxi and Bhikhu Parekh (eds), *Crisis and Change in Contemporary India*. New Delhi: Sage Publications, pp. 98–121.

_____. 2006. 'Religious Diversity and National Unity: The Gandhian and Hindutva Visions', in V.R. Mehta and Thomas Pantham (eds), *Political Ideas in Modern India*, New Delhi: Sage Publications, pp. 221–37.

Parekh, Bhikhu (ed.). 1974. *Colour, Culture and Consciousness*, London: George Allen & Unwin.

_____. 1999. *Colonialism, Tradition and Reform: An Analysis of Gandhi's Political Discourse*, Revised Edition, New Delhi: Sage Publications.

———. 2000. *Rethinking Multiculturalism: Cultural Diversity and Political Theory*, London: Palgrave.

Parvathamma, C. 1984. *Scheduled Castes and Tribes, A Socio-Economic Study*, New Delhi: Ashish.

Patterson, Orlando. 1982. *Slavery and Social Death*, Massachusetts: Harvard University Press.

Pelczynsky, Z.A. 1984. *The State and Civil Society, Studies in Hegel's Political Philosophy*, Cambridge: Cambridge University Press.

Phadke, Y.D. (ed.). 1991. *Mahatma Phule samagra wangmaya*, Mumbai: Maharashtra Sahitya Sanskriti Mandal.

Pillai, R.V. 1999. 'Manual Scavenging', in R.M. Pal (ed.), *Protection of Human Rights—A Critique*, New Delhi: Indian Social Institute, pp. 119–28.

Posner, Eric A. 2000. *Law and Social Norms*, Harvard University Press.

Postone, Moishe. 1996. *Time, Labour and Social Domination: A Reinterpretation of Marx's Critical Theory*, Cambridge: Cambridge University Press.

Power, Samantha. 2002. *A Problem form Hell: America and the Age of Genocide*, New York: Basic Books.

Pupavac, Vanessa. 2002. 'Patholizing Populations and Colonizing Minds: International Psychological Programs in Kosovo', *Alternatives*, vol. 27, no. 4, pp. 489–511.

Pyarelal, 1932, *The Epic Fast*, Ahmedabad: Navajivan.

Quinton, Anthony. 1997. 'Humiliation', *Social Research*, Spring, vol. 64, no. 1.

Rajagopalachari, C. 1946. *Ambedkar Refuted*, Bombay: Hind Kitabs.

Rawls, John, 1972. *Theory of Justice*, London: Oxford University Press.

Raz, Joseph, 2002. *Values, Respect, and Attachment*, Oxford: Oxford University Press.

Ripstein, Arthur. 1997. 'Responses to Humiliation', *Social Research*, Spring, vol. 64, no. 1.

Robinson, Rowena. 1998. *Conversion, Continuity and Change: Lived Christianity in Southern Goa*, New Delhi: Sage Publications.

Roediger, David R. 1999. *The Wages of Whiteness, Race and the Making of the American Working Class*, London, New York: Verso.

Roemer, John. 1986. 'Should Marxist be Interested in Exploitation?', in John Roemer (ed.), *Analytical Marxism*, Cambridge: Cambridge University Press.

———. 1996. 'Equal Shares: Making Market Socialism Work', in Erik Wright (ed.), *The Real Utopias Project*, London: Verso.

Rodrigues, Valerian. 1994. 'Between Tradition and Modernity: The Gandhi-Ambedkar Debate', in A.K. Narain and D.C. Ahir (eds), *Dr Ambedkar, Buddhism and Social Change*, New Delhi: B.R. Publishing Corporation, pp. 137–61.

———. (ed.). 2002. *The Essential Writings of B.R. Ambedkar*, New Delhi: Oxford University Press.

Rorty, Richard. 1979. *Philosophy and the Mirror of Nature*, Princeton: Princeton University Press.

Rousseau, Jean Jacques. 1973. 'A Discourse on Arts and Sciences', in G.D.H. Cole, J.H. Brumfitt, and John C. Hall (eds and trans.), *The Social Contact and the Discoures*, London: J.M. Dent and Sons.

Roychoudhury, Tapan. 2002. *Europe Reconsidered*, New Delhi and London: Oxford University Press.

Roy, Bhaskar. 1991. *Philosophy and the Idea of Freedom*, Oxford: Blackwell.

Saksena, K.D. 2002. *Dynamics of India's Textile Economy*, Delhi: Shipra Publications.

Sangvai, Sanjay. 2000. *The River and Life: People's Struggle in the Narmada Valley*, Mumbai: Earthcare Books.

Sangvai, Sanjay and Alok Agarwal. 1991. 'State Repression in MP-Target: Popular Movements', *Economic and Political Weekly*, 23 November.

Sarkar, Sumit. 1993. *An Exploration of the Ramkrishna Vivekananda Tradition*, IIAS, Shimla.

———. 1996. 'Indian Nationalism and the Politics of Hindutva', in David Ludden (ed.), *Making India Hindu*, New Delhi: Oxford University Press.

Sartre, Jean Paul. 1957. *Being and Nothingness*, trans. Hazel E. Barnes, New York: Philosophical Library.

Scary, Elaine. 1987. *The Body in Pain: The Making and Unmaking of the World*, Oxford: Oxford University Press.

Scott, James. 1990. *Domination and the Art of Resistance*, New Haven: Yale University Press.

Scruton, Roger. 1983. *A Dictionary of Political Thought*, London: Pan Books and Macmillan.

Seidler, J. Victor. 1986. *Kant, Respect and Injustice—The Limits of Liberal Moral Theory*, London: Routledge and Kegan Paul.

Seidman, Steven. 1994. *The Post-modern Turn, New Perspective on Social Theory*, Cambridge: Cambridge University Press.

Shah, Ghanshyam. 1997. 'Bureaucracy and Urban Development: Can it be made to Last? Post-plague Scenario in Surat', *Economic and Political Weekly*, vol. 32, no. 12, 22–28 March, pp. 607–13.

Shah G., H. Mander, S. Thorat, S. Deshpande, and A. Baviskar. 2006. *Untouchability in Rural India*, New Delhi: Sage Publications.

Sharma, Arvind. 2000. *Classical Hindu Thought: An Introduction*, New Delhi: Oxford University Press.

Sheth, D.L. 1999. 'Secularisation of Caste and Making of New Middle Class', *Economic and Political Weekly*, vol. 34, nos 34–5, 21–28 August, pp. 2502–10.

———. 2000. 'Caste and the Secularization Process in India', in deSouza (ed.), *Contemporary India*.

Shklar, Judith. 1984. *Ordinary Vices*, Massachusetts: The Belknap Press of Harvard University Press.

_____. 1990. *The Faces of Injustice*, New Haven: Yale University Press.

Siquiera, Alito. 2003. 'Gentios, Naturees e Casts: Notes on Conflict and Statistical Classification in Eighteen Century Portuguese India', Paper presened at the Seminar on 'Portugal India' at the Department of Portuguese and Brazilian Studies, Brown University, USA, 16–17 May.

Smith, Adam. 1966. *Theory of Moral Sentiments*, New York: Augustus M. Kelley.

Srinivasulu, K. 1996. 'Textile Policy and Handloom Industry Policy: Promises and Performance', *Economic and Political Weekly*, 7 December.

Taylor, Charles. 1985. *Philosophy and The Human Sciences*, Cambridge: Cambridge University Press.

_____. 1989. *Sources of the Self*, Cambridge: Cambridge University Press.

_____. 1997. *Philosophical Argument*, Massachusetts, Cambridge: Harvard University Press.

Temkin, Larry S. 1993. *Inequality*, New York: Oxford University Press.

Thakker, G.K. 1962. *Labour Problems of Textile Industry—A Study of the Labour Problems of the Cotton Mill Industry in Bombay*, Bombay: Vora & Co.

Thapar, Romila (ed.). 2000. *India: Another Millennium?*, New Delhi: Viking.

Thomson, E.P. 1963. *The Making of the English Working Class*, London: Penguin.

Tripathi, R.C. 1981. 'Machiavellianism and Social Manipulation', in Janak Pande (ed.), *Perspectives on Experimental Social Psychology*, New Delhi: Concept, pp. 133–87.

van Wersch, H. 1992. *Bombay Textile Strike, 1982–83*, Mumbai: Oxford University Press.

Verma, Vidhu. 1999. 'Colonialism and Liberation: Ambedkar's Quest for Distributive Justice', *Economic and Political Weekly*, vol. 34, no. 39, 25 September, pp. 2804–10.

Vora, Rajendra. 2002. 'Land Grabbing and Struggles of the Displaced in Maharashtra', in Ghanshyam Shah and D.C. Sah (eds), *Land Reforms in India: Performance and Challenges in Gujarat and Maharashtra*, New Delhi: Sage Publications.

Young, Iris Marion. 1990. *Justice and the Politics of Differences*, Princeton: Princeton University Press.

Walmiki, Om Parkash, Zootan. 2002. *Autobiography*, trans. Prabha, Kolkata: Samya Publication.

Walzer, Michael. 1983. *Spheres of Justice: A Defense of Pluralism and Equality*, Oxford: Basil Blackwell.

Westphal, Merold. 1984. 'Hegel's Radical Idealism: Family and State', in Z.A. Pleczynsky (ed.), *The State and Civil Society, Studies in Hegel's Political Philosophy*, Cambridge: Cambridge University Press.

Wester, Laura and Bill E. Lawson (eds). 2001. *Faces of Environmental Racism: Confronting Issues of Global Justice*, New York: Rowman & Littlefield.

Williams, Robert R. 1997. *Hegel's Ethics of Recognition*, Berkeley: University of California Press.

Wolff, Jonathan. 1998. 'Fairness, Respect, and the Egalitarian Ethos', *Philosophy and Public Affairs*, vol. 22, no. 2, pp. 97–122.

World Court of Women (WCW). 2002. *Singing in the Dark Times*, Bangalore: Asian Women's Human Rights Council; Tunis, El Taller.

Young, Iris Marrion, 1990. *Justice and the Politics of Differences*, Princeton: Princeton University Press.

Zelliot, Eleanor. 1986. 'The Social and Political Thought of B.R. Ambedkar', in Thomas Pantham and Kenneth L. Deutsch (eds), *Political Thought in Modern India*, New Delhi: Sage Publications, pp. 161–75.

———. 1988. 'Congress and the Untouchables, 1917–1950', in R. Sisson and S. Wolpert (eds), *Congress and Indian Nationalism*, New Delhi: Oxford University Press, pp. 182–97.

Zizek, Slavoj. 2000. *The Ticklish Subject*, London: Verso.

Contributors

UPENDRA BAXI is Emeritus Professor of Law, University of Warwick, United Kingdom.

NEERA CHANDHOKE is Professor, Department of Political Science, University of Delhi, Delhi.

PETER RONALD DESOUZA is Director, Indian Institute of Advanced Study, Shimla.

V. GEETHA is associated with Tara Children's Publication, Chennai.

GOPAL GURU is Professor, Centre for Political Studies, School of Social Sciences, Jawaharlal Nehru University, New Delhi.

ASHIS NANDY is Fellow, Centre for the Study of Developing Societies, Delhi.

SANJAY PALSHIKAR is Faculty, Department of Political Science, Central University, Hyderabad.

SUHAS PALSHIKAR is Professor, Department of Political Science, University of Pune, Pune.

THOMAS PANTHAM is a former Professor of Political Science, Maharaja Sayajirao University of Baroda, Gujarat.

BHIKHU PAREKH is Emeritus Professor at the Universities of Hull and Westminister, United Kingdom.

VALERIAN RODRIGUES is Professor, Centre for Political Studies, School of Social Sciences, Jawaharlal Nehru University, New Delhi.